ASH

ARCHIE MILES

ASH

ARCHIE MILES

FOREWORD BY DAME JUDI DENCH

Pearson Bark Books
Hill House Farm
Stoke Lacy
Bromyard
Herefordshire
HR7 4RE

First published by Pearson Bark Books, an imprint of Archie Miles, 2018

Copyright © Archie Miles 2018

The right of Archie Miles to be identified as the author of this work has been has been asserted by him in accordance with the Copyright, Designs and Patents Act 1988.

All photographs and illustrations © Archie Miles or © Archie Miles Collection, unless otherwise credited.

Every effort has been made to obtain the necessary permissions for the use of copyright material, but Pearson Bark Books apologise for any omissions in this respect and will be pleased to make the appropriate acknowledgements in any future editions.

All rights reserved. No part of this publication may be reproduced, stored in a retrieval system, or transmitted in any form or by any means, electronic, mechanical, photocopying, recording or otherwise, without prior permission of the copyright owner.

A CIP catalogue record for this book is available from the British Library.

ISBN 978 1 5272 2296 0

1 3 5 7 9 10 8 6 4 2

Designed by Chris Townsend at ABC Print Group, www.abcprintgroup.com

Printed and bound by L.E.G.O. S.p.A. , Vicenza, Italy.

Contents

Introduction 09

Ash Profile 14

Ash in the Landscape 30

Ash Place Names 40

The Raising of Ash 46

Ash Woods 54

The Uses of Ash 84

Ash Myth, Magic and Superstition 104

The Weeping Ash 120

Remarkable Ash Trees 130

Growing on Ash 162

Ash Dieback 178

The Inspirational Ash 190

Sponsors 208

Index 212

Acknowledgements 216

FOREWORD

When I first heard the news about the ash dieback epidemic sweeping across Britain, and began to understand what it might mean to lose the vast majority of our glorious ash trees and the dramatic changes that this loss would wreak on so much of our landscape, I was desolate, despondent, horrified. It seems that tree diseases are becoming an increasing and ever-present threat to so many of our native species, especially in recent years. Our majestic oaks; the sweet chestnuts, bearers of our Christmas delicacy; horse chestnuts with their candelabras of showy white or red flowers; alders that line the riverbanks and the feathery, swaying larches of emerald springs and burnished autumns are all fighting for their very lives.

I vividly remember the haunting spectre of Dutch elm disease in the 1970s and how millions of mighty elms were so speedily swept aside – all because of a tiny beetle. Very little was done at the time to record the passing of these trees that characterised so many of our quintessential British landscapes, so I was thrilled to learn that renowned tree author and photographer Archie Miles had embarked upon a project to redress that oversight with the elms by producing a comprehensive monograph about the ash tree … before it was too late!

His mission was to record the essence of our diverse ash landscapes with photographs taken throughout the seasons in almost every corner of the country – woodlands and hedgerows, mountains and gorges, parks and gardens, ancient and famous individual trees – but also to focus on the cultural and historical heritage that the ash has accrued down the centuries, along with its remarkable functional versatility and economic importance, and its place in the hearts and works of poets, writers and artists.

Ash dieback is unstoppable and it will probably eliminate almost all our ash trees, but there is no point in weeping and wailing about it for the die is cast. While we still have the ash, let us celebrate its grace and beauty, its distinctive contribution to so much of our landscape and its invaluable ecological and environmental roles in an ever-changing world. I believe that this book will stand for many years to come as the definitive record of one of our most valuable, admired and beloved native trees.

Dame Judi Dench

OPPOSITE:
Dramatic illumination of a lone ash in Borrowdale, Cumbria.

Introduction

The idea to produce a book about the ash tree began gestation about three years ago. I had seen the effects of Dutch elm disease in my teens and could just about remember what landscapes looked like with towering English elms gently swaying in the breeze: those gloriously distinctive tiered silhouettes in perfect evenly-spaced formation; sentinels along some old hedgerow with a burnished winter sun behind them. If you search for a book today to illustrate what our elm landscapes looked like fifty years ago, you will struggle to find one. One man, Gerald Wilkinson, wrote and illustrated a book called *Epitaph for the Elm* in 1978; indeed it was an epitaph, certainly for large mature elms in the landscape, and even he was almost too late to capture many of those with his camera. Although it was a hurriedly convened appreciation, Wilkinson was the only person with the foresight to produce a record before the loss.

With the knowledge that ash dieback had been officially recognised in Britain in 2012 (although it was almost certainly here many years previously), and judging by its progress in the three years up to 2015, I already had a deeply worrying image of an elm-like scenario unfolding. The great irony being that ash was the principal coloniser in the spaces that the departing elms had left behind. I set out on a personal crusade to get somebody interested in supporting my strong belief that we needed to have a record of our ash landscapes and most remarkable individual ash trees before ash dieback does its worst or the next deadly threat to ash, emerald ash borer, arrives here from foreign parts … as it surely will.

Like so many national disasters, it only remains that way for the majority of people while it is in the news headlines, so that when the topic fades from the media the public perception, particularly when the ash trees in their neck of the woods look fine and dandy, is that the crisis has all blown over. Well it will, literally, it really will; windborne spores will reach every corner of the land eventually. We are looking at a potential loss of 99 per cent of our ash trees, probably within the next ten to twenty years. If anyone doubts the severity of the situation even now, then a drive through the Kent, Sussex or East Anglia countryside will come as quite a wake-up call.

Initially I contacted several of my past publishers. No minnows in the publishing pond any of them, but my task was to convince them of the pressing nature of the project and moreover the potential saleability of a book on a subject that will affect millions of people; not just their local landscapes, but also the places that they love to visit or where they head for their holidays. The Yorkshire Dales, the Derbyshire Dales or the limestone gorges of the Mendips perhaps losing as much as half of their treecover just for a start. Cotswold hedgerows bereft of ashes; the famous ash roads of Northumberland denuded; massive ash coppice stools, some maybe 800–1,000 years old; and ancient ash pollards, some perhaps 500 years old, all lost for ever. I believed that creating a record of our ash trees, along with a complete cultural, historical and biological celebration, sounded like a pretty convincing and timely proposal for a book.

OPPOSITE:
Ash-lined road from East Grafton to Wilton, Wiltshire.

I detected the shuffling feet and muttering that it wasn't exactly a television tie-in, a brand-new diet or a cake-baking book (odd juxtaposition that) and certainly not another Attenborough blockbuster. I'd have to try my luck elsewhere.

I explored various avenues over about eighteen months, but to no avail. It seemed as if I just couldn't get people fired up about the importance of the subject and the urgency of the time frame and then I spoke to my two main sponsors that you see acknowledged in this book and suddenly a possibility began to emerge.

With the bit between my teeth in the spring of 2017 I set out to discover how the ash landscapes of Britain with their woods and their individual trees were faring. My findings were very varied. Probably the biggest jolt for someone coming down from the West Midlands was walking through some of the Kentish woods that looked rather like the aftermath of Dutch elm disease, with the bleached bones of whole stands of ash clattering together in the wind. Along the roadsides almost every sizeable ash tree appeared to be in some stage of decline. Britain's largest weeping ash – a tree on a private estate near Bedgebury, a glorious snapshot of which someone had sent me only a couple of years previously, looked for all the world as if it was succumbing to ash dieback. All in all, this was a pretty depressing vision of the future.

It wasn't all doom and gloom, though. As I travelled around the UK I saw signs of ash dieback in almost every place I visited, but I felt I had to overcome the initial instinct to feel downcast. After all, I was on a mission to find the very best landscapes and individual trees in order to ensure that this book is a celebration rather than an epitaph.

There were some wonderful moments on my travels: perched on the lip of Burrington Combe in Somerset at daybreak, watching the first rays of sunlight skim over the ash treetops below; being invited into the private gardens of Heanton Satchville, Devon, to see a remarkable woven ash arbour almost 200 years old; sitting beneath the Loweswater Ash, a recent discovery in Cumbria and a truly awesome tree; picking my way across limestone pavement above Malham Cove, Yorkshire, to find tiny bonsai-scale ashes in the grikes; bathed in the emerald light below an ash tunnel in a remote Northumbrian lane; discovering ancient ash wood pasture a few miles down the road from where I've lived for almost thirty years; and finally encountering one of my all-time favourite artworks – David Nash's *Ash Dome*.

I have met so many enthusiastic and immensely helpful and knowledgeable people as I worked on this book, all of whom are incredibly proud of their trees and concerned about what the future may bring, not forgetting all those specialists and craftsmen and women who have generously given me interviews, their valuable time and the benefit of their in-depth expertise and experience. Where would I have been without them?

It's not until you delve deeply into a subject that you start to find out how complex and extensive it actually is. I had thought that after writing about the oak a few years ago, when it was difficult to pack everything into a single volume, that the ash would be a lot simpler, but I arrived at the final phase of the editorial process wondering, yet again, how on earth I'd fit everything in.

My heartfelt wish is that this book will act as a permanent reminder to everyone of how important all our trees, not just ash, are to our everyday lives, to our own health and happiness and the ecological and environmental future of our planet. The loss of one species of tree will indeed be a disaster, but we need to learn lessons to care better for the trees we still have and to reduce, if not eliminate, the risk of introducing new pathogens into Britain. When politicians shuffle environmental issues to the back of the pack because 'it's not good for business', they need to be reminded of their duty of care.

I have tried to encompass all aspects of the ash tree in Britain and hope that this book will stand as a record of a time when we are still able to appreciate the splendour of our ashscapes. This is my personal homage to the magnificent and beautiful ash – the Venus of the Woods – and I sincerely hope that readers will enjoy my offering.

LEFT:
First rays of the morning sunlight glance across the ash woods in Burrington Combe, Somerset.

OPPOSITE:
Ash stand in Brockhampton Woods, Herefordshire. A typical view through the canopy of a loosely managed ash wood, a mixture of natural regeneration and planted trees.

Ash Profile

James Grigor in his book *The Eastern Arboretum, or Register of Remarkable Trees, Seats, Gardens, &c. in the County of Norfolk* (1841) introduces the ash with obvious admiration and affection:

> This lofty and beautiful tree is a general favourite in this country. It is prized in its living state as one of the greatest ornaments of the field, pre-eminent in the elegance of its structure, having an easy flowing spray, which, when seen in its perfection, not unfrequently hangs about it in loose pendulous masses … No individual of the forest kind makes a surer anchoring in the earth, and none spreads a more ample sail aloft. It is seldom seen prostrated by the tempest. Whilst the ash, then, is by the consent of many reckoned elegant, it is by no means deficient in stately bearing.

The ashes are one genus of the olive family (*Oleaceae*) and amount to some sixty-five species in the northern hemisphere. With one or two exceptions they are trees bearing pinnate-compound leaves, comprising six to twelve paired, elliptic-ovate, shallowly toothed leaflets plus a single terminal leaflet. The flowers lack petals and sepals and are pollinated by the wind. They bear winged fruits known as samaras. Common ash has a wide native range, being indigenous to most of Europe from the Mediterranean up to Norway and to the Caucasus and western Russia in the east.

The common ash tree (*Fraxinus excelsior*) is undoubtedly one of Britain's most familiar broadleaf trees, and readily identified by its pinnate-compound leaves, setting it apart from the other common broadleaf trees, such as oak, beech, birch, lime, sycamore or sweet chestnut, although not to be confused with the rowan or mountain ash, a completely unrelated species. It is our third most common broadleaf tree after native oaks and birch. The National Forest Inventory for Great Britain gathers the statistics for trees with a diameter at breast height (dbh) greater than 4 centimetres in all woods larger than 0.5 hectares. As of 2013 the NFI identified 1.3 million hectares of broadleaf trees, of which 142,000 hectares are ash; i.e., 11 per cent of all broadleaves or 5 per cent of all species, although in the southern counties of England and the East Midlands this latter figure rises to almost 13 per cent. Nationally, this equates to approximately 126 million ash trees. In addition, it was estimated that there were some 1.3 billion ash seedlings and saplings. In 2015 a survey of non-woodland ash trees carried out by the Tree Council for the Department of the Environment, Food and Rural Affairs (DEFRA) estimated that there were somewhere between 27 and 60 million more ash trees with more than 4 centimetres dbh. This broke down into 20 million hedgerow trees, 3.6–4 million urban trees, 17–34 million trees in woodlands and clumps of less than 0.5 hectares, and 4–4.4 million trees along roads and railway lines. Add to these figures an estimated 400 million seedlings and saplings, and it is incredibly challenging to arrive at a definitive answer. Verification of statistics on a countrywide scale will always be difficult; particularly with the gradual acceleration of ash dieback the losses versus the gains will alter the statistics all over again.

Ash is a tree that prefers base-rich, moist soils (ideally pH>4.2) – hence its proliferation in the valleys of the geologically more calcareous regions, typically in places such as the Derbyshire Dales and the Mendips – and yet it will grow almost anywhere, in extremis from solid rock faces or in the gutter. Ash is an opportunist and a survivor, although its greatest test is currently unfolding and it remains to be seen what the final outcome will be as the ash dieback epidemic runs its course.

RIGHT:
Profile of a mature ash in winter, with the commonly observed forking of the trunk.

ABOVE:
A huge multi-stemmed maiden ash in a Cornish pasture, shows exactly what a healthy tree should look like in the height of summer.

Ash species can be traced back to the Cretaceous period, but it is believed that some time around 7 to 5 million years ago common ash and narrow-leaved ash (*Fraxinus angustifolia*) began to become established as the principal ash species in Europe, common ash preferring the more temperate northern climes while narrow-leaved ash took to the southern territory around the Mediterranean. Common ash fossils have been found in interglacial beds at Hitchin, Hertfordshire, and in Neolithic deposits at Crossness, Essex. There are possibilities that ash survived in a few refugia along the west coast of Britain through the last Ice Age. However, evidence from post-glacial pollen analysis extracted from cores calibrated using radiocarbon dating shows that ash colonised much of the southern half of Britain by about 5,000 years ago, making it a relatively late arrival when compared to many other native broadleaf species. The source of these migratory ash trees was once thought to have been Sweden and Denmark, but genetic similarities of British ashes to those on the Iberian Peninsula would seem to indicate a greater likelihood that the tree migrated northward up the Atlantic coast, before crossing the land bridge into Britain.

There are, however, some genetic commonalities among British ashes with the Scandinavian gene pool, suggesting that these trees have also had an influence on our present-day stocks, although the principal origins are still thought to be the Iberian Peninsula. The isochrone contour maps of Professor H. J. B. Birks show an almost complete colonisation of Ireland by about 3,000 years ago, yet an unclear picture, due to lack of hard evidence, of how far into northern England and Scotland ash had spread naturally less than 5,000 years ago.

Ash has become so ubiquitous that it may seem like an odd assumption, but some nineteenth-century authorities asserted that it was not a native species in Scotland, having a status more akin to beech in northern climes as a very successful introduction that has become naturalised. Professor Robert Jameson, writing in his journal of 1830, claimed that although

> The Ash and the Beech have a place in the *Flora Scotica* of Lightfoot and Hooker, and they have long ornamented our woods and plantations … there is great reason

BELOW (CLOCKWISE FROM TOP LEFT): *Ash buds in winter, immature male flowers, male flowers, and pollen release.*

to doubt their being truly indigenous to this country, or having formed any part of the ancient forests. No traces of them appear in our peat-mosses; yet Ash-seeds and Beech-mast would in all probability have proved as indestructible as Hazel-nuts or Fir-cones [pine-cones] which are abundant in many peat-mosses.

This claim is countered by Robert Hutchison, writing in the *Transactions of the Highland and Agricultural Society of Scotland* (1880), who states that not only is it highly unlikely that ash would have grown in the sort of terrain that would become peat bogs anyway, but its presence is known from the 'earliest records', as it was used for 'deadly instruments of warfare' and 'peaceful implements of agriculture'.

In the depths of winter there are two distinct features that mark the common ash tree out from other species. In profile a mature ash may adopt a variety of forms. Tall, sinuous trees in woodland, often up to 30 metres in height, are usually the result of forestry planting where, growing in close proximity to each other, they thrust upwards seeking the light, putting out few lateral branches, or having them removed under the management regime, and developing the long, straight, knot-free butts that foresters prefer. Exceptional trees growing to over 40 metres are not unknown. Open-grown trees tend to be tall and domed with several principal boughs in a strongly ascending formation, while the lower boughs frequently arc downward or droop, but distinctively turn upwards at the ends. The other distinguishing characteristic is the velvety-black, squat, conical buds. The large terminal buds will produce the new stem growth for the following season while the lateral buds will produce the flowers. Quite often the central terminal bud dies, which stimulates the two small buds at its base to grow, creating a forked end to the twig, but eventually one will become the strongest and form the new main stem. Damage or dieback of the terminal bud sometimes occurs at an early stage of the tree's development, caused either from late spring frosts, drought, deer damage or wind, and then it may result in a maturing tree with twin leaders, thus creating a distinctly forked shape to the tree form, the junction of which will be a potential failure point in the future. It is not uncommon to see large forked ashes that have

18 ASH PROFILE

split in two either from high winds or perhaps the unduly heavy loading created by infestations of ivy.

Common ash usually begins to bear flowers at thirty to forty years of age. The dense axillary panicles of tiny, dark maroon or purple flowers, devoid of petals, on the shoots of the previous year's growth appear before the leaves flush, usually by mid April, but it can be as early as late March or, conversely, well into May. This results in communities of trees, some of which have barely broken bud, alongside others that are in full leaf and already forming clusters of fruits. The assumption is that this is a survival mechanism; the trees genetically programmed to flower over an extended period to allow for damage to the earliest inflorescence from late spring frosts. The male flowers appear first, resembling little clumps of dark coral and when fully opened bear clusters of twin-branched stamens. Hermaphrodite flowers appear next, and lastly the female flowers, each having a style tipped with a dark red stigma. These burst forth in exotic-looking feathery sprays on long green stems, each one a tiny sylvan, pyrotechnical explosion. Alan Mitchell describes ash flowering most succinctly as 'total sexual confusion'. Trees may produce male, female or hermaphrodite flowers, either on separate trees or all together on individual trees (trioecious or subdioecious). Studies carried out in 1991 revealed that there tend to be more predominantly male trees than females, and when hermaphrodite flowers are part of the array they manifest in three types: either purely hermaphrodite or alternatively with vestigial male or female organs, these latter two types still having the ability to function as either males or females or even as both male and female. Equally, some trees that bear predominantly male or female flowers will not necessarily produce pollen or seed.

Ash trees also have the remarkable capacity to change their sexuality from one year to the next. The reason is something of a biological mystery, but at some point in the evolution of the ash it became necessary for the tree to adopt this strategy. Possible explanations could be climatic variation, increasing the fecundity of the tree when conditions for seed germination seem more favourable, or perhaps some sense of competition (or lack of it) that stimulates the tree to produce more seed when the immediate

BELOW (FROM LEFT TO RIGHT): *Female flowers, mature ash keys, and ripened ash keys remaining on the tree throughout winter.*

ASH PROFILE

OPPOSITE:
The common Ash Tree, copper engraving from the 1st Hunter Edition of John Evelyn's "Silva" 1776.

BELOW:
Ash seedlings on the woodland floor indicate a lack of deer predation.

habitat is threatened by proliferation of rival species or, equally, when space opens up and there are increased chances of colonisation. In order to confirm or deny this theory it would be interesting to study ash trees flowering in situations where they are relatively confined, for example within dense woodland, and then clear felling or wind throw around these trees changes the surrounding habitat into potential colonisation territory or, conversely, to observe sexuality changes in open-grown trees that are absorbed into woodland stands. Obviously a dataset would have to be derived from a large sampling across a wide variety of habitats to come to any meaningful conclusions. A recent French study revealed an 86 per cent constancy of sexual phenotype from one year to the next in wild ash trees, but this was contrasted with clones grown in a seed orchard that maintained stable gender status within each clone, leading to the conclusion that sexual orientation was genetically controlled. However, this nursery-type habitat would be less likely to present any challenging environmental changes such as might be influential in a wild setting.

When ash seedlings develop their first leaves after the narrow cotyledons, they produce a single pair of simple leaves, broad at the base, toothed and tapering to a point. The following pair of leaves will have three leaflets each and thus a succession of larger and longer pinnate-compound leaves begins. The seedlings are quite shade tolerant, becoming less so as they mature, so that once they exceed about 50 centimetres in height they will require almost full sunlight to progress further. Seedlings, saplings and young coppice growth, particularly on the woodland floor, will flush as early as mid April, giving them the best chance to survive and thrive before the woodland canopy closes over for the summer. Young ashlings in woodland are often at great risk from deer predation.

Ash is a nitrophilous species with a high demand for soil nutrients. The root systems of ash are a combination of lateral woody arrays with bunches of fine rootlets in the top half metre of soil, while the original tap root, the tenacity of which is frequently discovered by anyone who would try and dislodge a two- or three-year-old sapling from

The common Ash Tree.

Publish'd Jan 1, 1776, by A. Hunter, M.D. as the Act directs.

ASH PROFILE 21

LEFT:
This exposed tree in Ling Gill, near High Birkwith, North Yorkshire, illustrates the tenacity of ash in harsh upland terrain.

its anchoring, remains along with several vertical sinker roots which may go down as much as 2.5 metres. Little wonder, then, that ash is such a windfast tree.

As leaves unfurl in spring they are a vibrant, fresh yellow-green, maturing to dull, dark greyish-green above with a paler underside – seen to best effect on a windy day. Studies in Germany have shown that, much like the extended season for flowering, leaf flush is also staged over a protracted period to allow for damage to some trees from spring frosts, and this has been observed to be a heritable characteristic, so each tree has its own stable ecotype. Each of the paired leaflets is either sessile or may have a very short stem of perhaps a couple of millimetres. The terminal leaflet has a stem of 1–2 centimetres. Close examination of the leaves reveals a white pubescence along the midrib beneath each leaflet. The rachis (main leaf stem) is also pubescent and, particularly at the base, is noticeably grooved, winged or U-shaped in cross section, opening out as and where the leaflets are attached. This groove is a useful way for the tree to maximise its water supply, as rainwater drains from the leaflets into the channel and may be held there for absorption by tiny hair-like structures over several days. Each leaf is generally 20–30 centimetres long, and the leaflets up to 12 centimetres.

Leaf morphology is remarkably diverse; a visual indication of the genetic diversity within the ash population. Leaflet shape varies from being very slender and elliptical, so that the tree might sometimes appear to be a hybrid between common ash and narrow-leaved ash, to ovate, with a decidedly rounded rather than sharply pointed tip. Crosses with narrow-leaved ash do occur with some frequency in southern Europe and it has also been established by a recent study in Ireland, so could well be more widespread, although narrow-leaved ash is far from common outside formal settings in much of Britain. Some leaves produce progressively larger leaflets towards the tip, while others are completely the opposite, developing smaller leaflets toward the tip. The degree of serration to leaflet edges varies greatly. Leaves lacking a terminal leaflet – i.e., ending in a pair – are often seen, and there are many other aberrations in leaflet layout and form, one of the more unusual being a bifurcated terminal leaflet. As research continues into the genetics of ash resistance or tolerance to ash dieback, and although it may seem an improbable factor, it will be intriguing to see if there is any relationship to leaf morphology.

Young stems and leaves of some ash trees have been observed with a purplish tinge, a tendency that appears specific to a few individuals. Another interesting characteristic of leaf growth is observed the first season after pollarding, when trees put out a particularly dark-hued and luxuriant flush of foliage which frequently remains until long after most other ashes have shed their leaves in the autumn, sometimes until late November. Bigger leaves and a longer season on the tree will help to reinvigorate a pollard that has just been cut back hard. The growing season of ash is notoriously one of the shortest of the native broadleaf species – generally within the parameters of 141 to 174 days, leading to the warning from John Evelyn in his *Sylva* (1664) that ashes are not a wise choice as a garden tree:

> for displaying themselves so very late, and falling very early, not to be planted for umbrage or ornament, especially near the garden, since, besides their predatious roots, the leaves dropping with so long a stalk, are drawn by clusters into the worm-holes, which foul the alleys with their keys, and suddenly infect the ground.

The Reverend William Gilpin, innovator and promoter of his theory of the Picturesque, takes a similar stance in his *Remarks on Forest Scenery* (1794), where, in his opinion,

> ash falls under the displeasure of the picturesque eye. Its leaf is much tenderer, than that of the oak, and sooner receives impression from the winds, and frost. Instead of contributing its tint therefore in the wane of the year among the many-coloured offspring of the woods, it shrinks from the blast, drops its leaf, and in each scene where it predominates, leaves wide blanks of defoliated boughs, amidst foliage yet fresh, and verdant. Before its decay, we sometimes see its leaf tinged with a fine yellow, well contrasted with the neighbouring greens. But this is one of nature's casual beauties. Much oftener its leaf decays in a dark, muddy, unpleasing tint.

Although, in mitigation, he adds, 'And yet sometimes, notwithstanding this early loss of its foliage, we see the ash, in a sheltered situation,

OPPOSITE:
A selection of remarkably variable ash leaf shapes.

BELOW:
Massive old ash pollard in the Lodon Valley, Herefordshire, illustrates how ash trees continue to repair the bark of their boles in pastures where they are nibbled and rubbed by livestock.

RIGHT:
Autumnal ash tree on the edge of a Worcestershire woodland.

ABOVE:
The extensive root system of a tree growing in shallow soil on rocky ground is clearly revealed in an old ash wood at Wasdale Head, Cumbria.

when the rains have been abundant, and the season mild, retain its green (a light and pleasant green), when the oak and the elm, in its neighbourhood, have put on their autumnal attire.'

This may be the opinion of an aesthete, but ultimately, perhaps unwittingly, close to the mark, for when there is abundant rainfall and mild temperatures ash is at its best and may well extend its leafing season.

In autumn ash leaves may occasionally turn a beautiful buttery yellow before they fall, but more often the trees, which are particularly sensitive to early frosts, either shed their leaves while they are still green or the leaves curl up and go brown (much as Gilpin observed). Some authorities believe that the yellow colour is caused by drought conditions, but this hardly explains why some trees in a dense stand will do this while others remain green. Personal observations and conversations with other tree people seem to indicate that it is the same individual trees each year that have a propensity to produce yellow autumnal colour. The fallen leaves break down and rot very quickly, and since worms are quite partial to ash leaves, they are often dragged down into their burrows (as Evelyn observed) – sometimes resulting in the strange sight of half-submerged ash leaves strewn across a closely mown lawn. Within a week or two of falling, ash leaves have turned brown and shrivelled up completely, leaving only an intricate cross-hatching of abandoned rachides – nature's game of Spillikins. The leaf litter of ash, much like that of limes, species with which it is often associated, is readily decomposable and rich in nutrients that in turn have a favourable effect on the soil chemistry.

The winged fruits, or samaras, often referred to as ash keys, which hang in clusters, each bearing a single seed, are about 3–5 centimetres long and slightly twisted much like a propeller blade that will help to extend the flight range of the samara when blown from the parent tree. The name 'key' supposedly derives from the shape of medieval keys for locks. The samaras are also occasionally referred to as 'tongues' because of their likeness to a bird's tongue. Samaras will also float on water and may be dispersed greater distances in this manner. Although the samara will be fully grown by early July, the seed will keep growing until August. They frequently remain on the tree over winter,

BELOW:
Hedgerow ash on top of the Cotswold escarpment near Cutsdean, Gloucestershire. Ash is one of the definitive species of Cotswold hedges.

when the desiccated brown clusters of keys may be observed. It is not clear whether this is a random occurrence in individual trees or whether some are genetically programmed to do this every year. Could it be possible that prevailing or predicted climatic conditions may have a bearing on this too? Production of seed varies greatly from year to year and since trees can also change their sexuality between seasons it is difficult to draw conclusions. Seeds generally take two years to germinate anyway, even if they fall from the tree in the first year, normally requiring two winters to stratify; however, there is a low occurrence (less than 5 per cent) of ash seeds germinating after one winter. The seeds do have the ability to lie dormant for up to six years, but ash is a tree that succeeds by creating a seedling bank rather than a seed bank. It seems that worms also have a taste for ash seeds, so that the keys are often drawn down into their burrows along with the leaves. This is unusual, as the seeds have been shown to have a high phenolic content which makes them unpalatable to small mammals – a useful survival strategy if you want to germinate rather than feature on a mouse's menu.

The bark of young ash trees is generally quite smooth and may be silvery-grey, or ash-like in colour, which some have suggested gave rise to its common name, or it may have a greenish tinge or be a yellowish-brown or fawn, although the actual colour of the bark is often masked by a blanket coverage of crustose lichens. In older trees the bark becomes fissured and ridged, exhibiting a finely latticed pattern. Twigs are flattened and usually grey or sometimes with a hint of green. For a tree that is normally very resilient in high winds, the new twigs are remarkably brittle and, after a high wind in springtime, a woodland floor will be littered with twigs and small branches. Some ash trees develop large bosses or burrs on their trunks that may be caused by the tree's reaction to some viral infection or perhaps a way of healing after some sort of physical damage. Ash has a phenomenal capacity to repair itself after loss of boughs from wind throw, lightning strike or human harvesting by pollarding or coppicing. In open pastures it is not unusual for livestock to browse the bases of ash trees, either for small shoots or bark, and use trees as scratching posts. Such trees continually produce 'repair' bark, causing the base of the tree often to appear as if it has been set in huge blobs of concrete.

28 ASH PROFILE

Mature ash trees are very demanding of light, water and nutrients, and many of the early writers warn of the perils of planting ashes too close to crops or gardens as the widespread shallow root systems will disadvantage any competing plants or trees. John Evelyn in his *Sylva* of 1664 observed:

> It is by no means convenient to plant Ash in plow-lands, for the roots will be obnoxious to the coulter [vertical blade fixed in front of a ploughshare]; and the shade of the tree is malignant both to corn and grass, when the head and branches over-drip and emaciate them; … The best Ash delights in the best land, which it will soon impoverish, yet grows in any, so it be not over stiff, wet, and approaching to the marshy, unless it be first well drained: By the banks of sweet and crystal rivers and streams I have observed them to thrive infinitely.

Evelyn's reference to the malignant shade of the tree was perhaps a little misguided, but undoubtedly the root system is notoriously demanding when it comes to water and nutrients, so perhaps James Grigor in *The Eastern Arboretum* was a little closer to the truth:

> In describing this tree, all writers agree in stating that it vanquishes every thing in its neighbourhood, and that it is unfit to surround fields of corn or grass, or, indeed, cultivated land of any description. We should recommend it, therefore, to be planted very sparingly as a hedgerow tree, and when raised for the purposes of its timber, that it should be the sole occupant of the soil; for even over other ligneous bodies placed beside it it maintains a most hurtful influence.

Weeping ash (*Fraxinus excelsior* 'Pendula') has long been a popular ornamental choice for parks and gardens and more details and history of the tree are covered in its own dedicated chapter (see page 120). Obviously, due to the current ash dieback epidemic, few ash trees of any description are now being planted, but in the latter part of the twentieth century the narrow-leaved ash cultivar 'Raywood', with its wonderful red, pink and purple autumn colours, was often a popular choice for parks, gardens and streets and, being a significantly smaller tree than common ash at maturity, it is rather better suited for such urban situations. Another popular ornamental ash has been the manna ash or flowering ash (*Fraxinus ornus*), introduced into Britain in 1710 by Dr Uvedale, a species that is native to southern Europe and Asia Minor. Seldom growing much higher than 18 metres, it has never had any utilitarian value in Britain, but in southern Europe the timber is of excellent quality and the foliage is often cut for animal fodder. The 'manna' of its appellation is the sugary sap tapped from the young trees, usually allowed to crystallise before collection, known as mannite, and was once used in many countries as a mild laxative or as a sweetener for less palatable medicines. In Britain the tree is planted in parks and gardens principally for its impressive displays of showy white flowers.

BELOW LEFT:
Fraxinus ornus 'Sarvar' – a manna ash cultivar at Westonbirt Arboretum, in Gloucestershire.

BOTTOM:
Fraxinus angustifolia 'Raywood' – until recently a very popular tree for parks, gardens and streets, largely because of the superb autumn colour.

OPPOSITE:
A remarkable survivor high above Ribblesdale in North Yorkshire, this tree grows from the limestone pavement and has thrived despite the harshest weather conditions and hungry sheep.

Ash in the Landscape

Ash appears in a wide variety of locations; in a range of different woodlands and hedgerows as well as park, street and garden trees in urban areas. Although intrinsically a lowland species, typically found along river valleys, it appears to be perfectly able to thrive in open, exposed, upland situations; frequently up to 350 metres above sea level. Ash is equally at home in coastal situations, a quality that William Cobbett notes in his book *The Woodlands* (1825), where he mentions observing 'thousands' of instances where coastal oaks have been bent and sculptured by high winds, a phenomenon known as thigmomorphogenesis, and yet ash trees remain resolutely unaffected. With a typical self-satisfied flourish, Cobbett derides the writings of William Gilpin (one senses that the principles of the Picturesque were something of an anathema to a pragmatist like Cobbett), who coined the 'Venus of the Woods' appellation for ash: 'He [Gilpin] called the Oak, the "Hercules of the Woods;" and, as I have shown, this Hercules flees at the bare approach of that which the Venus sets at defiance.'

Ash is usually associated with two principal woodland types, where it is often the dominant species: namely, ash/field maple woods in the base-rich soils of lowland Britain and farther north, often in upland situations on limestone, ash/rowan woods. The most archetypal, distinctive ash woods have to be those dramatic gorge woods of the Mendips, the ash-dominant valleys of the Derbyshire Dales of the White Peak and the strange, almost surreal ash woods, growing so improbably either from or semi-submerged in the limestone pavements of North Yorkshire. In lower concentrations ash will also be found in association with alder woods and with beech woods.
As A. G. Tansley succinctly observed in *Britain's Green Mantle:*

> Wherever, in fact, limestone soils occur, there we have – outside the beech region – ash as the natural dominant tree. Within the region where beech is dominant, ash usually precedes it in the woodland succession on limestone soils. Where calcareous soil is deep, however, oak comes into the woods and we get transitions to the ash–oak woods.

On the chalky soils of southern England ash will colonise the ground at first, but is often shaded out when beech grows up around it, only having a measure of resurgence when space is released by decline or collapse of dominant beech. In the eastern counties, on the boulder-clay, ash and hazel are often the principal underwood species in oak woods; the former two trees usually managed as coppice while the oaks are selectively thinned and left as standards. Native limes are often associated with ash in the woods of the Welsh Borders, while yew and whitebeam are the companions in many of the southern chalky woods of Surrey, Sussex and Hampshire. Hawthorn, blackthorn and hazel are usually the principal species of the ash-wood shrub layer, but in the southern counties it may also include dogwood, spindle, privet, alder buckthorn, elder and wayfaring tree. In the northern ash woods the presence of sycamore, wych elm and silver birch is usual; and on higher ground hazel and particularly downy birch become more prevalent among the ash. The ramping tendrils of traveller's joy or old man's beard, that feral clematis, surge unchecked and impartially over the southern ash woods, while in the north this role is taken by great gouts of ivy.

Because of the light, airy nature of the foliage, there is always a rich field layer below the ash. Tansley provides a comprehensive inventory of wild flowers in ash woods. Dog's mercury is a recognised indigenous species in the field layer common to almost all of these woods apart from alder stands, and is often accompanied by moschatel. Some of the more common early-flowering species, such

ASH IN THE LANDSCAPE

ABOVE:
Very early May morning view across the carpet of bluebells in predominantly ash woodland on the eastern slopes of Midsummer Hill towards the southern end of the Malvern Hills, Worcestershire.

as lesser celandine, ramsons and bluebells, have the light they need to put on magnificent displays while some of the more discriminating lime-loving plants, such as wild columbine, cuckoo-pint, sweet woodruff, great bell-flower, water avens, wood forget-me-not and butterfly orchid, all cleave to ash woods, and bloody cranesbill and green hellebore are two of the rarer species. Two plants most often encountered in more northerly ash woods are Jacob's ladder and globe-flower, although baneberry is particularly rare. Personally, I have seldom encountered any of these last three species, but dedicated botanists will know if they are still growing in these woods. On the drier, thinner soils associated with the sides of limestone gorges, plants such as ground ivy, wood sage and hairy St John's wort are typical, and occasionally lily of the valley.

Hedgerow trees exist as maidens, pollards and laid coppice, although ash will sometimes layer or throw up suckers. John Evelyn refers briefly to pollarded ashes in hedges and their propensity to regenerate speedily: 'Hedge-row Ashes may the oftener be decapitated, and will show their heads again sooner than other trees so used.' Sometimes veteran and ancient ash pollards are found in wood pasture settings, although these are seldom still actively managed as such. Where these landscapes are incorporated into old deer parks it's quite possible that the trees may once have been part of long-defunct hedgerows, most of which were grubbed out when creating the parks hundreds of years ago; looking for linear alignments of veteran trees, particularly pollards, in parks may confirm that likelihood. Ancient ashes in parkland situations are relatively unusual, as species such as oak and sweet chestnut and even beech are more commonly found. This might simply be down to the greater longevity of these species when compared to ash, so that in the past ash could quite possibly have been a major element in such parks.

Revisiting some of the nineteenth-century texts on trees, one finds several deprecating opinions upon the practice of pollarding, typically, and most specifically concerning ash, by John Leonard Knapp in *The Journal of a Naturalist* (1829):

This system of cutting off the heads of young trees in the hedge-rows is resorted to by the farmer for the purpose of forcing them, thus deprived of their leaders, to throw out collateral shoots, serving for stakes for fences [an incorrect assertion, as ash is a poor choice for such a use, and farmers would have known this] and for firewood … No trees suffer more in this respect than the Ash. Prohibitions against mangling trees are usual in agreements; but, with some exceptions in regard to Oak, little attention seems paid to the covenant, as is obvious on the most cursory view of the country in any direction … It is by no means an uncommon thing to observe every Ash-tree reduced to stumps by successive pollardings. I am not so silly as to enlarge upon the beauty of what has been called 'picturesque farming;' [undoubtedly a sideswipe at the likes of Gilpin and

LEFT:
Fine profile of a maiden ash in a Shropshire hedgerow.

BELOW:
Old ash coppice stools line a defunct hedgerow above Hilton, Dorset, with clear evidence of having been laid in the distant past.

ASH IN THE LANDSCAPE   33

RIGHT:
Pollard Ash from 'The Forest Trees of Britain' - Rev. C.A. Johns, 1847.

BELOW:
Tree Surgeon Dave Smith performing a crown reduction on an old outgrown ash pollard.

OPPOSITE ABOVE:
Ancient ash pollard near Purslow, Shropshire - 8.23 metres in girth.

OPPOSITE BELOW:
Long abandoned coppice stool near Lanhydrock, Cornwall - 11.1 metres in girth.

Uvedale Price] but when we cast our eyes over the country, and see such rows of dark, club-headed posts, we cannot but remark upon the unsightly character they present, and consider that it is neither laudable to deform our beautiful country by connivance at this practice, nor that it is proper attention to individual profit to allow the continuation of it. The Ash, after this mutilation, in a few years becomes flattened at the summit, moisture lodges in it, and decay commences, the central parts gradually mouldering away, though for many years the sap-wood will throw out vigorous shoots for the hatchet.

Such strong views might have prevailed among people from privileged backgrounds (which certainly included Knapp) unaffected by the utilitarian benefits, but for the hard-working country folk the produce from pollarded ash trees signified warmth and cooking in the home, the best material for implements, fodder for livestock and even potential income from selling wood to a variety of ash-dependent craftsmen and industries.

There was a grain of truth in Knapp's assertion that pollarding had the potential to signal the decline of an ash tree, but this was only if the regime was abandoned. Historically, there was a steady demand for the produce of the pollards that meant management was kept up on a regular

POLLARD-ASH.

rotation, and that in turn meant the trees remained vibrant, healthy and free of detritus. Although Knapp was writing (and moaning) 200 years ago about what he perceived as the depredation of the countryside, his claims, ironically, are now rather more pertinent. With little demand for ash-pollard produce, many old trees have been left to their own devices, and frequently this lack of intervention leads to their downfall. Long, outgrown branches have overextended the tree's capacity to safely maintain its structure. The massive cantilever effect of arcing boughs that all pivot on a circle of timber around the top of the bole of the pollard exerts

34 ASH IN THE LANDSCAPE

great amounts of physical stress on this part of the tree. Add to the equation detritus and rot within the head of the bole, as well as probable hollowing in many of the oldest trees, the ingress of wood-rotting fungi, the loading of ivy that sometimes occurs, and then they have to withstand the forces imposed by high winds. The recipe for disaster is obvious.

Dotted around Britain a handful of ancient ash pollards, possibly in excess of 300 years old, have survived, and there will be many more in excess of 200 years old. The problem now is making the right call for these trees in terms of management. Leave them alone and they will inevitably deteriorate. Pollard them too hard in one operation, when they might not have been touched for maybe fifty, sixty or eighty years, and the result could be totally counterproductive. The tree is totally traumatised and dies. Conversely, if the tree is resilient enough it might bounce back. If the tree does regenerate,

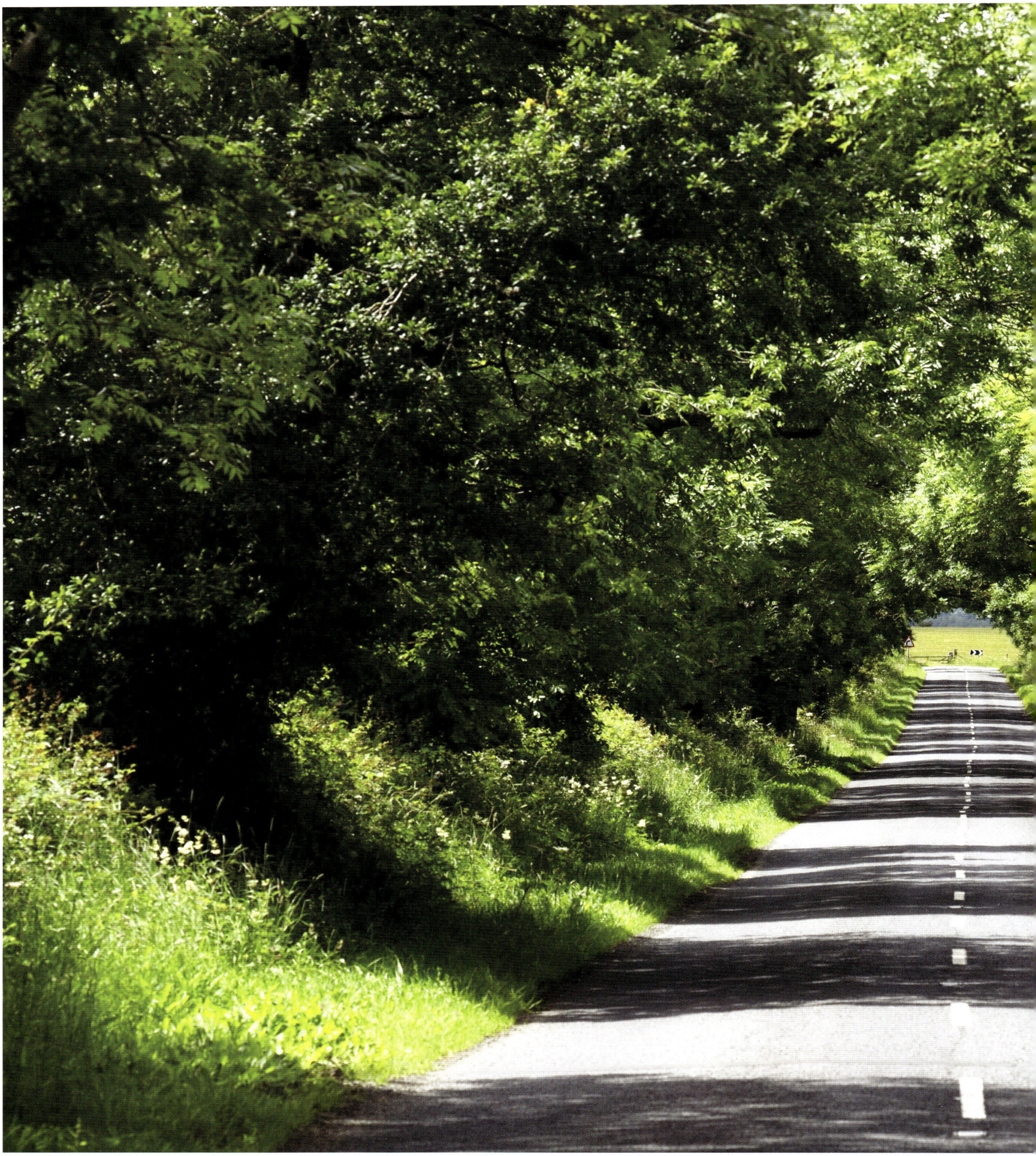

LEFT:
Ash tree tunnel on the B4343 between Hartburn & Scot's Gap, Northumberland.

ABOVE:
Ancient coppice stool in the Wye Valley.

there is now the risk that the new growth is particularly susceptible to ash dieback. So, what to do? Many tree surgeons have had successful outcomes from either performing crown reductions on old pollards – a sort of semi-pollarding – or simply cutting out perhaps a third of the boughs over three successive partial pollardings spaced a few years apart. Whichever route is taken, this still leaves the old tree some foliage to help sustain it through the process.

Some of the very oldest ash trees live on as massive coppice stools to be found in ancient woodland, often situated along old boundaries or wood banks, and those that have been laid or plashed into hedgerows, with amazing horizontal boughs sometimes reaching 5 or 6 metres from the original bole. Some of these coppice stools have been estimated to be at least 500 years old and, in a few very singular examples, as much as 800 or 1,000 years old, and yet it is impossible to be exact since the original wood of the parent tree is inevitably long gone. On reflection, some of these coppice stools could have been actively worked since the time of John Evelyn, himself an observer and advocate for the coppicing of ash ('being once well fixed, you may cut him as close to the earth as you please; it will cause him to shoot prodigiously, so as in a few years to be fit for pike-staves') and again, on coppice stools:

> From these low cuttings come our Ground-Ashes, so much sought after for arbours, espaliers, and other pole-works; they will spring in abundance, and may be reduced to one for a standard tree, or for timber, if you design it; for thus, Hydra like, a ground-cut Ash –
> 'By havock, wounds, and blows,
> More lively and luxuriant grows.' –
> Horace

Many ash coppice stools were traditionally cut a couple of feet above the ground, a custom that Oliver Rackham mentions, but fails to explain. Since it is well known that ash wood deteriorates quickly when in contact with the earth, and several early writers warn of ash stools rotting, it seems to make sense to cut them slightly higher, where there is less risk of detritus lodging, allowing excessive moisture to build up around recently cut stems, forming a damp, decomposing mass at ground level, and potentially hastening that rotting process. It's also possible that it could be sufficient height to minimise damage to new growth from rabbits, which habitually sharpen their teeth by gnawing bark.

Ash is an important and widespread element of the urban treescape. Crucially, it doesn't seem fazed by the challenges of high pollution levels in urban locations and, strangely, recent studies in Kent seem to indicate that urban trees are withstanding or avoiding ash dieback better than their rural counterparts. This has been put down to leaf clearance from where ash spores might develop and the isolated locations of many urban ashes rather than air pollutants having any effect on spores, although small urban-fringe woodlands do seem to become infected. In years to come the presence of ailing ash trees in urban environments is likely to become something of a headache for many cash-strapped councils. The hope is that if urban ashes stand a better chance of survival there won't be a kneejerk reaction by authorities to eradicate all of them before they do succumb to ash dieback, with the risk of losing potentially tolerant trees. The sheer cost of these type of exercises may well restrict such actions anyway. The urban ash just might be a beacon of hope in an otherwise gloomy scenario.

LEFT:
High cut coppice stool in Hayley Wood, Cambridgeshire.

BELOW:
Typical street tree shows the close proximity to people, traffic and houses. Possibly a source of concern with the advance of ash dieback.

ASH IN THE LANDSCAPE

OPPOSITE:
An extract from 'Abhainn Ashik to Yr Onnen' by Ackroyd & Harvey from the exhibition 'The Ash Archive' in 2018.

Ash Place Names

The first time that a comprehensive catalogue of place names was brought together in one place was at the completion of the Domesday Book in 1086 although, obviously, many place names were far older than this, some dating back at least to the Old English charters of the seventh century, and a few as early as the writings of Ptolemy in the second century. Names were influenced by the different languages of invaders and settlers, from the Celts, Anglo-Saxons and Norsemen to, later on, the Normans.

The etymology of place names is an extremely complex science, for in some cases very similar-sounding names have very different meanings. Nothing should be taken for granted; for example, the name Ashford may seem obvious – 'the ash-tree by the ford' or 'the ford where ash-trees grow' – and this would be true for those places in Derbyshire, Kent and Devon, but in Surrey it is derived from *Ecelesford* (969) and *Exeforde* (1086), meaning 'the ford of a man called Eccel'.

If not derived from the name of the landowner, place names were usually contrived from major topographical features such as hills, valleys, woods, rivers, etc. or from more intimate features in the landscape such as farmsteads, enclosures, churches, wells and, of course, trees. The ash and the thorn (either hawthorn or blackthorn) appear to be the most commonly occurring species for this purpose, which would seem to indicate their ubiquity. However, in some parts of Britain it may have been because they were relatively unusual species, which made certain individual trees into notable landmarks.

There are places in Kent, Devon, Dorset, Somerset and Surrey called Ash, and Ashe in Hampshire – quite simply 'the place at the ash-tree or trees' – and similarly Ashen in Essex, but ash is more often associated either with another physical feature in the landscape, such as the common Ashley – 'ash-tree wood or clearing' or with a settlement, again, commonly, Ashton (including Eshton in Yorkshire) – 'farmstead where ash-trees grow' – or Ashby – literally 'by where ash-trees grow' or indicating 'farmstead or village where ash-trees grow'. Ashbourne in Derbyshire derives from 'a stream where ash-trees grow'. Sometimes there are three elements to the place name: for example, Ashwellthorpe in Norfolk is 'the thorp or hamlet belonging to Ashwell', which in turn is an 'ash-tree spring or well'.

Another common conjunction of place names is when they become possessive in some form – the wood, field, hill, tree, etc. belonging to a landowner, often termed a 'manorial affix'. A typical example in relation to ash might be Ashbrittle in Somerset – originally *Aisse* in Domesday, but by 1212 had become *Esse Britel,* 'the ash-trees belonging to a man called Bretel', or again, Ashreigney in Devon denotes 'the ash-trees at a place belonging to the *de Regny* family', from the thirteenth century. The always flamboyant-sounding Ashby de la Zouch in Leicestershire was land recorded as held by Roger de la Zuche in 1200, clearly with attendant ash trees. Ashbocking in Suffolk was originally named Ash (recorded as *Esse* in 1198 and *Assh* in 1296), but by 1411 had become *Bokkynge Assh*, Charter Rolls showing that one Ralph de Bocking held the manor in 1338.

Place names beginning with the ash variant 'Ask', derived from Old English æsc and later Old Scandinavian *askr*, are to be found principally in Yorkshire, indicating the Norse influence in those parts: Askham ('homestead or enclosure where ash-trees grow'), Askrigg ('ash-tree ridge') or Askwith ('ash-tree wood'). The village of Escrick, also in Yorkshire, derives from Old Scandinavian *eski* and Old English *ric* ('a strip of land or narrow ridge where ash-trees grow'). While Esher in Surrey

ASH PLACE NAMES

42 ASH PLACE NAMES

simply signifies 'a district where ash-trees grow'. Aspatria in Cumbria is an interesting variation, for this means 'Patric's ash', a combination derived from *askr*, along with the Celtic name. Some other ash place names have more prosaic origins, many probably from the post-medieval period, and are simply called after ash trees associated with a settlement, such as Stoke Ash in Suffolk or Ashkirk ('the church near an ash-tree') in the Scottish Borders; while other settlements found their names from a group of notable ash trees in the vicinity: Three Ashes in Herefordshire; four Four Ashes (in Solihull, Suffolk and Staffordshire – twice!); Five Ashes in East Sussex; Six Ashes in Shropshire; Seven Ash in Somerset and Eight Ash Green in Essex. Several of these are also marked by the presence of a public house of the same name. Topping all these there's Monyash in Derbyshire, from the Old English *manig* and *æsc*, signifying 'many an ash' – a tree that still dominates the local landscape to this day, although that could all change in the near future. When the geographical parameters of country folks' lives were a lot more confined than they are today, something as basic as little and large were sometimes all that was needed to differentiate two places: hence the adjacent villages of Ash Magna ('large ash-tree') and Ash Parva ('small ash-tree') in Shropshire. However, large ash trees eventually die and small ash trees become large ash trees, so this surely represents a very specific place in time.

A cursory glance at almost any Ordnance Survey map will reveal numerous local landmarks such as crossroads, hills, woods, farms or homesteads with ash appellations. Again, it is the ubiquitous nature of the ash that makes it so readily available for this purpose.

In Welsh place names oak and alder occur most commonly, while ash is relatively unusual. The Welsh name for ash is *onnen*, found in such place names as Rhyd-yr-Onnen in Gwynedd (the 'ash-tree by the ford') or simply Onen, a crossroads hamlet in Monmouthshire just 3 miles south of another settlement at a crossroads called Cross Ash.

In Ireland the Gaelic names for ash ranged through *fuinnse*, *fuinnsean* and *fuinnsiog* (pronounced 'funsha', 'funshan' and 'funshog'), reflected in names such as the River Funcheon in Cork and settlements named Funshin and Funshinagh in Connaught.

In Scotland the Gaelic name for ash is *uinnse* (pronounced 'inshy') and Sir Herbert Maxwell in his *Scottish Land-Names; their Origin and Meaning* (1894) notes several ash-related place names: Inshaw Hill (Wigtownshire) is 'ash-tree hill' and Killyminshaw (Dumfriesshire) is 'ash wood'; alternatively *uinnseog* ('inshog'), as in Inshock (Forfar), Inshaig (Argyll), Inshog (Nairn), all mean 'ash-tree', while Drumnaminshog and Knockninshock (Kirkcudbright) are respectively 'the ridge and the hill of the ash-trees'.

Examining the roots of place names is a fascinating way to glean a far greater understanding of the interrelated historical threads of the settlement, often referring to elements that have long since disappeared.

Borrowash in Derbyshire appears to have had three slightly different names, all recorded in the thirteenth century; its earliest was *Burgh upon Derwent* in 1269, Burgh signifying a castle, fort, hill or mound, or perhaps a combination of two of these things – a fortified mound? By 1272 the name had become *Burysasch* and in 1275 it was recorded as *Burwishasshe*, 'the ash by the Burgh'. The difference being that within several years the presence of an ash tree had suddenly become significant enough to be mentioned or to reflect the identity of the location more precisely. Archaeologist Ian Parker Heath, who has done much research on the neighbouring village of Ockbrook, writes of a landmark to the east of the village, first recorded in 1826, called Giant's Hill. It appears on the first Ordnance Survey map of 1887 and a mound, quite possibly a tumulus, shown on the hill, is called Giant's Grave. A nearby enclosure was called Castle Field. Other mounds and earthworks at the site suggest either a defensive structure or perhaps burial mounds or barrows. So there is a suggestion that the name Burgh begins to become plausible if it was related to any of these features. Exactly why ash became part of the settlement's name is impossible to know.

Whitnash in Warwickshire is an ancient settlement that can trace its roots back to before the Roman occupation. In the Domesday Book it is entered as *Witenas*, but by 1236 in the Book of Fees it has become *Wihtenassh*, meaning '(place at) the white ash-tree'. Exactly what a 'white ash' was is debatable – perhaps a landmark ash tree with very pale bark, or a sport tree with a genetic aberration that produced particularly pale foliage, or maybe simply a dead tree that had become weathered and bleached.

Campsea Ashe, alternatively Campsey Ash, in Suffolk, can trace its name back to the time

OPPOSITE:
An Edwardian postcard of the ash tree at Barkston Ash, marking the centre of Yorkshire.

BELOW:
The latest generation of the Barkston Ash in a long line of succession stretching back over 400 years.

BELOW RIGHT:
The Ash Tree pub sign, Barkston Ash, North Yorkshire.

of the Viking colonisation of much of eastern England in the ninth and tenth centuries, when the Scandinavian language began to have a strong influence on place names. It is believed that the name derived from the combination of two adjacent settlements – *Kampi Ey*, which meant 'a camp and an island', and *Esca*, the 'ash-tree'. By 1086 the Domesday Book lists them as *Campeseia* and *Esce* – 'island (or dry ground within a marsh) with a field or enclosure' and 'ash-tree'. By 1211 it is *Campesse*, *Campese* by 1235 and, more recognisably, by 1254 *Campeseye Ass*. It is unusual that to this day the place has two slightly different, but equally accepted variants of its name, alongside a tradition that rather appropriately perpetuates hundreds of years of etymological morphology.

A famous oak tree at Lillington, a suburb of Leamington Spa in Warwickshire, that once marked the centre of England was relentlessly photographed from the late Victorian era onwards, being published by innumerable postcard companies well into the twentieth century. Estimated to be about 200 years old, it was eventually found to be unsound and had to be felled in 1970. A replacement was planted. Exactly why people were so fascinated by this definition of the geographical centre-point of the country is difficult to reconcile, but it was clearly a theme that travelled.

In the village of Barkston Ash, near Tadcaster in North Yorkshire, local tradition asserts that an ash tree that once grew on the village green not only gave the village its name, but also marked the centre of the County of Yorkshire. A bizarre local legend claims that anyone who spits at the tree (why would you?) will be struck by lightning a year and a day later – a story perpetuated because of a character known as Jack Foll who was reputed to have done exactly that and later suffered this very fate. As long as the locals can recall, there has always been an ash tree as a focal point in the village, but obviously not the same one.

Barkston was recorded in the Domesday Book as *Barchestune* and classified as a *Wapentac* (latterly *Wappentake* or *Wapentake*), meaning an area of jurisdiction, a name particularly associated with northern counties of England, and of similar status to a 'hundred' in other parts of the country. Clearly there had to be some focal point near the centre of the Wapentake, where everyone was accustomed to gather to make laws and administer justice. The name is believed to be derived from the Old Norse, literally translating as 'weapon + taking' – signifying a means for an assembly to vote with a show of weapons. In the case of Barkston it might have originally been a crossroads or some other noticeable feature in the landscape, as the

44 ASH PLACE NAMES

addition of 'Ash' to the name first appears in the West Riding Sessions Rolls of 1598 (*Wapentag de Barkston Ash(e)*), at which time it would appear that the meeting place was by now beneath a large ash tree. This would indicate that there has been a tradition of a landmark ash tree in the village for at least 400 years. It would be fascinating to know when the last official administrative gathering convened beneath the tree. The last large ash to fulfil this role was estimated to be about 150 years old when it was eventually deemed to be unsound and needed to be felled in 2000. However, local tradition insisted that it was immediately replaced with a sapling. This young tree is currently in good shape, but the local community hopes that ash dieback will not visit their eponymous tree, and only time will tell.

The nearby pub, just along the road, is called the Ash Tree and has a painted rendition of the Barkston Ash on its pub sign. Ash Tree pubs are something of a rarity, especially when compared to the plethora of Royal Oaks, but if King Charles II had hidden in the top of a great old ash perhaps history might have been very different.

Ash names are sometimes woven into the street grids of large towns and cities, and may often refer to landmark trees or woods that, in most cases, have disappeared under the relentless advance of urban sprawl many years if not centuries ago. One example is Burnt Ash Road, in the London Borough of Lewisham, a name that begs the question as to its origin. Early records, some of which go back to the fourteenth century, identify a wood nearby known as Crabland Spring that covered the crest of Burnt Ash Hill. In the eighteenth century there was also a Burnt Ash Farm. 'Crabland' might seem to indicate a wood containing crab apples; it may well have done, as Oliver Rackham does note that crab-trees were the third most mentioned species as boundary markers in Anglo-Saxon and Welsh charters. 'Spring' is an appellation from Old English meaning a wood under coppice management or, again, more particularly from Middle English, 'a plantation of young trees, especially one for rearing or harbouring game, a spinney, a copse'. Assuming that the 'young trees' in this instance might have been ash coppice regeneration, it would seem likely that the name 'Burnt Ash' was derived from the production of charcoal.

Another unforgettable place name has to be Knotty Ash, a district on the eastern edge of the City of Liverpool, brought into the entertainment spotlight in the 1960s by local resident and comedian Ken Dodd as the home town of his famous Diddy Men. The name is supposed to derive from a gnarled old ash tree that once stood near the former Knotty Ash public house. In Middle English *knot* usually refers to a hill (a name particularly associated with northern dialects), so whether there was once a hill with an ash tree here would be interesting to know.

BELOW:
Veteran ash pollard on the edge of Ashton Wood, above Ashton under Hill, Worcestershire.

OPPOSITE:
Etching of an ash tree by an unknown artist, published by Ackermann, London 1821.

The Raising of Ash

From the seventeenth century onwards numerous treatises and manuals devoted to woodland management and rural husbandry were published, and right up to the end of the nineteenth century they all place the ash and the oak as the premier tree species for cultivation, and of greatest value to foresters with such an abundance of ready markets for the wood. It is possible to pluck examples of planting, raising and harvesting from any one of these books, but perhaps one of the more entertaining accounts comes from William Cobbett in *The Woodlands – A Treatise* (1825).

Cobbett heralds the ash with a flourish: 'This tree is, on every account, one of those which is of the greatest consequence. The manner, therefore, of raising it, ought to have particular attention bestowed upon it.' He begins his detailed instructions of how to plant, manage and harvest ash trees under the subtitle 'Common English Ash: Fraxinus Exclesior [sic]' – a strange oversight for a man as exacting as Cobbett. He admires its potential magnitude and beauty and recalls how Gilpin famously described it as 'the Venus of the Woods'. Cobbett notes with regret that the big disadvantage of ash is that 'it puts on its leaves later in the spring, and loses them earlier in the fall [his time spent in America clearly influencing his text], than any other English tree.' Then, in a disparaging if not slightly lascivious tone, he suggests that 'Gilpin was thinking of a *naked* Venus, and then, indeed, the Ash claims the pre-eminence in our woods.' He continues with the virtues of ash:

> ... we have no tree of such various and extensive use as the Ash. It gives us boards; materials for making implements of husbandry; and contributes towards the making of tools of almost all sorts. We could not well have a wagon, a cart, a coach or a wheelbarrow, a plough, a harrow, a spade, an axe or a hammer, if we had no Ash. It gives us poles for our hops; hurdle gates, wherewith to pen in our sheep; and hoops for our washing tubs; and assists to supply the Irish and West Indians with hoops for their pork barrels and sugar hogsheads.

Cobbett stresses the ease of obtaining plentiful supplies of ash seed and proposes a financial illustration for the gentleman with planting intentions, aiming to produce a hundred thousand plants.

> The seeds for ten rod [a sixteenth of an acre] of ground could not, to any gentleman in the country, cost above a shilling; another shilling would mix the seed with sand; five shillings would dig the ground and sow it; another five shillings would be ample pay for the weeding of it; so that, unless a gentleman could talk of the rent of ten rod of ground ... the whole of the cost of this one hundred thousand plants would be only *twelve shillings*, much about three halfpence a thousand ...

Apparently this would provide enough young trees to plant up 40 acres of woodland.

He goes on to describe different methods of management – coppicing at various intervals to obtain underwood for specific purposes and the option to leave single stems from each stool to grow into mature trees, thinning as and where necessary. Coppice with standards is still a widely practised woodland regime today. However, he notes that 'by planting the trees close together, particularly at the first, you insure straightness, and also an absence of side shoots of any size. The plants draw each other up in a straight form, and, if thinned out gradually and judiciously, they become an uniform and most beautiful plantation.' He is most insistent that the best time to fell ash is in the winter, with all such work completed by the

THE RAISING OF ASH 47

BELOW:
Outgrown coppice stools near Middleton-on-the-Hill, Herefordshire.

BELOW RIGHT:
Brood chambers left by ash bark beetles (Hylesinus varius).

beginning of March, and, while he fails to identify any uses for the bark, he also insists that timber should be debarked as soon as possible to prevent the wood from rotting. An assertion reinforced by many authorities for at this time the timber is most at risk from attack by ash bark beetle, whose larval channels disfigure the sapwood of the tree. This insect was often simply referred to as 'the fly' by many rural craftsmen.

In conclusion Cobbett asserts: 'As a fuel, its wood is far better than any other tree that we have: its growth is almost the quickest: its various uses are all of importance; and its propagation, cultivation and management, are all nearly as easy as those of a cabbage plant.' A strange comparison, but then that's Cobbett!

Quite correctly, he stresses the need to protect young ash trees in plantations and coppice regeneration.

An observation which relates to Ash trees in general is this, that the greatest care should be taken to keep cattle out of the young plantations, and out of coppices, where the young shoots are yet low. A hungry cow, or a hungry horse, especially the latter, would destroy an acre in the course of a few days. When once cropped off, they can yield you neither pole nor hoop. The coppice if cropped all over, would yield you nothing but fagot wood. I therefore beg leave to press upon all those who have young plantations, or recently-cut coppices, the absolute necessity of keeping all sorts of cattle out of them, not forgetting those mischievous vermin, the rabbits, one of which will bark twenty, thirty, or perhaps fifty, young Ash trees in a night. In many cases, valuable coppices have been nearly totally destroyed, or at least a ten years' growth of them has been destroyed by the teeth of the rabbits and the hares, both of them fond of the bark of young trees in general; and this valuable tree, the Ash, happens, unfortunately, to be one of their favourite dishes.

In this latter assertion he was correct to some degree, but it is thought that most rabbit damage occurs because they are gnawing the bark to wear down their ever-growing teeth rather than seeking nutriment.

The management advice for ash woods varies relatively little among writers on forestry matters, but in the light of the current lack of management in so much woodland, largely down to the uneconomic prospects for produce sales, the observations of Prideaux John Selby in his *History of British Forest-Trees*, albeit over 150 years ago, could still be very relevant. While he recommends

48   THE RAISING OF ASH

'cultivating the Ash with a view to profit, and where it is intended to form the principal crop of timber, it is best planted by itself without admixture of other deciduous trees, as from its mode of growth it proves one of the worst of neighbours in mixed plantations.' Once ash is planted, Selby is quick to berate those foresters who might neglect their trees:

> It is from a want of attention to timely thinning, – one of the most important branches of Arboriculture, – that we see so many instances of unhealthy and stunted-looking plantations: these, whether as large masses or in the form of narrow belts, are, after the operation of planting, too frequently allowed to grow unheeded and neglected for many years, without any attempt to improve their condition by gradual thinning and the necessary admission of light and air.

After about twenty years the consequences are a familiar sight – overcrowded woodland with tufty-topped trees, bereft of lateral branches, with inadequate root systems, so that when they are eventually thinned the greatly weakened trees, once exposed to high winds, are very susceptible to wind throw and, as a result, often damaging other areas of the plantation in their path when they fall. James Brown in *The Forester* (1851) considers that 'smaller ash trees always yield much better timber'. He continues:

> A peculiar characteristic of this tree is, that the quality of the wood is always the better for being rapidly grown; at least in so far as regards its immediate use, it being always increased in toughness of fibre by the rapidity of its growth (but perhaps not the durability of its timber), the opposite of which is the case with most other trees.

There is a general agreement among forestry writers that raising ash trees is a simple, and relatively foolproof, process (viz. Cobbett and the cabbage). After detailed instructions of how to stratify the seed in beds of sand for eighteen months prior to planting, and stipulating exact spacing for transplanted seedlings, the consensus is that ash will grow very well from randomly (naturally) distributed seeds anyway. The best suggestions are often that anyone wishing to plant ash trees simply rakes over a bit of soil and sprinkles seeds before raking a tiny bit of earth back over them. Upon germination a little weeding out of the poorer plants will allow the others to thrive. Seedlings are generally thought to be big enough to transplant into the woods by three to four years.

Another common observation is that self-sown seeds usually seem to be more vigorous than planted seedlings. Henry Elwes, in *Trees of Great Britain and Ireland* (1909), noted that trees from seed in his nursery attained 7–8 feet after three years while those grown as transplanted seedlings were only 3 feet high at the same age. Surely the

ABOVE:
A twenty year old ash plantation that is ripe for thinning.

THE RAISING OF ASH 49

ABOVE:
Remarkably tall ashes at Cobham Park, in Kent – a photogravure plate from 'The Trees of Great Britain and Ireland' by Elwes and Henry. H.J. Elwes would appear to be in the centre of the group. Elwes and Henry were great advocates for growing the finest timber trees.

genetic lineage of self-sown seeds in the wild reflects their proven adaptation to a particular type of site. Introduced, planted trees may have their origins in a very different type of landscape and soil, making them less suited to their new location. As Richard Mabey has pointed out, trees from the Highlands of Scotland are hardly likely to thrive in the fens of East Anglia and vice versa. Again, Herbert Edlin in the 1940s, among other writers, strongly advised the planting of ash seed of known provenance in the same types of location as the parent trees to gain the best results.

Writing in his *Welsh Timber Trees* of 1931, H. A. Hyde refers to research information then recently received from Germany that had tried to explain why particular ash trees succeed in very different habitats. He describes the Welsh ash woods on Carboniferous Limestone, often with an admixture of oak, typical of the Gower Peninsula and the environs of Tenby in Pembrokeshire; and contrasts this with the less predictable flourishing of ash in wet ravines and along stream sides on non-calcareous soils. The thinking was that these two dissimilar types of ash populations were 'different strains' or 'local races', a factor that could now be confirmed or refuted with genetics. It was found that the so-called 'lime-ashes' were more adaptable, needed less moisture and could thrive on almost any soil, while the 'water-ashes', grown from stock associated with the damp siliceous soils, were much less adaptable. With these affinities in mind, Hyde recommends that planted ash trees should be sourced from local stock in order to get the best from tree growth and, ultimately, the timber. This theory of planting locally sourced ash trees still makes a great deal of sense today, for thousands of years of natural selection have refined a balance in the various regional ash populations, perfectly attuned to their very specific habitats.

Elwes and Henry considered that ash was the most profitable hardwood to cultivate in the early twentieth century, and of a far superior quality to the imported ash timber. They state that ash trees become most prized when boles reach about 3–6 feet in girth, around fifty to sixty years old, asserting that 'no other hardwood apart from sweet chestnut becomes so valuable at such an early age'. Other writers and foresters believed that ash timber reached its pinnacle around eighty to a hundred years of age, and an amusing anecdote from the Reverend C. A. Johns notes: 'When the woodpeckers are seen tapping these trees, they ought to be cut, as these birds never make holes in the Ash, until it is on the decay.' A little late by this time one would have thought.

There was often concern that older trees developed discoloured or 'black-hearted' timber – thought by some to be less desirable, albeit still structurally sound. This phenomenon does not indicate a stage of decomposition or a sign of disease, and is still not entirely understood, although it appears to be more prevalent in trees growing on particularly wet ground. Maiden trees much in excess of a hundred years are usually thought to be in decline, but coppice stools and pollards can attain much greater age. Coppice poles were often considered to be the most useful size for many applications, and stools have the ability to throw poles 6–7 foot long in a year, but after five or six rotations the stools may become hollowed and worn out. Nonetheless, bearing in mind there can be twelve to twenty years between each cutting, that is still a very productive life.

Elwes makes bold claims for ash timber: 'For all purposes in which strength, toughness and durability are required, [it] has no equal … In consequence it is now the easiest to sell, if not quite the highest priced, of all English timbers; and its growing scarcity seems to point to a great future for it.' The assumption was that increased demand and a reduction in availability would lead to higher returns for growers. Remarkable optimism in 1909, at a time when so many uses of ash, and wood in general, were about to be eclipsed by metals and later on by plastics.

Until relatively recent times ash was very much a part of the commercial broadleaf cultivation strategy. However, communications with the industries that still require high-quality ash timber result in rather downbeat responses, typically that the quality of ash they seek is not readily available in Britain, nor the conversion infrastructure to process the timber into the appropriate shapes and sizes for use. The result is that much ash for industry is now sourced from abroad. The arrival, or at least the official recognition of the arrival, of ash dieback in 2012 has put the brakes on any further planting and raising of ash trees, certainly in a commercial sense, for the foreseeable future. A moratorium has been imposed on all ash tree imports and nurseries have no reason to grow the trees if there are no potential buyers. All that can be done now is to observe the ash stocks that exist, monitor how they progress in the face of ash dieback, and hope that some will survive. Although the disease may not affect the timber during the early-onset phase, it will eventually cause basal rot which travels through the tree causing instability. For some while yet there will be ash available for a variety of industries and crafts, although one senses that ultimately the firewood trade will be the biggest beneficiary.

Close examination of a cross section of an ash log reveals the structure of the annual rings of wood laid down in the tree. It is clearly defined as two phases of annual growth. The early-wood, or springwood, is made from thin-walled cells with larger cavities, facilitating the rapid ascent of sap up the tree and a higher rate of growth during springtime and early summer. It is clearly lighter in colour and the width within each

BELOW:
Ash regeneration outside Stoke Woods, Rodger Stoke, Somerset, shows how quickly young trees can colonise open ground, as long as they can avoid the predations of herbivores.

THE RAISING OF ASH 51

RIGHT:
Cross section of a 64 year-old ash tree shows clearly defined ring width variation depending on prevailing climatic conditions. The two very narrow rings in the middle refer to the extreme drought of 1975/76. The broad ring a little further on in 1985 was a particularly wet summer. The outer seven rings, just before the tree was felled in 2010, where there is hardly any summer growth, show that the tree was fighting some sort of stress conditions or disease. This pattern is very typical of other ash trees that have been felled and were suffering from ash dieback.

BELOW:
Black heart in a cut section of ash timber.

OPPOSITE:
Pete Fordham at work in a recently felled compartment of oak and ash coppice with standards in Bradfield Woods, Suffolk.

annual ring tends to be relatively consistent. The late-wood, or summerwood, manifests as a much darker line, since the cells are much smaller and have much thicker walls and the later growth phase is most highly influenced by the variability of rainfall during this period. Other factors such as late frosts, the immediate aftermath of pollarding or coppicing, and any tussles the tree may have with disease also tend to be reflected in the summerwood layer. The larger pores of the springwood which are so well defined in ash means that it is known as a ring-porous species, contrasting with other hardwoods (known as diffuse-porous species) where there is little visible difference in pore size throughout the growing season.

It is this disparity in form and strength between the springwood and summerwood of ash, along with its tendency to grow with extremely straight grain, that makes it such a good wood for cleaving. With the skilful use of a froe (a metal blade with a handle set at right angles) and a wooden maul or club, ash will cleave easily, either radially (straight across the annual rings) or tangentially (at an angle diagonally across the rings). Gentle pressure on the froe in different directions eases the cleave to stay straight and even. These are the raw materials, the blanks so to speak, that will be worked with draw-knives, spoke-shaves or turned on the lathe to make a multitude of useful, often beautiful products.

The other critical assessment of ash timber relates to the speed of growth, a factor easily measured across the annual growth rings. Twenty or more rings per inch indicates quite slow growth, while less than ten rings per inch is considered fast grown, so for optimum toughness where products are tested to the limit, typically something like an axe helve, growth rates of four to sixteen rings per inch are preferable. In the modern era power tools and intricate, computerised lathes may have superseded the artisan's hand tools, passed down through the generations, but the eye of the true craftsman or craftswoman is still indispensable.

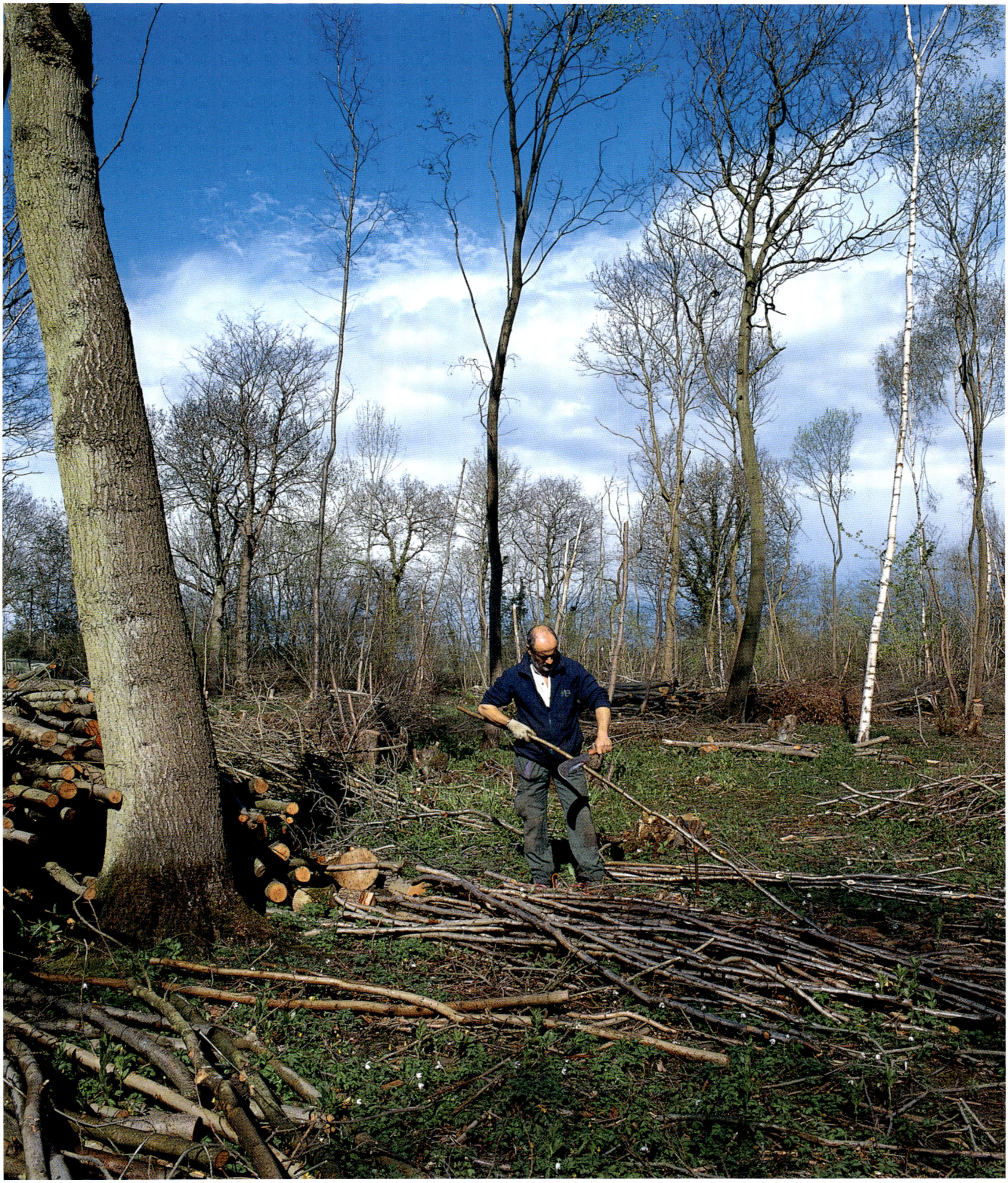

BELOW:
Inside Rassal ash trees grow along the rocky terraces.

Ash Woods

Ash may be a contributory species in a wide variety of woods throughout Britain, but it is on limestone in particular that it often becomes the dominant or climax species, shaping the landscape as well as the specific habitat for a distinctive range of flora and fauna. These woodlands, clearly defined by ash, are just a representative selection of such sites and provide a vivid indication of the magnitude of the losses to the treescape that are likely to occur in the wake of the ash dieback epidemic currently sweeping across Britain. Try to imagine all of these places devoid of ash trees.

Rassal Ashwood and the Dundonnell River valley

A few miles to the north of the Kyle of Lochalsh, at the head of Loch Kishorn in Wester Ross, one finds a most unusual and totally unexpected wood in this remote corner of Scotland. Ash trees are by no means thick on the ground in this region, but Rassal Ashwood, regarded by many authorities as the most northerly ash-dominant wood in Britain, has been deeply rooted here on top of a remarkable limestone outcrop for many centuries, perhaps even millennia.

The first sight of ash trees as one drives up the nearby country road is of somewhat ragged old specimens clinging to the limestone crags immediately above and, in the spring, the damp flushes beneath harbour clumps of the wild iris or yellow flags – bold, exotic-looking plants somewhat out of character in this relatively barren landscape. Pick a way up the rocky slope and, once over the rise, the main bulk of the wood swings into view. Like many dense woods, it's hard to appreciate the complex nature of the structure from the outside, but once within the stock-proof fences the wood begins to reveal itself.

Rassal became a National Nature Reserve back in 1956, and two years later the first trial exclusion of sheep by fencing off one part of the wood resulted in a remarkable regeneration of wild flowers and young trees. The process was then repeated in a different area in 1975, with the addition of some experimental planting. Again, the results were very positive and by 1991 it was thought best to fence off the whole wood. The evolution of Rassal has been moulded by a balance based on human need for grazing livestock beneath the trees, providing the animals with shade in summer and shelter in winter, and feeding them with ash fodder, as well as for the cultivation of crops and woodmanship. Evidence of outgrown ash pollards reveals that the site was managed as wood pasture, and ring counts from some of these older trees dates most of them back to the late eighteenth or early nineteenth century, although one has been dated back to at least 1739.

The lie of the land is a diverse mixture of little outcrops and ridges of limestone pavement, occasionally littered with large moss-clad boulders. The rockiest areas, perhaps less accessible for hungry animals to reach, seem to support the biggest trees, and not just ash, as rowan, hazel and willows are all part of the mix, and almost everything is well mantled with mosses and lichens. It may not be immediately apparent to the casual viewer, but woodland historians believe that some of the clearings and terraces within the wood have almost certainly been utilised for cultivation of crops in the distant past. The trees that do grow near these clearings are usually the younger, smaller ones, since the cultivated areas would have needed to be kept clear of overshadowing larger trees.

The setting is magnificent – a raised stage of historic woodland, its vibrant, purposeful role in the Highland community virtually abandoned, but held in trust by its own natural vitality (with a little human assistance), surrounded by an ever-watchful mountain amphitheatre.

Make a bold statement and there will always be someone waiting in the wings to query it and striving to set matters straight. In this instance the owner of an estate set in the Dundonnell River valley, some 50 miles further north, felt slightly aggrieved that his ash trees had long been overlooked by the charters of trees and woodlands. With the relative scarcity of ash in the north-west of Scotland one would have to wonder how many of them naturally pioneered their present territory. In the environs of Dundonnell the obvious indigenous broadleaf treescape principally revolves around birch and alder, with sessile oak and, to a lesser degree, wych elm, rowan, holly, hazel, wild

ABOVE:
Mountainous backdrop beyond Rassal Ashwood.

RIGHT:
Early morning sunlight strikes a lone ash in the Dundonnell River valley.

ASH WOODS

ABOVE:
Poised above the river the extensive roots of this ash consolidate the bank.

cherry and crab-apple. Small numbers of beech and sweet chestnut are certain introductions.

Ash trees are evident in some order in the valley, though never presenting the appearance of ash-dominant or even ash-prominent woodland. Most are maiden trees, either standing in glorious isolation or in small groups, and generally in the valley bottom, closer to the river. Some trees, in a couple of locations, are very obviously planted in closely spaced lines along the riverside, almost certainly as an attempt to create a strong network of roots to stabilise the banks.

Rassal, on its limestone outcrop, is an obvious haunt for ash, but the Dundonnell River valley lies mainly on siliceous schists of what are known as the Moine Series – a complex layering of rock sheets caused by tectonic thrusting and mountain formation around 430 million years ago. A recent survey of the area's lichens revealed the surprising evidence of many calcareous springs emanating from rocky clefts clearly bearing calcite deposits.

The run-off from such sources was shown to influence the lichen flora, but will obviously also influence selective colonisation of vascular plants and trees and, most particularly, creating the base-rich soils that ash prefers. Soil tests around the existing ashes would make an interesting study.

One of the largest ashes that fell in a storm in 2008 had an annual ring count taken from a cross section at about 2 metres above ground. The 281 rings, plus a few more, allowing for the height of the cut sample, revealed that it had started life a few years prior to 1725. For a tree with a girth of almost 3 metres this was quite a remarkable age, so clearly growth was relatively slow in these colder northern climes with long winters and shorter growing seasons. As far as foresters would have been concerned, this was not the best recipe for growing high-quality ash timber, which normally comes from fast-grown trees less than half the age. Another issue with these ash trees is the almost total lack of evidence of either pollarding or coppicing. Even the dendrochronology failed to show any signs of ring-width variation usually associated with pollarding cycles. If these were meant to be working trees, this seems very strange. Sadly, there are no historical estate records of tree planting at Dundonnell, but a sole surviving ash with a 5-metre girth may potentially hold the secret of the earliest planting in this remote valley. One senses that this may date back to around 1600.

An interesting comparison with the impressive age of the wind-thrown ash was the felling of an almost identically girthed ash on my land in Herefordshire a few years back. A ring count for this tree revealed it to have been 160 years old, making it a little over half the age of the Dundonnell tree, and a vivid illustration of how growth rates can vary in different climes.

Some strange growth traits appear on a couple of ashes at Dundonnell – notably one tree that appears to have fasciated or coalesced boughs that form a kind of large burry excrescence with three branches emerging from it (see page 170). Exactly what has caused this is something of a mystery. A virus? Some kind of insect-induced gall?

LEFT:
A row of planted ash trees along the Dundonnell riverbank.

BELOW:
A typical solitary tree above the valley. The pale grey crustose lichen is Ochrolechia subviridis and gives the appearance of having been painted onto the bark.

ASH WOODS 59

ABOVE:
Ash colonises even the most precipitous and precarious situations in Cheddar Gorge.

The Mendip Gorges

The Mendip Hills of Somerset are formed by a long ridge of Carboniferous Limestone running east to west across the north of the county, overlooking the Levels to the south and deeply bisected by several deep gorges, which have long been havens for ash-dominant woodlands with their accompanying rich array of calcicolous plants. These gorges were formed by summer melt-waters during various Ice Ages over more than a million years, when the subterranean caverns carved out during the intervening climatically warmer eras were blocked by permafrost.

Cheddar is the most famous of these gorges and a long history of tourism has resulted in a detailed pictorial record stretching back to the middle of the nineteenth century. Early photographs show a landscape that is apparently almost devoid of trees, which may seem surprising to today's visitors who see verdant woodland on both sides of the gorge and many small stands and solitary trees clinging to rocky outcrops. The inference here is that a combination of more intensive livestock grazing coupled with tree felling or coppicing led to the Victorian vistas looking so treeless. With the decline in the demand for wood during the post-war period one begins to chart a distinct increase in the levels of vegetation. Postcards of the 1950s already show views that contrast quite noticeably with those of the late Victorian and Edwardian periods.

At present there are so many trees in Cheddar Gorge that feral sheep and goats have been introduced to keep some of the regeneration at bay. The idea is to make more open grassland available for some of the rare wild flowers that grow here, such as the Cheddar pink, known only in the gorge, the nationally rare little robin geranium, and Cheddar bedstraw and several other nationally scarce species. However, since recent studies have concluded that eight species of indigenous whitebeams also grow here, three of which are known only in the gorge, the voracious appetites of these introduced animals now puts pressure on the natural regeneration of these rare trees, which illustrates how manipulating the habitat for one range of species doesn't always succeed across the board.

On the north edge of the Mendips another well-wooded gorge is Burrington Combe; not quite as dramatic as Cheddar Gorge, maybe, but containing a rich array of trees, again dominated by ash. On the northern-slopes yew, wild privet, wayfaring tree and whitebeam find precarious purchase on the crags and screes, while on the south side oak does well, particularly where the woodland thins beyond the dense stands of ash and gives way to the open moorland of Black Down, where some impressive rowans flourish among the bracken, interspersed in spring with fine displays of bluebells.

Ebbor Gorge in the hills above Wookey Hole is a lot more peaceful than either Cheddar or Burrington, since no road carves through the natural splendour of this wooded chasm and it is a fairly rugged path down from the car park above into the bosky depths below. Here ash is, yet again, the dominant tree, but accompanied by a diverse array of other species, including oak, wych elm, field maple, beech and sycamore, with an understorey of hazel, dogwood, spindle and hawthorn, and the very unexpected presence of a circular group of what would appear to be an old plantation of hornbeams. Although these must be too far west to be a natural colonisation, they do seem to have settled in very well with other apparently self-sown trees in the wood. It's the towering ashes that take star billing in this wood, though, as their tall, sinuous trunks compete and stretch skyward to find the sunlight. There have been over 150 lichen species recorded here as well as more than 100 different mosses and liverworts. For the most determined of scramblers making it to the top of the limestone cliffs there is the reward

ABOVE:
Early morning view across Burrington Combe towards Black Down.

RIGHT:
Young ashes find purchase on the limestone ledges of Cheddar Gorge.

BELOW RIGHT:
Ancient coppice stool in Little Stoke Woods.

OPPOSITE:
Ash dominant canopy above Little Stoke Woods.

of breath-taking, bird's-eye views across the gorge treescape and on towards the Somerset Levels, with small buckthorns and whitebeams clinging to the cliff edge.

Not all of the most remarkable Mendip woods are to be found in deep gorges, and perhaps one of the best of the rest is the woodland of Rodney Stoke National Nature Reserve. To view the dense ranks of trees that make up Big Stoke and Little Stoke Woods from the village below, it seems incredible to think that they were almost completely clear-felled after the Great War and partially felled again in 1939. The whole wood complex had long been managed as coppice and the evidence for this is still strongly reflected, principally by ash and oak stools, but also by small-leaved lime. Here and there the occasional wild service tree flourishes, along with buckthorn and guelder rose, and yet hazel dominates the understorey. The wood lies on two south-facing spurs and comprises a mixture of mounds and clefts. Some of the most picturesque ash stools are found grappling with life on the thin soils atop the rocky ridges, their serpentine roots snaking this way and that across the woodland floor. The abundance of natural regeneration of ash, both within the wood itself and the grassland above (see page 51), suggests that deer, which normally browse off all young seedlings and saplings, are not that numerous and livestock have not grazed the open grassland for some time. It would be an interesting experiment to see if the ash woods can burst through their old boundary at the top of the hill and colonise new ground with mature trees; however, one cycle of intensive grazing could stall that very quickly.

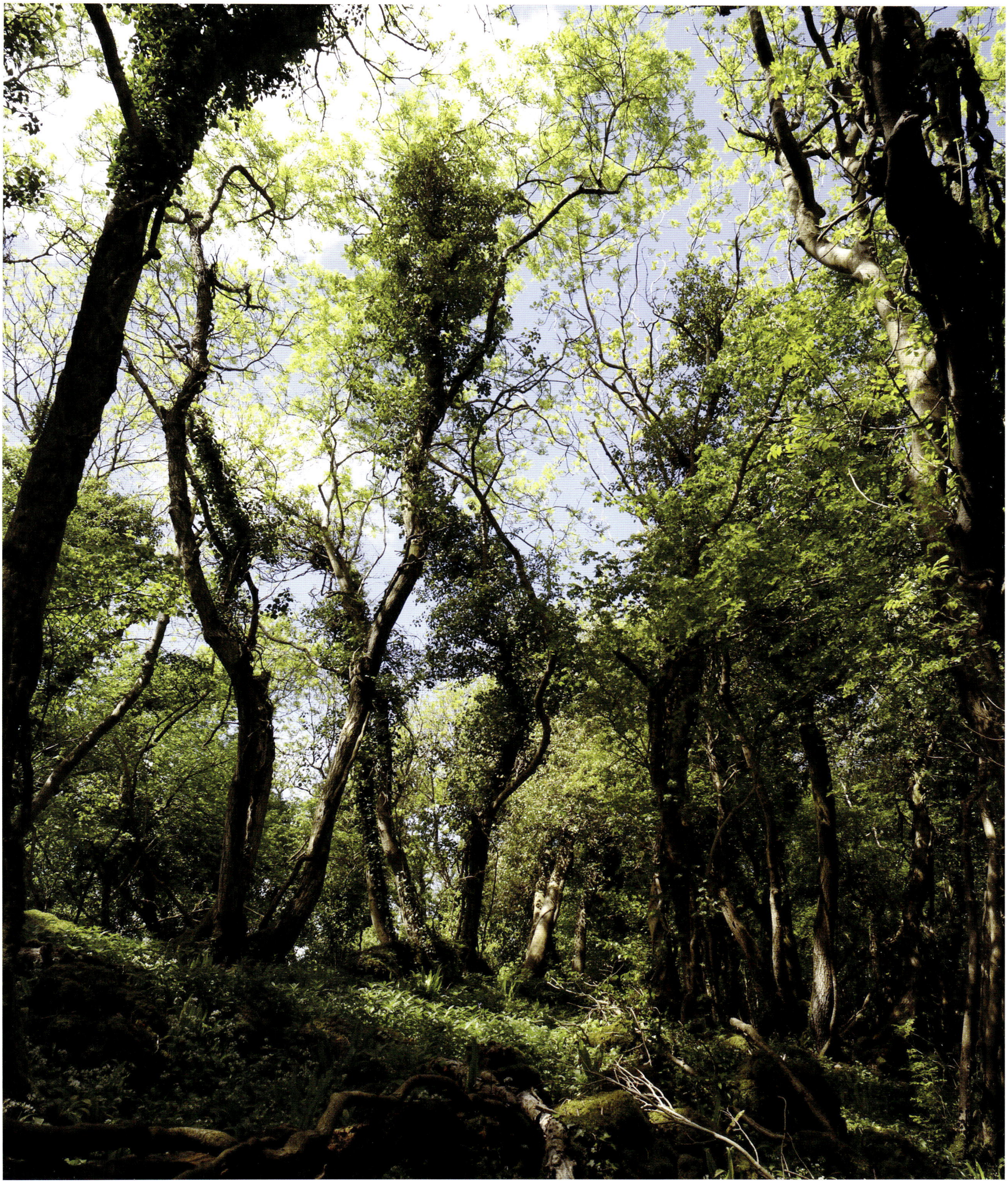

BELOW:
A distinctive group of ashes on the approach to Dovedale.

The Derbyshire Dales

With the impending threat of ash dieback sweeping the land, probably the single most vulnerable ash-defined treescape, and arguably the largest area of Britain that could be changed almost out of all recognition by the loss of ash trees, has to be the Derbyshire Dales. Especially across the limestone geology of Derbyshire, the area known as the White Peak, ash has long been the pre-eminent tree species, and not just in woodland, but lining the river valleys, as field trees, as well as alongside walls and in hedgerows. However, it is the deep river valleys, below limestone crags and screes, that will potentially look the most denuded should the worst-case scenario come to pass.

Dovedale has been a tourism honeypot since the Victorian era. This was a tamed wilderness; safe, but imparting something of a sense of adventure to the early tourists who were lured to the romantic beauty of the valley. Here they could ramble in a genteel fashion along well-trodden paths and marvel at the rock formations of pinnacles and caves carved out by glacial melt-waters, and the verdant woodland on every side, much in the same way as visitors still do today. Although a high proportion of the tree cover immediately along the riverbanks is alder, ash is by far the most dominant tree throughout the ravine. However, it's not just the actual river valley that contains fine ashes. Approaching Dovedale from the village of Thorpe, there is a classic view from the hilltop, perennially arresting, before the gentle descent into the valley below, where signature clumps of ash trees with the conical hill of Thorpe Cloud or the sweep of the valley as backdrop have featured in so many photographs. All around, the fields abound with small groups or fine individual ash trees, many traditionally used as shelter for livestock and probably for cutting ash 'hay' to feed them. Ashes reveal the lines of boundaries both current and defunct, often with the evidence of horizontal boughs laid in antiquity. Worryingly, during a visit in 2017 the signs of ash dieback could be observed in several different places.

LEFT:
Ash dominant woodland in Dovedale with Thorpe Cloud rising in the distance.

BELOW:
Reflections in the River Dove.

ASH WOODS

RIGHT:
Looking down on the ash canopy from high above Lathkill Dale.

BELOW:
Ashes quickly colonise and thrive on the limestone screes.

About 10 miles north of Dovedale, and just to the south of Bakewell, Lathkill Dale is another steep-sided valley dominated by hanging ash woods. Here the landscape is even more visibly moulded by sheep, for where they cannot reach on the steep valley sides trees grow in profusion, but on the hilltops above, on the plateau grassland, the sheep hold sway amid the undulating networks of dry-stone-walled enclosures. A broad footpath makes access easy for people of all abilities and walking upstream from below the village of Over Haddon one encounters flower-rich meadows on the south-facing north side of the valley. Mossy saxifrage grows here and further on, as the woodland closes in, drifts of wood anemone, primrose, red campion, forget-me-not and yellow archangel, and sporadic displays of lily of the valley and nettle-leaved bellflower. The rare Jacob's ladder grows in the upper reaches. Wych elm is still to be found in these woods even though Dutch elm disease has severely reduced its presence. In addition to the ash, oak and sycamore are the other principal broadleaf species, while dogwood, hazel, bird cherry and whitebeam complete the understorey. There are many places where limestone scree still appears to be very much in a state of flux, but ash bravely protrudes from among the rock-strewn slopes. Clearly, as the landscape slowly moves it opens up new fertile territory for the ever-exuberant ash keys to find a safe harbour. The view of the dale from the top of the crags above reveals a solid green carpet of tree canopy stretching out below, in places exclusively of ash; a sobering reminder of exactly what is at stake here for habitat and landscape character.

BELOW:
The emerald splendour of Lathkill Dale in spring.

ABOVE:
Plenty of vigorous regeneration in a group of recently pollarded trees.

Borrowdale and Watendlath Wood Pastures

Borrowdale in Cumbria is a paradoxical mixture of modern forestry in the shape of conifer plantations, usually on the lower slopes, interspersed by oak-dominant semi-natural ancient woodland, often mixed with ash and wych elm, that has been managed either as coppice wood or coppice with standards for hundreds of years, usually found on the higher, more inaccessible terrain. Add to this mixture the ghosts of wood pasture, a woodland type that has all but disappeared due to changes in farming practice. Ash pollards still stand, randomly distributed along the valley bottom and with increasing abundance as one travels higher up towards the valley end around Seathwaite, which is officially the wettest inhabited place in Britain, with records of around 330 centimetres of rain annually.

Here one finds Seatoller Wood, a long, straggling wood that ranges across the north-western slopes of the valley, containing a fascinating mixture of broadleaf trees growing on the steep, boulder-strewn hillside. Ash and oak predominate in different areas, and there is also birch, wych elm, holly, hazel, rowan, blackthorn, hawthorn, yew and bird cherry. Ancient ash pollards abound, most noticeably on the lower slopes that would have been more accessible for livestock. Sheep graze here now, but the reason for the pollards would have been to keep regrowth out of reach of cattle, horses and possibly wild deer. For a long time these pollards were allowed to grow unchecked, but because many of them became top-heavy they split and tumbled or lost boughs, so decisions were taken by the National Trust some forty to fifty years ago to bring them back into management – not really for any practical agricultural purpose, but simply to keep them alive and vibrant, functioning as habitat for epiphytes and invertebrates, providing nesting sites for birds and roosts for bats, and maintaining them as a cultural landscape feature. The initial worry was that cutting these trees back after so many years of management inactivity might traumatise them and they would die. Quite the opposite – the new pollarding regime, whereby trees are given a regular trim every fifteen to twenty years, has worked extremely well, and regeneration is excellent. Not only do the trees thrive, but so too do the attendant colonies of lichens and bryophytes perfectly suited to this wet, sheltered microclimate. The pollards also provide anchorage for aerial trees, with the bizarre sight of sometimes quite substantial yews, rowans, hollies or sycamores bursting forth from the crowns, although this phenomenon is not always welcomed by the conservation team as the success of the aerial trees could eventually lead to the loss of the pollards as they are split asunder by the invader.

Travelling south into Borrowdale, near the southern end of Derwent Water, a narrow lane

LEFT:
Looking into Seatoller Wood with an ash pollard in the foreground that is ready to be cut once more.

BELOW:
A National Trust forester pollarding one of the veteran ashes in Borrowdale.

Limestone Pavement Ash Woods of North Yorkshire

BELOW:
The great limestone arc of Malham Cove, North Yorkshire.

It is perhaps difficult to define the ash trees of the upper Yorkshire Dales as woodland, since they frequently occur either in very small stands or have a diminutive physical presence. For centuries the ash trees, along with all the other vegetation, have been embroiled in a battle for survival with sheep and the harsh weather conditions, but principally with the sheep. Not only do sheep find ash foliage very palatable, but they are remarkably tenacious and agile creatures, often scrambling up and down precipitous hillsides, traversing narrow ledges and, risking broken legs, nimbly navigating their way across the deep grikes of the limestone pavements, to reach their chosen meal.

Malham Cove has long been a popular tourist destination as a dramatic spectacle, both from below and above, as well as proving a challenging

years ago to bring them back into management – not really for any practical agricultural purpose, but simply to keep them alive and vibrant, functioning as habitat for epiphytes and invertebrates, providing nesting sites for birds and roosts for bats, and maintaining them as a cultural landscape feature. The initial worry was that cutting these trees back after so many years of management inactivity might traumatise them and they would die. Quite the opposite – the new pollarding regime, whereby trees are given a regular trim every fifteen to twenty years, has worked extremely well, and regeneration is excellent. Not only do the trees thrive, but so too do the attendant colonies of lichens and bryophytes perfectly suited to this wet, sheltered microclimate. The pollards also provide anchorage for aerial trees, with the bizarre sight of sometimes quite substantial yews, rowans, hollies or sycamores bursting forth from the crowns, although this phenomenon is not always welcomed by the conservation team as the success of the aerial trees could eventually lead to the loss of the pollards as they are split asunder by the invader.

Travelling south into Borrowdale, near the southern end of Derwent Water, a narrow lane

LEFT:
Looking into Seatoller Wood with an ash pollard in the foreground that is ready to be cut once more.

BELOW:
A National Trust forester pollarding one of the veteran ashes in Borrowdale.

forks left and climbs steeply through ancient oak woods named, rather inappropriately, Ashness Wood (indicating ash growing on a ridge or promontory), but perhaps ash was previously more prolific here. The lane shadows the course of the Watendlath Beck for about 5 miles, the adjoining fields dotted with whiskery old ash pollards, until the farm and tarn at the end of the valley are reached. Straight away, within a few metres of the farm, ancient ash pollards are evident crouching above the beck and, casting an eye to the distant hills, it becomes immediately apparent that these trees are a defining feature of Watendlath – there are scores of them. The name appears to be derived from Old Norse and means 'hill at the end of the lake', and Watendlath Fell looms large at the end of the tarn.

If the Borrowdale pollards are impressive, then some of the Watendlath trees are truly exceptional. Many are completely hollowed out, some boles have split into two or three outstretched shards, while others have fallen and yet continue to thrust out new growth. Aerial trees are frequent, but the abiding vision is of ancient trees completely and utterly smothered in mosses, liverworts and lichens to the point where hardly any bark is visible on some of the crusty old boles. Although they are far from the biggest ash trees in the land, they will have grown incredibly slowly in this environment, and best guesstimates for their ages range from 200–350 years old, although quite recently some authorities have speculated that they could be as much as 500–700 years old. As Maurice Pankhurst from the National Trust points out, 'We have pollarded trees at Watendlath with ring counts of more than a hundred years for some cut material,' which would suggest the period at which pollarding was last widely practised in the valley. He continues:

> The major problem with these trees is knowing when to pollard, as it is no longer a simple rotation; many need individual treatments depending on the integrity of the bollings. Currently some require pollarding on five-year cycles while others may shift towards every ten to fifteen years.

On early twentieth-century postcards of Watendlath the ash trees along the beck behind the farm can clearly be seen, looking almost exactly the same as they do today, but a hundred years ago they were still being regularly cut over to service the needs of stockmen. At present, bringing these pollards back into management shows the trees responding remarkably well. It seems odd to think that the reason to retain these ancient ashes today is driven by nature conservation and the preservation of the wood pasture – a rare cultural landscape – rather than agricultural necessity. Such considerations would have been of little concern to the farmers of old; for the pollards were simply working trees with practical purposes.

ABOVE, LEFT & OPPOSITE: *A selection of some of the many ancient ash pollards at Watendlath, wreathed in mosses and lichens.*

ASH WOODS

Limestone Pavement Ash Woods of North Yorkshire

It is perhaps difficult to define the ash trees of the upper Yorkshire Dales as woodland, since they frequently occur either in very small stands or have a diminutive physical presence. For centuries the ash trees, along with all the other vegetation, have been embroiled in a battle for survival with sheep and the harsh weather conditions, but principally with the sheep. Not only do sheep find ash foliage very palatable, but they are remarkably tenacious and agile creatures, often scrambling up and down precipitous hillsides, traversing narrow ledges and, risking broken legs, nimbly navigating their way across the deep grikes of the limestone pavements, to reach their chosen meal.

Malham Cove has long been a popular tourist destination as a dramatic spectacle, both from below and above, as well as proving a challenging

BELOW:
The great limestone arc of Malham Cove, North Yorkshire.

prospect for experienced rock climbers. The great arc of the limestone cliffs was formed by glacial melt-water at the end of the last Ice Age some 12,000 years ago, but the impressive cataract of years gone by is seldom seen today as the river flowing down from the cove emanates from subterranean waterways deep underground. On 6 December 2015, after particularly heavy rainfall, for a short time water did flow from the lip of the cliffs so that very briefly, with a height of 80 metres, it became the highest single-drop waterfall above ground in England. This was thought to be the first time that this had happened for many centuries. For the last twenty-five years peregrine falcons have bred on a ledge in the middle of the cliffs and rock climbing is suspended while they rear their young.

The trees that grow close to the base of the cliffs, up the valley sides and even from the cliff face are largely ash and sycamore. Climb to the top of the cove to discover a whole new landscape of limestone pavement: blocks or slabs known as clints criss-crossed by deep crevices known as grikes, a formation that was caused when the glaciers retreated. This surface demands that visitors really do watch where they are going, as it's too easy to miss your footing and suffer a nasty injury.

Within the protective grikes grow a rich array of calcicolous plants and trees, with ash being the most frequent broadleaf species. Where and how

ABOVE:
Ashes of bonsai proportions thrive in the rocky grikes.

ASH WOODS 73

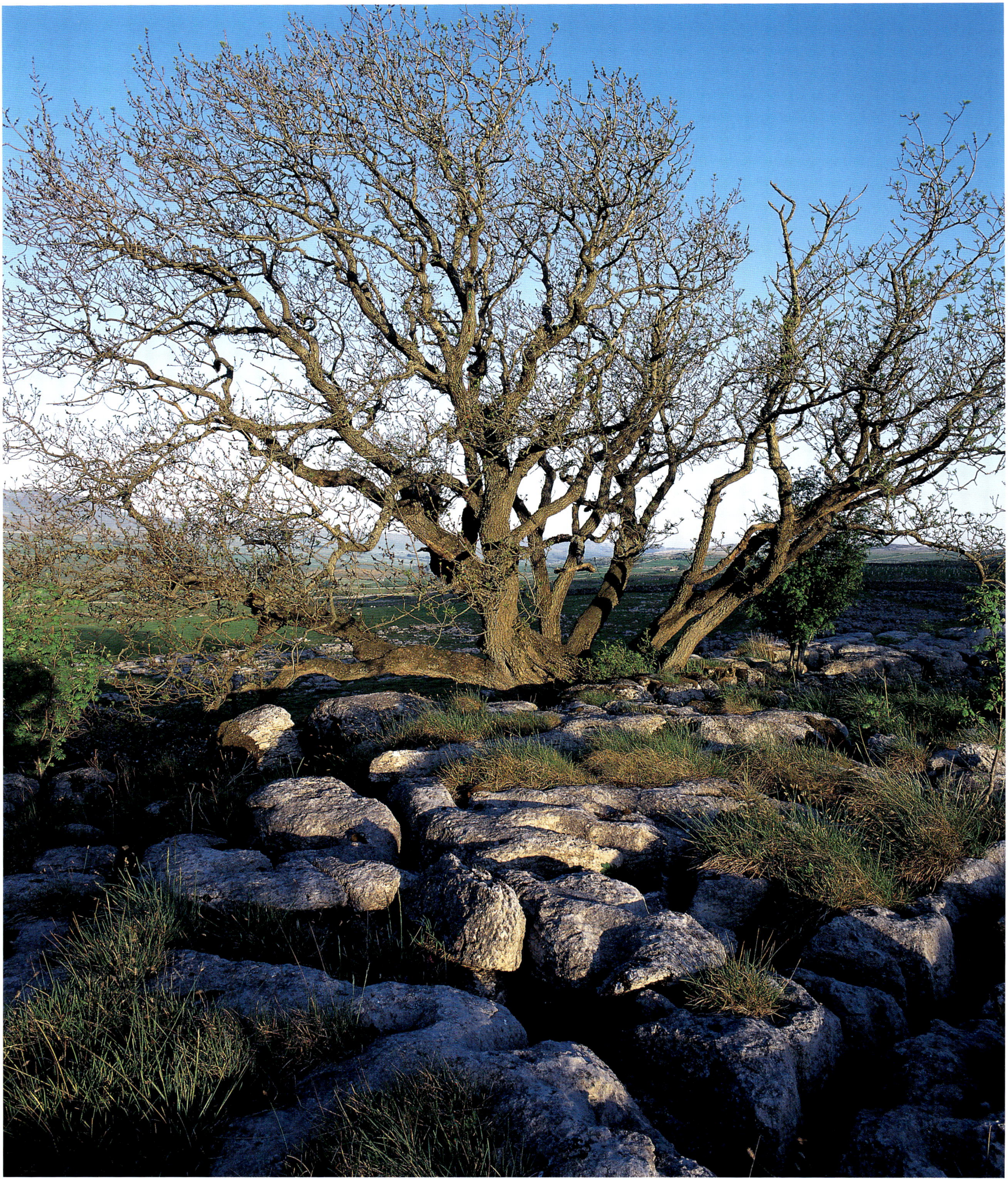

they obtain their nutrients and water from these seemingly bottomless fissures is something of a mystery, but the root systems find a way. The going may be precarious, but the predations of sheep are readily visible on some of these naturally bonsaied ashes. Nonetheless, most survive this regular pruning and they are also well protected against icy gales and driving snow in their rocky clefts. These ash trees may be very small, but growth in such conditions will be remarkably slow so their size may belie their age.

Similar limestone formations occur in a variety of places through North Yorkshire, the northern tip of Lancashire, Cumbria and, famously, the Burren in the Republic of Ireland. All are notable sites for their rich flora. Another wood of a slightly different character, still within the bounds of North Yorkshire, is Colt Park Wood at the top of Ribblesdale. Near the village of Selside, on the western slopes of the valley, it can be viewed from a distance as a long row of trees resembling an outgrown hedge. At the front of the wood the trees safely sit atop a sheer wall of limestone that drops some 5 metres into the pasture below. All the sheep can do here is gaze longingly at their prize, while at the back of the wood a dry-stone wall also keeps them at bay. The 6.5 hectare wood is a very small site when put in the context of the surrounding sparsely tree-clad fells, but it does offer a glimpse of what upland ash woods in this part of Britain might have looked like several thousand years ago. The ashes may be extremely old, but most are fairly small and stunted, often twisting or semi-collapsing above convoluted roots that fold around and into the rocky woodland floor. There is evidence that many of these trees were regularly coppiced in the past. Colt Park must have been enclosed for a long time, to protect the ash stools used to provide wood for a variety of purposes as well as foliage for fodder, an important consideration in these barren uplands. Closing the wood off also spared farmers from losing their sheep to serious injuries or even a painful demise.

In late spring the whole woodland floor is a superb rock garden decked with lime-loving plants: wood anemones, primroses and early-purple orchids abound, but there are also specialities such as mountain pansies, the delicate white mossy saxifrage, and in summer the bright yellow nodding orbs of the globe-flower. Ash is definitely the dominant tree, but wych elm, sycamore, downy birch, rowan, hazel, hawthorn and bird cherry all find their place too. I quoted a couple of lines from Richard Mabey's *The Wildwood* in my *Hidden Trees of Britain* book some years ago, and I have no compunction in repeating them here: '… the more inhospitable the terrain, the more specialised the plantlife to be found there. The more specialised the plantlife (and the longer it is left to do as it wishes in any one spot), the more striking, bizarre and memorable the beauty that results.' This sums up a place like Colt Park perfectly.

OPPOSITE:
Limestone pavement in Colt Park Wood, Ribblesdale, North Yorkshire.

BELOW:
Ash on a boulder in Brow Gill Beck, near High Birkwith, across the valley from Colt Park Wood.

ABOVE:
Ash wood pasture near Whyle, where the old pollards are growing over medieval earthworks.

Herefordshire–Worcestershire Borders Wood Pastures

After living in Herefordshire for almost thirty years I like to think that I know my local treescape pretty well. In the time I have lived here I have travelled to almost every corner of the county either in search of trees or following leads given by other tree people. At gatherings and lectures one is always being approached and told about some new tree that has just been discovered. So it was with eager anticipation that I set out with landscape historian David Lovelace, in March 2018, to look at what he had described as one of the finest ash wood pastures he had ever seen.

Pollarded ash trees are not uncommon in the Herefordshire hedgerows, as well as a few crusty old individuals in open pastures, and some of them are of prodigious size – massive fists of vibrant growth towering over squat, burry boles. Very few are ever pollarded any more and their outgrown poles, which have become substantial boughs of perhaps fifty to a hundred years' growth, may eventually pose problems for the integrity of the tree's structure.

As we pulled off the country lane near Middleton-on-the-Hill into the farm entrance, I could see straight away that this was something out of the ordinary. The large expanse of open pasture before us was covered in small groups and numerous individual pollarded ash trees – a few having been recently trimmed back, while others had probably not seen a cut in thirty or forty years, maybe longer.

There were trees in all manner of forms: hollowed shards, probably rent open by loss of boughs at some long-forgotten time; low-spreading, forked trees; fine, upright trees; small, stumpy, characterful, burr-ridden trees and the odd phoenix tree – a wonderful assortment creating a truly diverse range of habitats in one historical landscape. On the slope down into the valley there was a plantation of tall, sinuous ash trees, which initially looked like a fairly recent introduction, but closer study revealed that many of these trees were single stems arising from significantly old coppice stools, some perhaps 150–200 years old. There was no obvious fenced protection for the coppice regrowth so clearly these young shoots must have avoided the predations of sheep a very long time ago (see page 48).

Down to the farmhouse, and a short walk along the valley, we came to yet another remarkably similar scene. A score or more of ash pollards dotted across an open pasture, with some of the trees morphing into the edges of the adjacent woodland. It appeared that very few of them had been cut in recent times and the ground was littered with fallen boughs. None of the ashes here were of great size – generally with girths of 2–4 metres – and yet they reeked of antiquity. Counting the annual rings in fallen trees would make a fascinating study, for the overriding suspicion is that, rather like their peers in Cumbria, their size belies their true age. This one location also offers more evidence of other ancient trees: mighty oak pollards with 10-metre girths and native lime stools running along historic wood boundaries, including among them the unusual 'Rubra' – a red-twigged variant of large-leaved lime.

It was difficult to drag ourselves away, but wending across country, down a tiny single-track lane that neither of us had ever navigated before, we spotted yet another ash wood pasture on the far side of a remote valley near Whyle. The setting sun brilliantly highlighted about a dozen old pollards in a field that also clearly revealed earthwork patterns of medieval strip farming. Another story of how this landscape evolved appears to lie in wait.

THIS PAGE:
Various characterful pollards in a rare landscape. Many of these trees have not been managed for decades. Some exhibit very strange forms – the 'snail' tree and the 'dancing' tree!

ASH WOODS 77

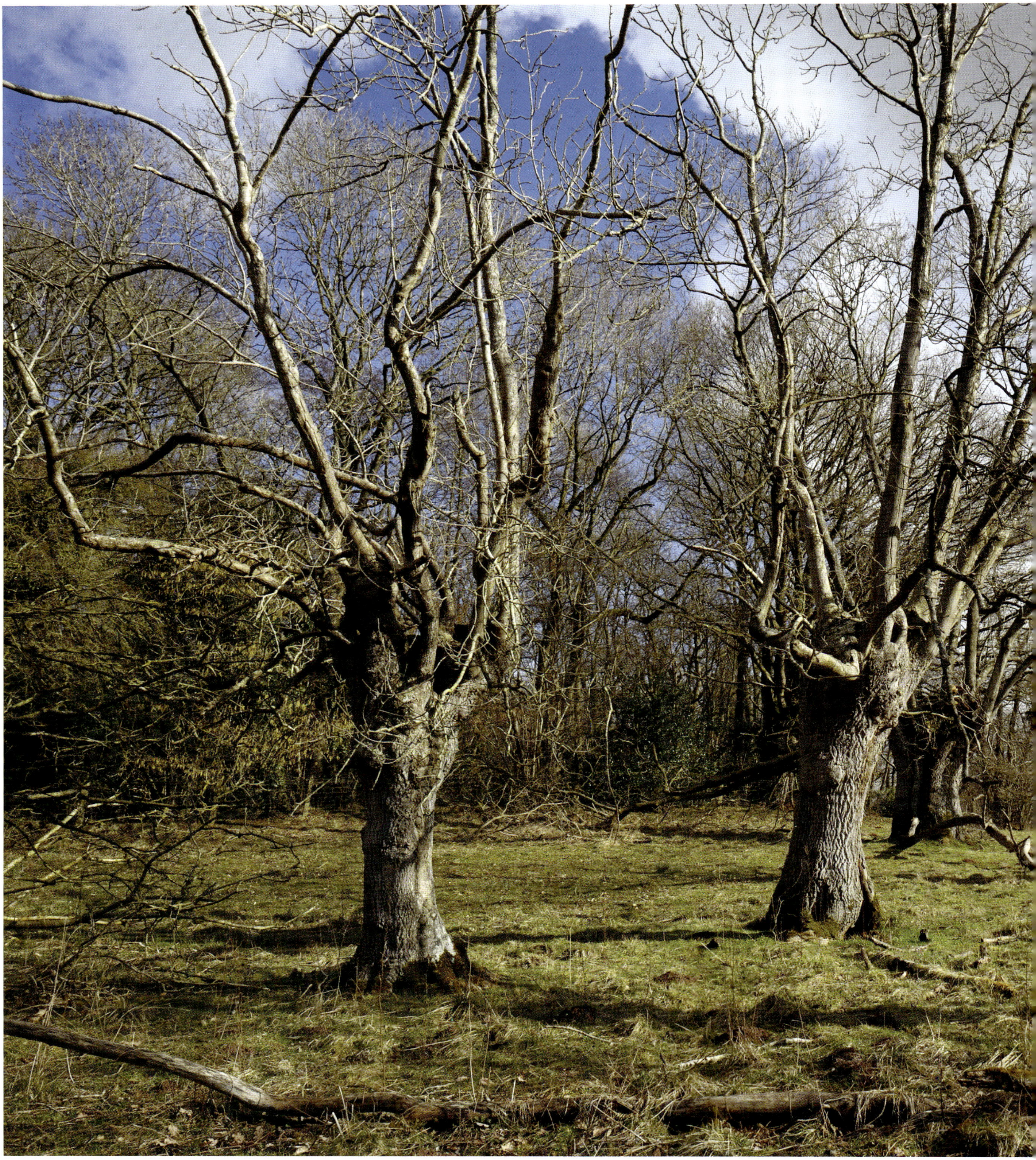

LEFT:
Perfect illustration of a historical wood pasture landscape.

ASH WOODS 79

BELOW:
Extravagant growth of an abandoned stool near Holtye, Kent.

OPPOSITE:
Ancient coppice stool recently revived near Ivy Hatch, Kent.

OPPOSITE BELOW:
Outgrown stool on top of a boundary bank in Hayley Wood, Cambridgeshire.

Coppiced Ash Woods

Kent

The progress of ash dieback is now well advanced in the south-east corner of England and few if any woods containing ash trees have escaped its inevitable spread. Many of the semi-natural ancient woodlands of Kent have been managed as coppice since time immemorial, although due to a decreasing demand over the latter half of the twentieth century this exploitation has now tailed off considerably. This has resulted in many woods containing large, outgrown coppice stools so that the conundrum now is whether or not to cut them over again with the knowledge that this is a disease that appears to have a preference for young trees or coppice regrowth.

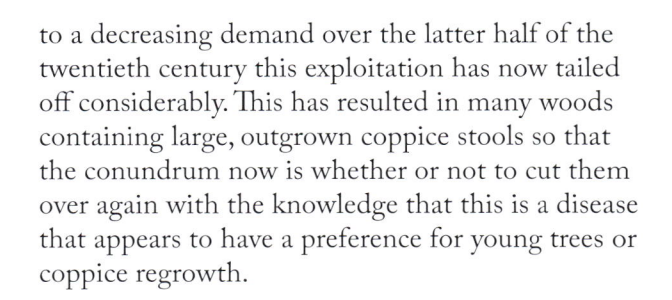

A walk through the interconnected woods south-east of Holtye uncovers some outstanding, long-neglected ash coppice stools, probably untouched for a century, and usually located on the outer edges or boundaries. From the outside the woodland canopy gives the impression of many mature ash trees growing in close proximity, only dispelled when one walks underneath and realises that these are towering stems of the long-abandoned coppice stools.

East Anglia

One of the most famous coppice woods in the whole of Britain would have to be Hayley Wood in Cambridgeshire, an ancient wood that had a precarious future ahead of it back in the 1960s, but was fortunately acquired by the local Wildlife Trust in 1962, thus assuring its conservation and access to all. The celebrated landscape historian Oliver Rackham researched the wood and revealed a highly detailed history stretching back to the thirteenth century, and even suggested that it was mentioned in the Domesday Book. Extracts from the *Ely Coucher Book* of 1251 referred to coppicing in Hayley Wood (or *Boscus de Heyle*, as it was then called), the use of its underwood for fuel and hurdle-making, and the protective earth bank around the wood's perimeter.

The woodland is now managed in separate compartments on regular rotations and a walk in springtime reveals the beneficial effect of this practice. Where there is a fairly dense cover of mature trees, the ground flora is relatively sparse and only the early-flowering species thrive before the sunlight is closed out. Where trees have grown up for several years, the flowers are evident, yet concentrated in the sunnier clearings. It's in the areas that have recently been coppiced that the carpets of wild flowers are most spectacular, and particularly the second summer after the coup, the plants having used that first season to gather their strength before bursting into their full glory the following year. The floral star of Hayley Wood is the oxlip, originally thought to be a hybrid between the primrose and the cowslip, now known to be a species in its own right and highly specific to ancient woods on the boulder clays of north Essex, west Suffolk and Cambridgeshire. It is only because the wood has been meticulously fenced to exclude deer that the plant survives, for in some neighbouring woods where this hasn't happened barely a single one is to be seen.

Hayley is an ash, field maple and hazel wood with a few oak standards, but it contains some very impressive ash coppice stools that may well date back to the medieval period, the largest of which are found along the old boundary bank, most noticeably in the south-west corner of the wood. Until very recently, nobody had thought it wise to recoppice these ancient stools, with the uncertainty as to whether such harsh management after maybe more than a century could be fatal. They are stunning memorials, reminders of a management regime long since ceased that was once a vital element of the rural economy. However, elsewhere in the wood smaller, younger

ASH WOODS 81

BELOW:
Ash coppice at Powerstock Common, in Dorset.

ashes are being high-cut coppiced once again (or is it low-cut pollarding?). Protective fences seal off compartments of regeneration as the ravenous deer still need to be kept at bay.

Another nearby coppice-with-standards wood is Bradfield Woods in Suffolk, noted for its unbroken history of management dating back to the mid thirteenth century. Like Hayley, Bradfield Woods is a vibrant, living treescape and, although there is probably more oak in this wood, ash is still very much one of the principal species here, including ancient stools that Rackham surmised might even be a thousand years old. For a tree normally considered outstanding if it reaches 300 years, this is certainly pushing the boundaries, but then that is the potential of coppicing, as one only has to consider recent re-evaluations of ancient native lime stools – some now thought to be in excess of 2,000 years old.

Dorset

Nestled among the hills, a few miles inland from Bridport, Powerstock Common is a very special place in the caring hands of Dorset Wildlife Trust. Until the mid nineteenth century it appeared on the maps as Poorstock, and is still pronounced thus locally to this day. The reserve is an interesting collection of diverse habitats: large open meadows with rich arrays of wild flowers, grasses and butterflies, and several different types of woodland, interwoven with old hedges and boundary banks.

There is much oak, both standard and coppice, with hawthorn and holly in the understorey, while the more calcareous soils tend to support ash and hazel along with occasional oak, field maple, spindle, privet and wayfaring tree. Willows and alders predominate in wetter flushes and around ponds. Ancient ashes with moss-clad boles line many of the old boundary banks, with their horizontal boughs reminiscent of long-forgotten hedging activity. Ash has always been a reliable and obliging subject for the hedge-layer, with a life force that springs straight back into action within a few weeks of pleaching.

Herefordshire

As a finale I have to mention a wood that I have known for almost thirty years and probably the one that is closest to my home. I have walked in it through every season, in every sort of weather, dodging the heat of midsummer beneath peerless blue skies, battling up muddy banks listening to raindrops pitter-pattering off soaking foliage or slithering back down through a snow-hushed, bitter chill of a winter's day. Broxash Wood, as its name implies, still has badgers and ash trees. Many of the ashes, as well as other trees such as the oaks and huge small-leaved limes, are very old outgrown coppice stools. I had walked the wood for twenty years before my partner Jan asked me if I knew about this huge ash coppice stool. How had I missed it? I've no idea, but I felt rewarded to think that Jan found it and knew instantly that it was special.

The wood is seldom managed in any way and I feel that really I should disapprove of this, as I'm always banging on about how well-managed woodlands have better-quality trees, are more vibrant and have increased biodiversity, but I'm happy to make a compromise with Broxash. I'm rather fond of its rambling, shambling constancy, its immutability, and yet its perpetual state of flux, its natural disorder and random progression. Woods are paradoxical places, sometimes surprising, occasionally disturbing, but more often reassuring, comforting; the primeval psyche kicks in, struggling to reconcile whether certainty and safety lies within or without the forest. It's a fascination, and it's why they enrich our lives.

BELOW:
A phenomenal stool in the depths of Broxash Wood, Herefordshire.

The Uses of Ash

Ash and oak have always been considered to be Britain's two most important timber trees. In some spheres their uses may have overlapped – for example, both oak and ash were traditionally needed by wheelwrights: the ash for the felloes (wheel rims) and the oak for the spokes; coopers needed oak for barrel staves yet raising the cask was performed with ashen trusses; and furniture is equally beautiful and functional made from either wood – but in other fields the two had their own very specific uses ordained by their different qualities. Great ships and timber-framed buildings were almost always the preserve of the oak, for oak timber reigned supreme for its load-bearing capacity and its ability to withstand immersion in salt water, trading across continents or defending the nation. Ash, while it is not the best wood for outside uses, particularly when in contact with the earth, is eminently preferable for such applications as implement handles, where its shock-absorbing qualities are required, and where the wood must be bent into some quite extreme shapes without compromising its strength: vital for coach-builders, chair-makers and coopers. In the twenty-first century many uses for ash have simply disappeared and, in those areas where it was once indispensable, it has been superseded by metals, plastics or lately by material such as carbon fibre.

In 1949 Herbert Edlin wrote a masterly work entitled *Woodland Crafts in Britain*, in which he examined every craft and industry that employed the produce of woodlands in minute detail. Many of these skills were limited to particular counties, sometimes to specific villages, or individuals working in a single woodland or workshop, where traditional methods of manufacture had been handed down through families for many generations. In some cases these crafts and their associated industries had changed remarkably little for several hundred years. In 1973 Edlin was asked to write an updated preface for a new edition of his original book and made the point (seemingly with a heavy heart) that many of the crafts he had written of only twenty-four years previously were now defunct and even those that had survived appeared to have a precarious future. 'Since 1949, when this book was completed,' he opined, 'the surviving crafts have declined with decisive speed. Only a handful survive in the real commercial sense, though others remain for valid artistic reasons.' Edlin noted that the only crafts that still thrived to any degree were the cleaving of chestnut and oak for fencing, hazel hurdle manufacture and some turnery. He recalled meeting the last in the line of the Chilterns beech bodgers, the makers of hazel barrel hoops and weavers of oak spelk baskets. They (and probably Edlin himself) agreed that 'none can believe that newcomers will ever take up such trades again.' Clearly this dramatic decline and change had been preconceived by Edlin in 1949, vindicating his exhaustive survey, yet he obviously took little pleasure in the outcome, other than the knowledge that he had acted soon enough to 'preserve an authentic, first-hand record, in words and pictures of all that the old skilled workers did'. It is to the credit of many of the talented craftspeople still working today up and down the land that the renaissance that Edlin could not envisage has to some degree kept a handful of these crafts alive.

John Evelyn in his *Sylva* of 1664 promotes the usefulness of ash with some vigour:

> the carpenter, wheel-wright and cart-wright find it excellent for plows, axle-trees, wheel-rings, harrows, bulls; it makes good oars, blocks for pullies and sheffs, as seamen name them: for drying herrings no wood is like it, and the bark is good for the tanning of nets; and like the Elm, for the same property, (of not being apt to split and scale) is excellent

for tenons and mortises; also for the cooper, turner, and thatcher; nothing is like it for our garden palisade-hedges, hop-yards, and poles and spars, handles and stocks for tools, spade-trees, &c. In sum the husbandman cannot be without the Ash for his carts, ladders, and other tackling, from pike to the plow, spear and bow; for of Ash were they formerly made, and therefore reckoned amongst those woods which, after long tension, has a natural spring, and recovers its position; so as in peace and war it is a wood in highest request: In short, so useful and profitable is this tree, next to the Oak, that every prudent Lord of a Manor should employ one acre of ground with Ash to every twenty acres of other land, since in as many years it would be more worth than the land itself.

John Worlidge, writing in his wonderfully titled *Systema Agriculturae, Being The Mystery of Husbandry Discovered and Laid Open* in 1669, echoed the claims of Evelyn in recommending the multifarious uses of ash:

> The use of the Ash is almost universal, good for Building, or any other use where it may lie dry, serves the occasion of the Carpenter, Plough-wright, Wheel-wright, Cart-wright, Cooper, Turner, &c. For Garden-uses also no wood exceeds it; as for ladders, Hop-poles, Palisade-hedges, and all manner of Utensils for the Gardiner or Husbandman. It serves also at Sea for Oars, Handpikes, &c. and it is preferred before any other.

BELOW:
The supreme utility of ash, 'The Husbandman's Tree', meant that it was often planted or encouraged around settlements.

BELOW:
The Penny Bridge Ash in Cumbria is an ancient pollard that may have gradually split apart over many years, but still produces a vibrant crop of young poles after every repollarding.

Worlidge's claim that it is good for building seems a little odd as ash would never be used as a major structural component – it could never compete with oak, but it was employed in some low-status buildings or for non-structural purposes such as panelling.

J. C. Loudon in *Arboretum et Fruticetum Britannicum* (1838) resurrects many of the uses listed by the old writers, but also notes some domestic applications for ash wood: 'It is highly valued for kitchen tables, as it may be scoured better than any other wood, and is not so liable to run splinters into the scourer's fingers. Milkpails, in many parts of England, are made of thin boards sawed lengthwise out of the tree, each rolled into a hollow cylinder, with a bottom affixed to it' – an application that strikingly illustrates the elasticity of the wood. Loudon recalls Evelyn's claim for the wood of the roots and burrs of ash which 'are in demand by cabinet-makers, for this curious dark figures formed by their veins, which make a singular appearance when polished'. In Evelyn's words, 'Some ash is so curiously cambleted and veined, that skilful cabinet-makers prize it equally with ebony, and call it green ebony.' This description can only refer to what is now known as black heart – resembling one of the slightly lighter ebonies, such as Macassar ebony, rather than the more familiar jet-black wood. Today black heart is often referred to as 'olive ash', and it does to some degree resemble olive wood.

Before Edlin wrote about woodland crafts, a fascinating but obscure little volume entitled *The Rural Industries of England and Wales*, a survey made on behalf of the Agricultural Economics Research Institute in Oxford, was compiled by Helen E. FitzRandolph and M. Doriel Hay and published in 1926. This was a revealing and exhaustive survey of timber and underwood industries across the land, focusing on the woods and various tree species, their conversion, the various manufacturing processes and tools, markets and the economic prospects for each. The book presents a catalogue of industries that were then part of a vibrant rural economy, although the authors hint at the early signs of decline in many areas, due in no small measure to cheaper imports from abroad, lack of cohesion and co-operation among innumerable individual craftsmen often working in isolation, and the advances and changes brought about by new materials and manufacturing methods. Many of these once vital rural industries are now reduced to the level of specialist crafts or hobbies.

'Ash,' the authors say, 'is one of the most useful of the underwoods; it is valuable for its peculiar quality of suppleness combined with strength, which makes it in general demand wherever riving or bending has to be done.' The list of ash uses includes gate hurdles, although hazel was used for making wattle (woven) hurdles; the heads, bows, teeth and the stales (handles) of rakes; barrel-hoops made from very thin cleft strips and usually curved using rollers or jigs; walking sticks – seemingly most prevalent in Surrey.

The handles of walking sticks could be made by steam-bending, but the stick-makers took a pride in growing exactly the right type of ash for the job, whereby the trees 'grow with the root at right-angles to the plant, and this will make a cross-head handle to the stick. The art of causing the plant to grow in this manner is regarded as a great secret.' The ash was ready for walking sticks after seven to eleven years. The authors reveal that the cost of cultivating an acre of ash for this purpose would run to about £250 – a substantial financial investment in the 1920s.

The section of the book on ash hoop-making comprehensively covers a variety of methods of manufacture, regional variations and commercial applications, including the levels of income derived from the industry. Hoops were required for making barrels to hold all manner of goods, from fish to cement powder, as well as items such as sieves or the tops of dolly-tubs – the manual precursor to the washing machine. This fascinating insight is tempered by dark shadows looming over the industry's future. 'Although there were said to be several hundred men employed in hoop-making in Kent, Surrey and Sussex, no apprentices were found, and every employer says that he cannot get boys to learn.' The days of young men accepting a seven-year apprenticeship with minimal wages had gone. 'Even sons of hoop-makers do not learn if their fathers can find anything better for them … In Furness [Cumbria] only middle-aged or elderly men were found making hoops, and there had been no apprentices for some years.'

The making of hay rakes was still a vitally important industry in the early years of the twentieth century as mechanisation had barely started to move into the agricultural world. For the vast majority of farming folk the seasonal use of hay rakes was a fundamental part of the annual workload. Rake-making was frequently just one strand of the business for carpenters, joiners, wheelwrights or cartwrights, although there were a few specialists. FitzRandolph and Hay noted: 'Some makers have estimated that there are from fifty to sixty processes from the cutting of the wood to the finishing touches,' so it was quite labour intensive even though machines were beginning to speed up certain tasks such as making the teeth. The agricultural role of the hay rake has become virtually redundant in the twenty-first century, but one firm, Rudd's Rakes of Dufton in Cumbria, are still in business after almost 130 years. John and Graeme Rudd, third and fourth generations of their rake-making firm, make about 10,000 ash rakes (with birch teeth) every year & whereas a few will still be used in conservation sensitive hay meadows many find employment for levelling soil, raking leaves or gravel, golf course bunker smoothing or even a recently added design used by Japanese Zen garden enthusiasts.

A rather unusual yet specific use of ash has been its employment for the making of paddles and most particularly for those used for steering the tiny one-man craft known as coracles. The coracle is one of the earliest types of boats known in Britain,

LEFT:
Ash hoop bending from 'The Rural Industries of England and Wales' by FitzRandolph and Hay, 1926.

RIGHT:
Peter Faulkner making an ash coracle paddle.

BELOW:
Finishing off a coracle in his workshop at Leintwardine.

dating from well before the arrival of the Romans, its name derived from the Welsh *corwgl*. The tradition of making and using coracles is especially associated with the rivers Teifi, Towy and Wye, as well as the Severn around Ironbridge; each area having slight regional variations in shape. Designed for a single person, they are extremely lightweight (around 15 kilograms) which makes them very portable. The principles of the design are generally the same: hazel rods are interwoven to make the framework, the ends being pulled upwards and secured in a woven gunwale of willow laths or, alternatively, unsplit hazel rods. A woven floor is also made from willow. This rather large basket-like structure is then covered with hide or calico, which is painted with pitch. A bench seat made of ash is secured inside and a short, large-bladed paddle is also made of ash. At this point the coracle is ready to venture on to the water, but mastering the skill to manoeuvre it with ease and accuracy takes a little while to perfect.

A complete overview of woodland crafts is a substantial book in its own right, as both FitzRandolph and Hay and later Herbert Edlin proved, but a cross section of those applications that were dominated by the use of ash, most of which are consigned to history, but a few of which have either survived or been revived, still makes an impressive inventory.

LEFT:
Men with coracles on the riverside at Ross-on-Wye, Herefordshire. Original photograph by Francis Bedford c1865.

THE USES OF ASH

RIGHT:
An early-twentieth-century advert for a wheelwright, wagon, van, cart and lorry builder reflects the transition from horse-drawn transport to the internal combustion engine.

BELOW:
A simplistic version of events at the Battle of Crécy in 1346 from a nineteenth-century account, but it does show archers from both sides, the French with crossbows, which took longer to reload and the English with longbows. Ash was used for both the French bolts and the English arrows.

Arrows

One of the earliest uses of ash refers to weaponry rather than utility. Both the Greeks and the Romans knew that the strongest and finest spears were made from ash; they also employed the wood for agricultural implements as well as being aware of the medicinal virtues of the tree. It is said that the spear of Achilles had a shaft made of ash and that Cupid's arrows were also of ash. The Saxon name for the tree was aesc, the same as their word for a spear, and very likely the derivation of the name ash. The use of ash for pikes in the British army lasted right up to the end of the seventeenth century when they were replaced by bayonets that could be attached to the ends of muskets. The longbow can be dated back some 5,000 years, but its heyday in conflict was during the medieval period. Ash was the prime wood used for arrows during the Hundred Years War (1337–1453) with France and this is well documented in Exchequer Rolls of the period, listing the various supplies received by the national armoury. With massed ranks of archers at battles such as Poitiers, Agincourt and Crecy launching volley after volley of these lethal missiles to rain down on their French adversaries, the thought of the resulting carnage makes one shudder. It is said that each archer could fire twelve arrows a minute; multiply that by 5,000 – the number of archers at Crécy – and the effects are truly terrifying. Roger Ascham in his *Toxophilus* of 1545 recommends ash as the best wood for sheaf arrows used in warfare. Because the grain of ash usually runs straight and even, it is the ideal wood for arrows and a few specialist arrow-makers are still working it today, although many modern arrows are now made from aluminium, fibreglass or carbon fibre. Ash has also been used for making bows. Traditionally, the best timber was yew, but supply could not always satisfy demand, so ash was also widely used, and in Wales wych elm was the usual substitute for yew.

Wooden Wheels

The construction of spoked wooden wheels stretches back over 3,500 years to the ingenuity of the Egyptian wheelwrights, although the specific use of ash by wheelwrights in Britain can be traced back at least two millennia to the Iron Age. Wheels from Roman chariots that have been excavated in Scotland were found to have rims of ash – in some cases, quite remarkably, a single piece of wood had been steam-bent into a complete circle. Traditionally, cart and carriage wheels have long been made using three different timbers. Elm was used for the nave (the hub of the wheel) as it was the only timber that could maintain its integrity when mortised with a dozen or more spokes, drilled through the centre for the axle, and yet still withstand all the stresses and strains imposed upon it by the rough, unsurfaced roads. Oak was usually used for the spokes, its innate strength best utilised when cleft with the heartwood to the rear of the wheel where the strain would be the greatest, although sometimes ash was used. Ash was reserved for the felloes, or fellies (as they are correctly pronounced) – the rim of the wheel which was divided into sections that each accommodate two spokes, and joined to each other by dowels. It is the supreme elasticity of ash, its excellent shock-absorbancy, that makes it the perfect timber for this demanding purpose. Rather than being flat, wheels were always of a dished form, giving a slightly conical shape inwards when viewed across the wheel, as this added strength. Cart and carriage axles, also commonly made of ash, were designed to point downward slightly at the ends so that the weight of the vehicle was loaded perpendicularly to the ground through the wheel. The whole wheel

THE USES OF ASH

would have an iron tyre around the outside that would be heated up, dropped on and then quickly doused with cold water to make it contract firmly and evenly around the wheel, thus drawing in the whole structure tightly together.

Since the early twentieth century the need to make spoked wooden wheels has steadily declined to a point where only a handful of highly skilled craftsmen are still operating. Phill Gregson is one of that select band – fourth generation in his family's business near Southport in Lancashire. His workshop is housed in an unassuming shed, nestling among a conglomeration of yet more sheds, shacks and outbuildings, some for storing timber, others housing the power machinery he needs to cut and turn his timber, and yet more with projects in progress. The workshop is chock full of specialist tools, jigs and all the paraphernalia of wheelwrighting accumulated over more than a century. Phill might seem to be something of an anachronism in the twenty-first century, but nothing of it. If anything, business has never been brisker. Not only does he get called upon to restore museum pieces, carriages used for sport and leisure, brewery drays, barrows and shrimping carts, and gypsy wagons (Phill and his wife have their own too), but he is constantly in demand for entire restoration projects, such as the ash bodywork of a 1960s fire engine currently on the road to completion. He's even made wooden wheels for bicycles.

Sourcing the timber he needs to make wheels can be challenging. Since the demise of most large elm trees in Britain, the timber is seldom readily available to make the naves, so Phill often uses utile – an African hardwood that has similar properties. Although ash is still common in Britain, he generally finds it easier to buy high-quality imported American white ash, much of which has already been kiln dried en route, but if the right timber comes up locally he will buy it, mill it himself and then put it in stick (stack the boards with one-inch spacers in between) to season. Before use this will have to be seasoned for one year for every inch of thickness, plus an extra year for good measure.

The felloes are first marked out on the chosen board before being planed on one side and passed through a thicknesser to make sure the sides are perfectly parallel. Each felloe is then cut in the flat on a monstrous old band saw, so no bending necessary, then the felloes are assembled around the 'spider' or 'speech' (the nave with spokes attached) clamped horizontally on a 'wheel stool', and marked up for drilling for the outer end of the spokes. After much refinement with spoke shave and sander, each felloe is ready to be gently but firmly tapped into place on the waiting speech with the aid of a spoke-dog, a sort of brace that squeezes each pair of spokes into exactly the right position for assembly. Once the iron tyre has been attached to the outside the job is complete.

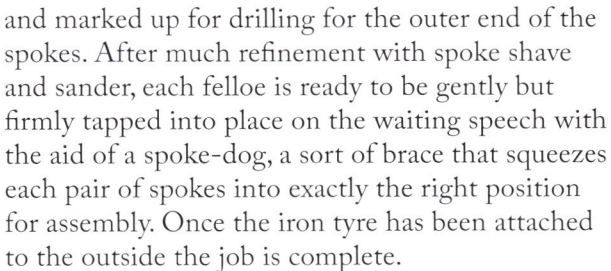

ABOVE & LEFT:
Phill Gregson, Master Wheelwright, preparing one of the felloes and locating it on to the spokes with the aid of a spoke-dog.

THE USES OF ASH 91

TOP RIGHT:
Building London Omnibuses with ash in 1905.

BELOW FAR RIGHT:
Wheel arches are the only wooden component of a Morgan car that are bent. Three thin sheets of ash are glued and laminated together in specially designed clamps.

BELOW RIGHT:
From the mid-seventeenth century to the late-nineteenth century the stage coach was the usual mode of long distance travel, slowly eclipsed by the advance of the railways. Huge quantities of ash were used to build coach bodies and soon this was extended into the construction of railway carriages.
A plate from 'The Word in Miniature' by W. H. Pyne, 1827.

The skills of the wheelwright often overlapped with those of the cartwright and the coach-builder. All had to have a deep understanding of the properties of different timbers, the sort of knowledge not quickly learnt, but acquired by immersion in their trade, passed down through the generations. Coach-building required large quantities of ash for the construction of the frames of the coach bodies, and it was a craft that took on industrial proportions as it survived the transition from horse-drawn vehicles to those powered by the internal combustion engine. The finest ash was supposedly grown in the Midlands, yet in 1901, due to a shortage of quality ash timber, the Coachbuilders Association appealed to the President of the Board of Agriculture to try and encourage landowners to grow more ash, as home-grown timber was deemed to be of far better quality than imported ash. Grants of £4 an acre were made available to people planting hardwood species. Railway carriages, omnibuses, trucks and motor cars all started out with ash frames; even a few components of early aircraft utilised ash. Famously, parts of the wing frames of the de Havilland Mosquito multi-roll combat aircraft were made of ash, although many other different timbers, including much balsa and spruce, were also utilised for 'the Wooden Wonder'.

Morgan Cars

One would have thought that such uses of ash have long been consigned to history, or at least the occasional resurrection for restoration projects, but this is not the case. The Morgan Motor Company of Malvern was originally founded by the Reverend H. G. Morgan's son – always referred to as 'H.F.S.' (Henry Frederick Stanley) – who designed and built his first experimental cars in outbuildings behind his father's rectory in Stoke Lacy, Herefordshire before taking his first model into production in 1910. It is reputed that some of the first frames of these early three-wheelers were originally built using North American tulipwood, but ash was soon to become the first choice. These early cars, right through to the 1930s, would have had some components of the frames steam-bent to accommodate the rounded tail sections.

Over a century later, ash is still very much to the fore with today's prestige, bespoke Morgan sports cars. Apparently this is a huge selling point for Morgan enthusiasts – they revel in the handcrafted aspect of the car ... and they pay for it handsomely! To visit the erecting shops at Morgan's Malvern factory is to take a step back in time, for here is a car-construction workshop that has changed relatively little since the first Morgans rolled off the production line. Granted, there are now power tools and some very high-tech adhesives in use, but the whole process is timeless. Apart from one component, the rear wheel arch, which is formed by laminating three glued sheets of ash in a special clamp, the whole frame is assembled from pieces of ash cut to shape

92 THE USES OF ASH

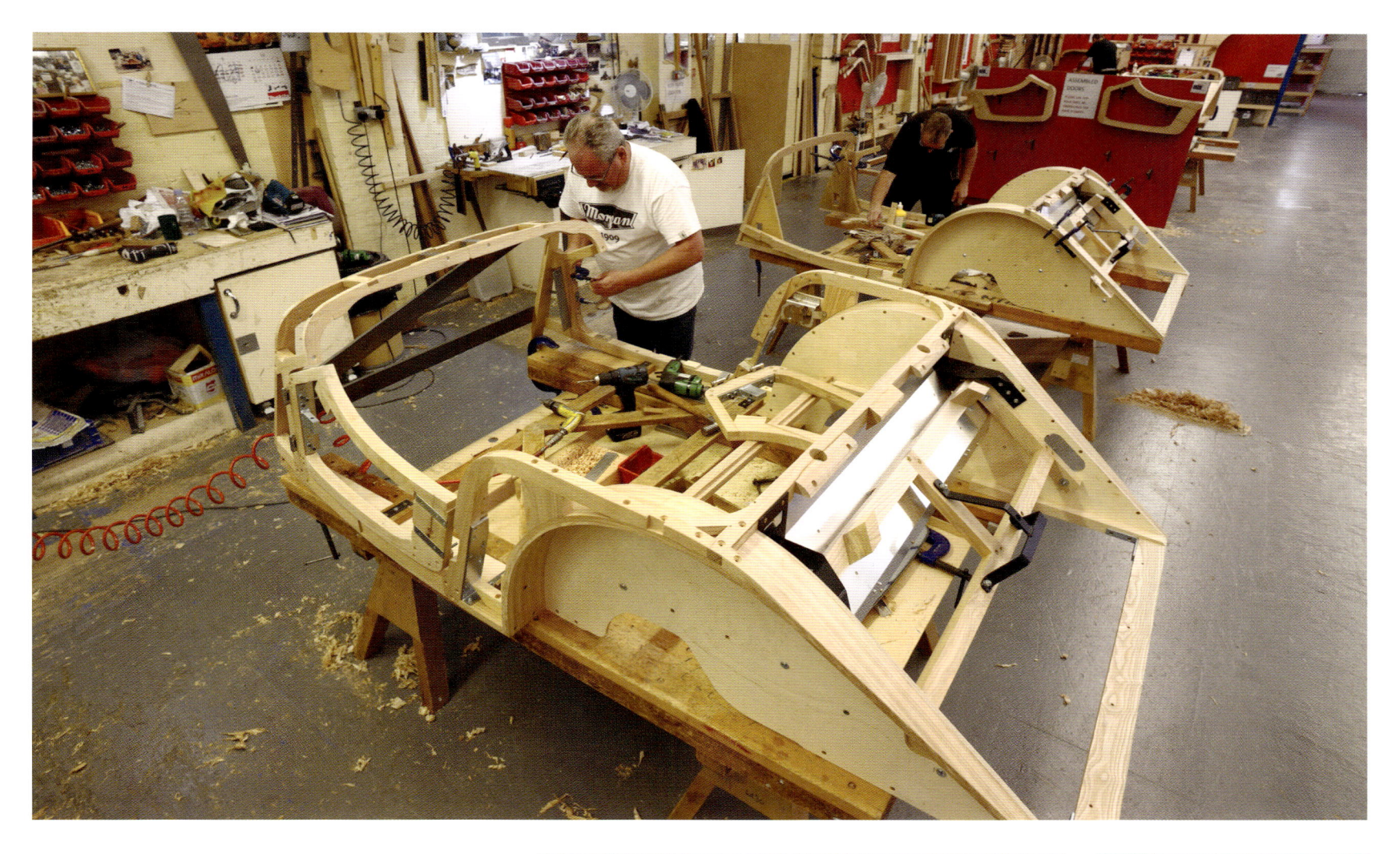

rather than bent or formed. It takes between thirteen and fourteen hours to build the body of a roadster, which is then dipped into a tank of wood preservative, before it is trundled into the next workshop to have the metal body panels fabricated. There could be an issue about the continuing availability of ash timber after ash dieback, but Morgan seem confident that their main suppliers in Lincolnshire have matters in hand. If the worst does happen they may have to look abroad, but finding another timber with the special qualities of ash will be quite a challenge.

Many other cars, right through until after the Second World War, were partially built with ash body construction, and one of the most fondly remembered must be the Morris 1000 Traveller, in production from 1952 to 1967; with its timber-framed external appearance it was the motor engineer's counterpart to the building vernacular of Olde Englande. Fine examples are now avidly sought by enthusiasts, and specialist restoration companies have set themselves up to bring less-than-pristine examples back to perfection, replacing those old ash members that didn't survive the climatic rigours of being on the outside rather than the inside of the bodywork.

ABOVE:
The recognisable shape of a Morgan in the workshops at Malvern.

LEFT:
Roger Orford has completely rebuilt the ash frame for the restoration of a 1930s three-wheeler.

BELOW LEFT:
The home of the Morgan – Stoke Lacy rectory, with the whole Morgan family ready for a days motoring, c1912.

THE USES OF ASH 93

RIGHT:
Having cleft the pieces of ash he needs to make a chair, Mike Abbott begins to work the various components on the shave-horse with a draw-knife.

BELOW RIGHT:
Philip Clissett in his workshop at Bosbury around 1900, from an old postcard published by Tilley & Son of Ledbury.

Chairs

If the joys of motor-car travel in the early years were the prerogative of the well-heeled or the adventurous, there is one use of ash, but not exclusively of that timber, that has been utilised throughout the land for eons – the chair. *Britain at Work*, an illustrated tome published in 1905, provides a portrait of the chair-making town of High Wycombe in Buckinghamshire at a time when factories and mechanisation were eclipsing the cottage industry and the woodland bodgers. Beech poles cut from the coppice stools of the Chiltern beech woods were used in vast numbers, but ash and elm wood was also employed, elm most commonly for the chair seats. Hugh B. Philpott introduces the reader to the ubiquitous chair:

> The chair plays such an important part in our modern social economy that it is difficult for us to imagine a chairless state of society. A throne, which is but a glorified chair, is the symbol of the most exalted rank; to invite a man to take the chair is to pay him a recognised compliment, and to invest him, for the time being, with almost despotic authority over some section of his fellows; while the offer of a chair is one of the commonest forms of conventional politeness.

94 THE USES OF ASH

In the nineteenth century High Wycombe was indisputably at the epicentre of British chair-making, but the craft was also carried on by a multitude of rural-based artisans all over the country, satisfying the local demand for these essential items of furniture, using coppice wood harvested from nearby woodland. Many are unsung yet gifted craftsmen who seldom even bothered to put their names to their work, but one or two became celebrated during their lifetimes, and their legacy has inspired a revival in traditional chair-making in the modern era. One such was Philip Clissett, born in 1817 into a Worcestershire family who had been making chairs since the mid eighteenth century.

The chairs of Philip Clissett are most commonly divided into two types: spindle-back and ladder-back frame-built chairs, often with woven rush, but sometimes with solid elm seats. Construction was usually from cleft green ash, the various elements worked with a draw-knife and spoke-shave on a shave-horse, and then parts such as spindles, legs, stretchers and seat rails turned on a pole-lathe in the workshop behind his cottage on Stanley Hill, near Bosbury, in Herefordshire. The rear legs which run up into the backs of the chairs and the back slats have a gentle curve to them, a form that was thought for a long time to have been achieved by steam-bending (a technique that certainly could have been used), but more recent thinking is that Clissett bent these pieces in special setting jigs and then warmed them in an oven, by the fire or simply left them out in the sun. Some components were joined together with wooden dowels, but most parts were assembled using tenons tapped firmly into drilled, marginally smaller mortises. No glues were necessary – simply expansion and friction – although nails were used to attach solid seats.

Clissett's chance meeting with the Scottish architect James MacLaren, while he was working at Ledbury Court in Herefordshire during 1886, led to a brief collaboration to produce some ladder-back chairs, based on the existing design by Clissett, but with minor 'improvements' suggested by MacLaren. Not long after this pivotal meeting MacLaren joined the Art Workers' Guild and within a short period an order was placed for Clissett chairs for the guild's meeting hall in London – eighty examples survive there to this day, made between 1888 and 1914. In 1890 the renowned Arts and Crafts designer Ernest Gimson spent several weeks with Clissett learning how to make chairs, the essence of which he took away with him, later to go into partnership with Edward Gardiner, making very similar chairs to Clissett.

There are several present-day disciples of the Clissett designs and methods of chair-making and perhaps none better known, or more appropriately located, than Mike Abbott. He's a man with a long and distinguished career as a green woodworker and teacher and an original founder member of the Clissett Wood Trust – a partnership that bought New Hill Wood (later renamed Clissett Wood) in Herefordshire in 1994. Although Mike later moved on to work in another wood, Clissett Wood continues to provide many courses for aspiring green woodworkers, now under the tutelage of Gudrun Leitz. Mike has become renowned for his greenwood courses as well as the beautiful

BELOW:
After steaming a piece of ash, Mike bends it in a clamp.

Construction of the chair frame with the aid of a sash cramp, which tightly engages the mortise and tenon joints.

Sanding down the finished chair before the woven seat is applied.

THE USES OF ASH 95

ABOVE:
One of Gudrun Leitz's ash chairs, with an organic detail in the back using a piece of yew.

BELOW:
Steam, jigs and clamps are the order of the day for making chairs in David Colwell's workshop.

Clissett-style chairs that he still makes in the small workshop behind his cottage (some things never change!). He now utilises the benefits of a few power tools, which he never used to, typically for cutting his mortise and tenon joints, but his chairs are still essentially handcrafted using very similar techniques to those employed by Clissett.

Gudrun Leitz, one of Mike's original partners in the Clissett Wood Trust, works with all manner of timber, but oak and ash predominantly. Her style is very much her own, a fusion between the traditional and contemporary designs that are led by the wood, her hand guided by its natural shapes and directions. If the wood Gudrun selects naturally forks or bends then she might build that into the design of a chair; if part of its intrinsic charm is the waney, rough edges of a board, following the original contours of the tree, then that might also be incorporated in a table, bringing a very organic feel to the finished pieces.

With the brief to produce something as simple as a chair, an item required for the most basic of needs, it is truly remarkable how many different forms it can take. David Colwell of Presteigne in Powys is a modern chair-maker who uses ash in what would be considered a radically different way to the traditional craftsmen working in the Clissett idiom. David was originally involved in designing and moulding furniture out of plastics and then it struck him that the bendable capability of ash, moreover its plasticity, might provide a different route to making furniture. If the chair-makers of old could harness the strength of steam-bent ash, then surely it could be used for contemporary designs. Not only could ash be pushed, pulled and twisted into quite complex shapes after it had been steamed, and still retain its innate strength, but it was ecologically sustainable and from renewable sources. He invented a new method of connecting the elements of his furniture with a tubular rivet system, and his 'O Range' was born – a unique style, an intriguing geometry, combining comfort and utility with a striking structural presence.

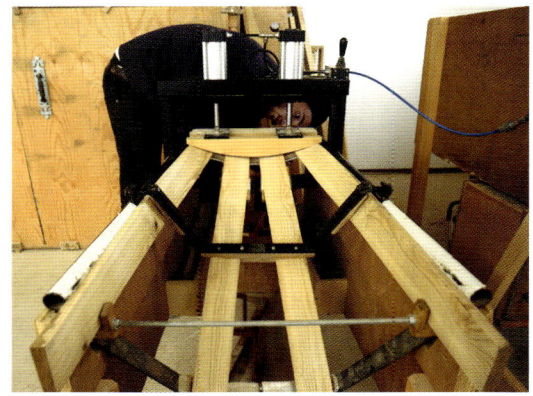

LEFT:
Making ash frames for tennis rackets.

BELOW:
An automatic lathe tapers ash rods into billard cues.

Both plates from 'Woodland Crafts in Britain' by H. L. Edlin, 1949.

Sport

The sporting world would have been, and still would be, the poorer without the benefit of ash. Until the 1930s all tennis rackets were made of ash, but by the 1950s wooden rackets began to be made from laminates, although still incorporating ash. Aluminium and steel frames had taken over by the 1970s and then, from the early 1980s onwards, carbon composites. However, even today the asymmetric frames of rackets used for the archaic game of real tennis are still manufactured from ash. The hurleys used in the fabulously fast and furious game of hurling, almost a religion in Ireland, have always been made from ash, the flared bases of twenty-five- to forty-year-old trees being especially selected for the purpose. While much of the ash required is sourced in Ireland, the huge increase in demand in recent years, with reputed sales figures topping 450,000 hurleys annually, has meant that several suppliers in England and Wales are now also growing ash for this market. Remarkably, as Rob Penn points out in *The Man Who Made Things Out of Trees* (see page 197): 'The array of increasingly sophisticated materials [in the modern era] have so far been unable to equal the properties of ash, including weight, appearance, price, performance, game-handling, elasticity and strength.' The great masters in the world of snooker still trust in ash for their precision-made cues. The very first poles used in the sport of pole-vaulting in the first modern Olympic Games of 1896 were made of ash, although carbon fibre has replaced this in the modern sport. Ash is still used for the parallel bars used by gymnasts and witnessing the extreme stresses placed on these by the participants perfectly illustrates that renowned flexibility of the wood. Top-quality cricket stumps and bails are usually made of ash, and the firm of A. S. Lloyd & Son, near Bridgend in South Wales, is one of the few producers still making these for the cricketing world.

THE USES OF ASH 97

RIGHT:
Richard O'Sullivan sets up an automatic four spindle copying lathe to turn axe helves.

BELOW RIGHT:
Mike Morgan works on a handle on a 42 inch variety turning machine.

Tool Handles

The Lloyd company is famed for a far more diverse catalogue of turned-wood items than simply stumps and bails. John Lloyd and his wife Julie are the present proprietors of the business that dates back to the early years of the twentieth century. After working as an apprentice to an iron monger in Merthyr Tydfil in the late nineteenth century, and seeing the strong demand for tool handles, John's grandfather took a trip to America to see how their tool handle industry prevailed, and soon discovered that there was a range of lathes that could machine copious quantities of turned items in double-quick time. He purchased some and brought them back to Swansea, establishing the company to manufacture ash tool handles, principally for the mining industry. Not only this but he also forged trading partnerships with American suppliers, importing tool handles into Cardiff Docks, before selling them on. The numerous privately owned companies of the mining industry were the main customers, and Lloyds thrived purely on this local trade. John

98 THE USES OF ASH

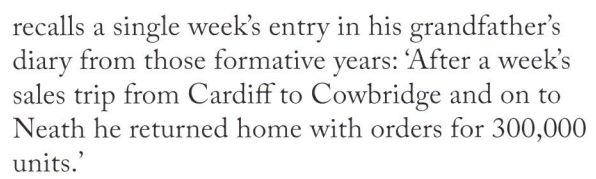

recalls a single week's entry in his grandfather's diary from those formative years: 'After a week's sales trip from Cardiff to Cowbridge and on to Neath he returned home with orders for 300,000 units.'

H. A. Hyde in his *Welsh Timber Trees* of 1935 stated that, 'The best miners' pick, mandril [mandrel] and shovel handles are always made of this wood [ash]; it is worthy of record that such handles of the finest quality are being cleft and finished by hand in Cardiff today.' This was a reference to John's grandfather G. P. Lloyd. Hyde also mentioned that 'the fossilised handle of an iron implement of Roman workmanship (c150–200 AD) found at Caerleon proved to have been made of ash.' So Lloyds were and are quite simply the latest generation of such craftsmen working in Wales for the last two millennia. By the end of the Second World War there were still forty-four companies in Britain who were members of the Tool Handle Manufacturers' Association. Today A. S. Lloyd is just one of two companies left in the industry.

John is immensely proud of the family tradition of producing high-quality turned items not just from ash, but also beech, a great deal of hickory imported from America and some very specialised products such as mallets turned from lignum vitae imported from Paraguay. Once upon a time the ash might have been sourced in Britain, but times have changed. John bemoans the fact that, although we have plenty of ash in the country, the quality of much of it is indifferent and there are no longer the sawmills that can process it for his requirements. Instead he buys his ash in dowel form from America, Belgium, Germany and Eastern Europe. In a nutshell, John explains that his use of ash is usually for non-striking tool handles while the hickory, which is a bit stronger and tougher yet heavier, is reserved for striking tool handles. The workshop is a cacophony of numerous machines turning, dowelling, sawing and sanding – ear defenders essential! In the midst of the uproar a small group of highly experienced craftsmen, much more than simple machinists, calmly select and minutely examine each raw piece of wood, setting up and nursing their machines through their paces. Undoubtedly the original business was founded on handles for picks, shovels and axes, but Lloyds can offer all manner of implement handles, including hay forks and rakes, scythes, mattocks, a huge selection of hammers and mallets, woodcarving and woodturning chisel handles, right down to little dibbers for the garden.

ABOVE LEFT:
Turning the old-fashioned way. Self-employed bodgers worked on pole-lathes in the woods or in workshops behind their cottages. They made all manner of turned items, in this instance a chair leg.

ABOVE:
A selection of different hammer handle patterns at A. S. Lloyd & Son.

A container full of ash cricket stumps.

THE USES OF ASH 99

ABOVE:
Country woodshed with plenty of logs in store for the coming winter.

Firewood

After so many valuable and useful applications for ash wood, it seems like something of an anticlimax to praise its virtue as probably the very best firewood – notoriously combustible whether green or seasoned. John Evelyn in *Sylva* calls the firewood 'the sweetest of our forest fuelling, and the fittest for Ladies chambers' and in 1717 Moses Cook, in *The Manner of Raising, Ordering and Improving Forest-Trees*, states, 'Of all the wood that I know, there is none burns so well green, as the ash.'

After describing the variable combustion virtues of a dozen or more firewoods, the last four triumphal lines of 'Logs to Burn', a well-loved poem written by Honor Goodhart in 1926, leave the reader in no doubt:

> But Ash logs, all smooth and grey,
> Burn them green or old;
> Buy up all that comes your way;
> They're worth their weight in gold.

Celia Congreve wrote her 'Firewood Poem' about the same time, in which she also extols the virtues of both green and seasoned ash wood.

> But ash green and ash brown
> Is fit for a queen with a golden crown.

And Walter de la Mare in his poem 'Trees':

> Of all the trees in England,
> Her sweet three corners in,
> Only the Ash, the bonnie Ash,
> Burns fierce while it is green.

Even though it is possible to burn ash logs green, it is perhaps not advisable if it can be avoided. The moisture content of freshly felled ash is about 33 per cent, admittedly lower than other hardwoods, but for the best heat output 20 per cent or lower, typical of seasoned ash wood, is well worth the wait.

100 THE USES OF ASH

ABOVE:
Ash leaves were once widely used for feeding livestock, but this practice has now been virtually abandoned. However, when animals can reach ash foliage they will devour it with gusto.

Fodder

The burning of ash was sometimes at odds with other rural necessities. The Reverend C. A. Johns in his *Forest Trees of Britain* recalls:

> The Romans are known to have used Ash leaves as fodder, as it was considered the best feed for cattle after Elm, and they must certainly have brought this practice over with them. For it is said that in Cumbria during the reign of Queen Elizabeth the farmers were at odds with the iron founders because all the 'loppings and croppings' of ash were consumed by the forges, leaving them little to feed their livestock.

He notes that even then [1847], 'Ash was still fed to cattle in the autumn in the north of Lancashire.' William Gilpin also says of ash: 'Its leaf and rind are nutritive to deer, and much used in browsing them in summer. The keepers of the forest therefore seek out all the Ash-trees they can find, which are for this purpose mangled and destroyed.' It is assumed he meant pollarded!

J. C. Loudon in *Arboretum et Fruticetum Britannicum* (1838) mentions that the ashes of ash wood make excellent potash, a claim echoed by several writers, and continues with an odd belief associated with ash leaves, used 'in some places, for feeding cattle in autumn, and in others in spring, and for adulterating tea. The leaves and shoots, eaten by cows, are said to give the milk and butter a rank taste; but this does not appear to have been considered a great evil by the Romans, as they recommended the leaves of the ash, next to the leaves of the elm, for fodder.'

Loudon's correspondent, Mr Sydney, communicator of the Cowpen Ash in Northumberland (see page 123), dismissed this notion as rubbish, as much butter was made in his ash-rich neighbourhood around Morpeth and he had 'never met with a farmer's wife or dairy-woman who had ever heard of the supposed injury done to butter'.

THE USES OF ASH

Sallading

John Evelyn recommended the culinary properties of the green ash keys, 'which, being pickled tender, afford a delicate sallading'. He avers that 'Ashen keys have the virtue of capers', and they were often substituted for them in sauces and salads.

Loudon echoes Evelyn's assertion, explaining that the aromatic, but quite bitter-flavoured keys were pickled in salt and vinegar and made into a kind of sauce, which is the so-called 'sallading'.

Ash Medicine

The herbalists of the sixteenth and seventeenth centuries were firmly of the opinion that all plants were under the direct influence of the planets and that for their medicinal properties to be efficacious they must be harvested when their governing planet was in ascendancy in the heavens – for, as John Aubrey opined, if they 'be not gathered according to the rules of astrology, it hath little or no virtue in it'. In ancient Greek and Roman mythology ash was dedicated to the planet Mars. Allocation of each plant to a particular planet was ordained by its physical characteristics, or the Doctrine of Signatures; the same manner in which many of the plants' virtues were deduced. Plants assigned to Mars had

> Leaves: hard, long, somewhat heavy, pointed and pendulous, harsh and hot to the tongue, not of good appearance. Flowers: Of a colour between yellow, vermilion, or blue, green, purple, red, changing quickly, abundance of flowers and seeds. Roots: Highly fibrous and creeping underground. Odour: Oppressive to the brain, potent, sharp, acrid.

Not all of these are relevant to the ash and many of these qualities are so wide-ranging among plants that it is difficult to grant much credibility to their curative potential.

Nicholas Culpeper in *The Complete Herbal* of 1653 offers cures and caution:

> The young tender tops, with the leaves taken inwardly, and some of them outwardly applied, are singularly good against the biting of viper, adder, or any other venomous beast; and the water distilled therefrom being taken, a small quantity every morning fasting, is a singular medicine for those that are subject to dropsy, or to abate the greatness of those that are too gross or fat. The decoction of the leaves in white wine helps to break the stone, and expel it, and cures the jaundice. The ashes of the bark of the Ash made into lye, and those heads bathed therewith which are leprous, scabby, or scald, they are thereby cured. The kernels within the husks, commonly called Ashen Keys, prevail against stitches and pains in the sides, proceeding of wind, and voideth away the stone by provoking urine.

He then rails against the much-quoted belief that ash is efficacious against the venomous bite of snakes.

> I can justly except against none of all this, save only the first, viz. That Ash-tree tops and leaves are good against the bitings of serpents and vipers. I suppose this had its rise from Gerrard or Pliny, both which hold, that there is such an antipathy between an adder and an Ash-tree, that if an adder be encompassed round with Ash-tree leaves, she will sooner run through the fire than through the leaves: The contrary to which is the truth, as both my eyes are witnesses.

It seems that myth and superstition were inextricably entwined with medicinal virtues. John Evelyn in his *Sylva* delves into medicinal attributes of ash:

> There is extracted an oil from Ash, by the process on other woods, which is excellent to recover the hearing, some drops of it being distilled warm into the ears; and for the caries or rot of the bones, tooth-ache, pains in the kidnies and spleen, the anointing therewith is most sovereign.

Dr Hunter in his 1776 amended and enlarged edition of the *Sylva* remarks that Evelyn's claim for the cures attributed to the oil derived from ash 'are not to be depended on'. Evelyn also quotes a popular belief that, 'The chemists exceedingly commend the seed of Ash to be an admirable remedy for the stone; but whether by the power of magic or nature, I determine not.' He sounds unconvinced.

J. C. Loudon records:

> M. De Perthuis states that the sap of the ash is an excellent remedy for the gangrene. For this purpose, the sap is extracted from the leaves by maceration; and from the green wood by putting one end of a branch or truncheon of it

into the fire, and gathering the sap, as it rises from the other end, with a spoon.

This latter aspect also relates to an ancient Scottish custom where ash sap from the fire is administered to newborn babies (see page 112).

Mrs Grieve in *A Modern Herbal* from 1931 asserts that both ash bark and leaves have medicinal virtues. The bark is taken from both the trunk and the roots – the latter much preferred. 'The bark contains the bitter glucoside Fraxin, the bitter substance Fraxetin, tannin, quercetin, mannite, a little volatile oil, gum, malic acid, free and combined with calcium.'

> Medicinal Action and Uses: Ash bark has been employed as a bitter tonic and astringent, and is said to be valuable as an antiperiodic. On account of its astringency, it has been used, in decoction, extensively in the treatment of intermittent fever and ague, as a substitute for Peruvian bark. The decoction is odourless, though its taste is fairly bitter. It has been considered useful to remove obstructions of the liver and spleen, and in rheumatism of an arthritic nature. A ley from the ashes of the bark was used formerly to cure scabby and leprous heads. The leaves have diuretic, diaphoretic and purgative properties, and are employed in modern herbal medicine for their laxative action, especially in the treatment of gouty and rheumatic complaints, proving a useful substitute for Senna, having a less griping effect. The infusion of the leaves, 1oz to the pint, may be given in frequent doses during the twenty-four hours. The distilled water of the leaves, taken every morning, was considered good for dropsy and obesity. A decoction of the leaves in white wine had the reputation of dissolving stone and curing jaundice. The leaves should be gathered in June, well dried, powdered and kept in well-corked bottles.

The fruits of the different species of ash are regarded as somewhat more active than the bark and leaves. Ash keys were held in high reputation by the ancient physicians, being employed as a remedy for flatulence.

Linnaeus suggested that ash bark was useful to treat malaria and recent research gives this assertion credence. Soluble glycocide extracts from ash seeds and fruits have been highly effective in reducing blood glucose levels without significantly affecting insulin levels, making them ideal for the treatment of hypertension, obesity and diabetes. Extracts are also known to inhibit bacterial and fungal growth. Claims have recently been made connecting the curative properties of mistletoe grown on ash trees in combating certain cancers, but so far little scientific evidence exists to substantiate this.

BELOW:
Common Ash, a hand-coloured copperplate engraving from a drawing by C. Mathews for 'British Phaenogamous Botany' by W. Baxter, Curator of The Oxford Botanic Garden, 1840.

OPPOSITE:
'Yggdrasil', a wood engraving by Simon Brett, in which the ash is clearly recognisable.

Ash Myth, Magic and Superstition

The ash – along with its constituent parts: leaves, twigs, bark and even the sap – has historically been a tree of good omen and of great practical use for the physical benefit of the human frame, while it has also attracted a host of rather more metaphysical virtues, reflected by a long and varied catalogue of often ritualistic, sometimes bizarre, customs and traditional beliefs.

The World Tree

One of the earliest mythological representations of the ash tree stems from the thirteenth-century *Poetic Edda*, popularly understood to be the Norse World Tree 'Yggdrasil'. Many accounts of the ash tree and its symbolic significance are perpetuated over the ensuing centuries, right up to the present day, all emanating from the original thirteenth-century epic. Unravelling the *Edda* is no simple task; for the language is so archaic, and the interpretations of the narrative sometimes so obscure, as to be more the fare of the mythologists and scholars of ancient Scandinavian culture, with its bewildering cast list of characters and creatures. Although most etymologists have agreed that Yggdrasil is a representation of an ash tree, another interpretation by F. R. Schroder in the 1930s found an etymological route to it being a yew tree, or more accurately 'yew pillar', and Fred Hageneder elucidates in his *Yew: A History*. Reference to early Icelandic texts also reveals the World Tree described as *barraskr* (needle ash) or *vetgronstr vidr* (wintergreenest tree). There are several references to the ash in the *Edda*, and Hageneder makes comparisons with references to Yggdrasil in *Voluspa* – an epic poem from Iceland, where it says of the World Tree:

> An ash I know there stands.
> Yggdrasil is its name,
> A tall tree, showered
> With shining loam.
> From there come the dews
> That drop in the valleys.
> It stands forever green over Urdr's well.

This last line certainly seems to indicate a yew tree, or maybe some other evergreen tree – surely not an ash. Although yew trees have never grown in Iceland and, in reality, little apart from birch and dwarf willows since the last Ice Age, yews would have been familiar to more southerly Norse communities. Hageneder firmly believes that the current popular belief that Yggdrasil was, or is, an ash tree is simply a misconception that has been perpetuated for the last 200 years to the point where it has passed into an accepted, unquestioned folkloric tradition with little factual backbone. He believes that the references to *askr* in the *Voluspa* refer to a wooden bowl rather than an ash tree. One is, after all, dealing with myth, legend, hearsay and a vast time frame where contortions and interpretations of stories told and retold may easily have lost or changed original meanings.

A World Tree or Tree of Life makes an obvious spiritual totem for many cultures, as trees are not only ubiquitous, but also embody that mystical quality of mimicking the human lifespan in the space of every annual rebirth – from the death-like torpor of winter, bursting into life, bearing flowers and fruit, creating the next generation, before returning once again to the 'death' of winter. It's not hard to believe that this eternal cycle must understandably have been perceived

ASH MYTH, MAGIC AND SUPERSTITION 105

BELOW:
A commonly held perception of the World Tree as depicted in 'Plant Lore, Legends and Lyrics' by Richard Folkard, 1884.

as a kind of magic, entrancing early civilisations and engendering a spiritual reverence. Moreover, in the material world humans were hugely reliant on the trees around them for fuel, food, fodder, shelter, tools, weapons and medicines. With this dependence on trees, a fundamental resource to ensure survival, and seemingly an endlessly renewable one, provided by some unseen power or deity beyond human comprehension, it's easy to understand how and why they became so revered.

A rudimentary description of Yggdrasil is of a tree beneath which the gods were wont to hold court, presided over by Odin, the supreme deity. It reaches far into the heavens, its branches covering the surface of the earth and linking the nine worlds of Norse cosmology, while the roots penetrate deep down into the underworld or 'infernal regions'. Again, Hageneder remarks upon the 'recurring theme of ninefoldness' that is common to *Voluspa*, with the nine yew root mothers, and also a feature of so many other cultures throughout Eurasia. An eagle sits atop Yggdrasil watching over the world, while a squirrel runs up and down the trunk reporting all matters that the great bird might have overlooked or, alternatively, with tales of mischief, creating strife between the eagle and Nidhogg, a serpent, sometimes described as a dragon, which lies beneath the tree chewing at the roots. Four harts run through the branches, biting the buds, and represent the four cardinal winds. Two fountains spring from the roots of the tree: wisdom lies concealed in one while the other contains knowledge of the future. Three virgins, the Norns or Fates (Past, Present and Future), attend to the tree, gathering water from the fountains to sustain it. Thomas Carlyle called it the 'Tree of Existence' and described how, 'Its boughs, with their buddings and dis-leafings – events, things suffered, things done, catastrophes – stretch through all lands and times. Is not every leaf of it a biography – every fibre there an act or word?'

It does seem very strange that, if the ash tree was at the epicentre of Norse pagan beliefs, relatively few recognisable images of specific trees, let alone any that are vaguely representational of an ash, have survived in the early illustrated manuscripts or on the stone crosses with which the Vikings marked their sacred sites in Britain. Perhaps, after their arrival at the end of the eighth century, they were won over by the Christian beliefs that prevailed in Britain, albeit still a relatively new religion among the masses. Thousands of years of tree veneration certainly wouldn't have ground to a shuddering halt in the immediate aftermath of St Augustine's mission from AD 597, but it might be that the World Tree gradually became sublimated to the image of the cross. However, old engrained images from their Norse roots must have endured, for a very stylised representation of a tree exists on the base of the renowned Viking cross at Gosforth in Cumbria, and yet it is impossible to decipher this as an ash tree. The theme of the other carvings on the cross is understood to be the victory of Christ over the heathen gods and so, all told, this carved narrative may reflect the blending of faiths and cultures, and might explain the eclipse of the Vikings' spiritual iconography. Carvings of Trees of Life continue to appear in the churches of the Norman era, but yet again they are incredibly stylised and one can only ponder on what specific species of tree the individual stonemasons had in mind at the time. Ash does not appear to have been one of them, but the essence and the image of some kind of a Tree of Life, derived from whatever indecipherable species, occurs historically in almost every corner of the globe. An illustration from *Edda Oblongata*, an Icelandic manuscript from 1680, also depicts an image of Yggdrasil with absolutely no resemblance to an ash or, for that matter, a yew. Ultimately there seems a lot more credence in the yew rather than the ash being the World Tree, with its phenomenal life expectancy, traditionally recognised by so many cultures as the symbol of eternal renewal and immortality of the soul. Maybe, in the greater scheme of things, we should cease to argue about the validity of one species of World Tree over any other. A tree is a tree and it fulfils its symbolic role, species known or unknown, to those who believe, trust and revere its spiritual significance.

Snake Bite

The association of serpents with the World Tree, or certainly Nidhogg, that biter of the roots, might explain the many accounts of snakes exhibiting great antipathy towards the ash. The earliest references to this stem from Pliny the Elder, in the first century, who claimed that snakes would rather creep into a fire than shelter among the branches of the ash tree, a claim which John Evelyn regarded with some derision: 'I am astonished at the universal confidence of some, that a serpent will rather creep into the fire than over a twig of Ash; this is an old imposture of Pliny, who either took it upon trust, or we mistake the tree.'

The Greek physician Dioscorides, also in the first century, claimed: 'The leaves of this tree are so greate virtue against serpents as that they dare not so much as touch the morning and evening

106 ASH MYTH, MAGIC AND SUPERSTITION

ABOVE:
A twelfth-century rendition of the Tree of Life on the tympanum above the south door of St. Mary's, Dymock, Gloucestershire. This style of carving is reproduced by the Dymock School of Norman stonemasons in several other churches in the area, but they resemble palms much more than ash trees.

shadows of the tree, but shun them afar off as Pliny reports.' On the principle that the predations of the serpent are repulsed by the overwhelming power of the World Tree to survive in the face of evil, perhaps this is how the ash tree came to be seen as a powerful antidote to snake bites. The sixteenth-century herbalist John Gerard echoed Dioscorides, asserting that 'the juice of the leaves or the leaves themselves being applied or taken with wine cure the bitings of vipers'. The seventeenth-century herbalist Nicholas Culpeper was not convinced, and cast derision upon such claims (see page 102).

The poet Abraham Cowley (1618–67) must have been familiar with the texts of the herbalists of the day, as he included this, by now, widespread superstition in one of his verses:

> But that which gave more wonder than the rest
> Within an Ash a serpent built her nest,
> And laid her eggs; when once to come beneath
> The very shadow of an Ash was death.

D. C. Watts in his *Dictionary of Plant Lore* cites several ash associations thought to keep snakes at bay. Ashes were planted around houses to repel adders. In Devonshire it was believed that a circle drawn round an adder with an ash stick would kill it. A floral wreath hung on an ash would protect nearby people and livestock from adders for the year. On Dartmoor and in Dorset it was customary that when dogs (or people) were bitten by adders they were dosed with a decoction made from young ash leaves. Quite what happened if it was late in the year is uncertain. In Somerset it was believed that, after someone was bitten by a snake, the wound must be sucked out three times; each time with the accompanying rhyme:

> Ashing-tree, ashing-tree
> Take this bite away from me.

In Wales carrying a piece of ash bark in the pocket was a popular amulet to keep snakes away. A strange tale is related in Richard Folkard's *Plant Lore, Legends and Lyrics* of 1884.

> There exists a popular belief in Cornwall, that no kind of snake is ever found near the 'Ashen-tree,' and that a branch of the Ash will prevent a snake from coming near a person. There is a legend that a child, who was in the habit of receiving its portion of bread and milk at the cottage door, was found to be in the habit of sharing its food with one of the poisonous adders. The reptile came regularly every morning, and the child, pleased with the

ASH MYTH, MAGIC AND SUPERSTITION

BELOW:
The Shrew Ash of Richmond Park was clearly an ancient hollow pollard when this photograph was taken in 1856, by Dr. Arthur Farr, for Sir Richard Owen. The 'witch-bar' appears to be across the hollow on the right side of the tree.

beauty of his companion, encouraged the visits. So the babe and the adder thus became close friends. Eventually this became known to the mother (who, being a labourer in the fields, was compelled to leave her child all day), and she found it to be a matter of great difficulty to keep the snake from the child whenever it was left alone. She therefore adopted the precaution of binding an Ashen-twig about its body. The adder no longer came near the child; but, from that day forward, the poor little one pined away, and eventually died, as all around said, through grief at having lost the companion by whom it had been fascinated.

Ruptures, Shrews and Witches

There is little doubt that the ash tree does provide many effective cures and tonics, as promoted by many modern herbalists, but there are a plethora of strange and sometimes unaccountable curative qualities ascribed to ash, perhaps none more widely reported by writers during the eighteenth and nineteenth centuries than that of infirm infants being passed through open clefts in ash trees to cure their maladies – usually infantile hernia. In *Sylva* John Evelyn notes:

> the rupture, to which many children are obnoxious, is healed, by passing the infant thro' a wide cleft made in the bole or stem of a growing Ash-tree; it is then carried a second time round the Ash, and caused to repass the same aperture as before. The rupture of the child being bound up, it is supposed to heal as the cleft of the tree closes and coalesces.

Evelyn's account was probably communicated via a third party, but for a more intimate description one need look no further than the diaries of the renowned naturalist the Reverend Gilbert White, writing about ash trees in his village of Selborne, Hampshire.

> In a farm-yard, near the middle of the village, stands at this day a row of pollard-ashes, which, by the seams and long cicatrices down their sides, manifestly show that in former times they have been cleft asunder. These trees, when young and flexible, were severed and held open by wedges, while diseased children, stripped naked, were pushed through the apertures, under a persuasion, that by such a process the poor babes would be cured of their infirmity. As soon as the operation was over, the tree in the suffering part was plastered with loam, and carefully swathed up. If the parts coalesced and soldered, as usually fell out, where the feat was performed with any adroitness at all, the party was cured; but where the cleft continued to gape, the operation, it was supposed, would prove ineffectual.

White, being the village vicar, then ameliorates his account of ancient pagan practice by announcing:

> Having occasion to enlarge my garden not long since, I cut down two or three such trees, one of which did not grow together.

ABOVE:
Surviving remnant of the Shrew Ash after the storm of 1875. A photograph taken in 1891.

We have several persons now living in the village, who in their childhood were supposed to be healed by this superstitious ceremony, derived down, perhaps, from our Saxon ancestors, who practised it before their conversion to Christianity.

Was the spiritual White keen to obliterate these pagan remnants? Did he consider the well-being or potential displeasure of those fellow villagers? Perhaps he considered these trees merely as symbols of an outmoded religious culture and unfounded tradition. Because *The Natural History of Selborne*, widely regarded as a classic text, has never been out of print since it first appeared in 1789 (around 300 editions to date), this ash story, which might easily have been lost with other folklore traditions, has been kept alive in a diverse catalogue of publications ever since.

A correspondent to *The Gentleman's Magazine* in 1804 related an instance of ash healing from Warwickshire.

On Shorley Heath in Silhill [Solihull] parish … there stands a young ash-tree, close to the cottage of Henry Rowe, whose infant son Thomas Rowe was drawn through the trunk or body of it, in the year 1791, to cure him of a rupture, the tree being then split open for the purpose of passing the child through it. The boy is now 13 years and 6 months old. I have this day, June 10, 1804, seen the ash-tree and Thomas Rowe, as well as his father Henry Rowe, from whom I have received the above account; and he superstitiously believes that his son Thomas was cured of the rupture, by being drawn through the cleft in the said ash-tree, and by nothing else.

A little later in 1804 another correspondent corroborates the above account, reporting that the tree was 'healthy and flourishing', a good omen for young Thomas. He adds:

ASH MYTH, MAGIC AND SUPERSTITION 109

BELOW:
This strange old tree in Bettws Dingle on the Welsh borders bears scars that have a passing resemblance to partially healed apertures, but this may be fanciful conjecture.

Thomas Chillingworth, son of the owner of an adjacent farm, now about 34, was, when an infant of a year old, passed through a similar tree, now perfectly sound, which he preserves with so much care that he will not suffer a single branch to be touched, for it is believed the life of the patient depends on the life of the tree, and the moment that it is cut down, be the patient ever so distant, the rupture returns, and a mortification ensues, and terminates in death.

The correspondent goes on to remark that sometimes the trees are left to heal themselves, but on other occasions nails are used to speed the process, so that wood-cutters often encounter trees full of nails. 'This belief is so prevalent in this part of the country, that instances of trees that have been employed in the cure are very common.'

Several similar accounts of these rituals have come down from the nineteenth century. Roy Vickery in his *Dictionary of Plant Lore* mentions two of these. One from Sussex in 1878 relates how an afflicted child must be passed nine times every morning through a cleft ash, and for nine consecutive days. Nine people must be in attendance and each passes the child through the cleft from west to east. Upon the final morning the tree must be bound up and, as it healed, so would the child. This account came from a clergyman's wife who, very sensibly, appears to have respected these antiquated local customs. Another incidence of this ritual was recorded in Somerset in 1886, with no mention of the ninefold

110 ASH MYTH, MAGIC AND SUPERSTITION

stipulation, but a notice that the naked child was passed through the ash cleft without touching the sides and with its face held heavenward, the whole event having taken place at sunrise. And from 1902 come Cecil Torr's Devonshire reminiscences, in *Small Talk at Wreyland*, after he had heard of a couple passing their ruptured babe through a cleft ash at daybreak. Torr asked the father of the child why they had done this. 'Why, all folks do it,' was the reply. Torr persisted, enquiring as to whether the man thought it would be beneficial for the child. To which the father replied, 'Well, as much good as sloppin' water over'n in church.'

Whether or not White's writings had a universal influence that manifested in such rituals being performed in many other places, or whether the knowledge of these superstitions was so widespread that it was already well established in other regions, it is difficult to know, but one senses the latter. However, another curious account of very similar events was recorded in the *Folk-lore Society Quarterly Journal* of 1898. In 1888 Sir Richard Owen, who had lived near Sheen Gate on the edge of Richmond Park since 1852, had related to the Journal's correspondent how he had observed a specific ancient ash tree in the park being used for very similar rituals and that

> he first encountered early in the morning a young mother with a sick child accompanied by 'an old dame,' 'a shrew-mother,' or, as he generally called her, a 'witch-mother.' They were going straight for the tree; but when they saw him, they turned off in quite another direction till they supposed he was out of sight. He, however, struck by their sudden avoidance of him, watched them from a distance, saw them return to the tree, where they remained some little time, as if busily engaged with it; then they went away. He was too far off to hear anything said, but heard the sound of voices in unison on other occasions.

Owen was later told by one of the park-keepers that 'mothers with "bewitched" infants, or with young children afflicted with whooping cough, decline, and other ailments, often came, sometimes from long distances, to this tree. It was necessary that they should arrive before sunrise.' There was a bar set in the tree known as the 'witch-bar' – whether an aberration of nature or placed there for a purpose does not seem obvious, but it was used for the ritual.

The important part of the ritual was performed at the tree. The 'shrew-mother' took the child from its mother, and giving directions to the parent according to the malady under treatment, passed the child slowly under and over the bar nine times, muttering charms or singing verses as the case might require. [The number nine featuring in this procedure is strangely reminiscent of the nine worlds of Norse mythology.] ...The passing of the child round the bar used to be timed to meet the rising sun. Whether only one or both women uttered the charm does not appear, but the failure to use the proper word at the exact moment when the first ray of sunrise broke over the horizon was given as the cause whenever the ash, with the intervention of the 'shrew-mother,' did not effect a cure. Many children were said to be cured at the tree.

The tree was badly damaged during a storm in 1875 and more than half of it was lost; however, the remaining portion thrived, largely as a result of an aerial root that must have already been growing inside the hollow bole. Because of the ongoing visits to the tree for the magical cures it bestowed, there was obviously still enough tree left to affirm its efficacy. Exactly when it was last used for this ritual is unknown, but great secrecy was usually observed when this was undertaken anyway. The gnarled vestige of the original tree survived until 1987 when it was blown down in the Great Storm.

The Richmond Park tree's appellation would seem to link it to another custom from antiquity, and maybe that is how its powers were originally intended. It was widely believed, according to the Reverend Gilbert White, that 'a shrew-mouse is of so baneful and deleterious a nature, that wherever it creeps over a beast, be it horse, cow, or sheep, the suffering animal is afflicted with cruel anguish, and threatened with the loss of the use of the limb.' The exact nature of such lameness is ill-defined, the assumption being that it equates to some form of neuropathy or a rheumatic condition. Historical accounts vary somewhat, for sometimes only cattle are under the charm, but the protection afforded has occasionally been extended to human subjects too, which may again relate to the Richmond Park tree. A shrew ash was made by boring a hole in the tree, placing a live shrew within, and then plugging the hole to imprison the poor little creature; most likely with some special incantation accompanying the ceremony. It was firmly believed that this would protect any of the livestock in that village or on that farm from affliction. Gilbert White remembered mention of an aged shrew ash in Selborne, some years prior to his incumbency, which had been much venerated. Often a stick would be cut from the tree which could be passed over any livestock, either to prevent or to cure an affliction.

Cures for very specific maladies were attributed to the ash, although because so many of them were recommended and practised in the distant past there is little evidence to maintain their efficacy. A lot of superstitions rested on the successful transferral of the malady to the tree. For example, pinning a lock of a sufferer's hair to an ash tree was supposed to cure whooping cough. In Wiltshire a popular belief for the cure of neuralgia was to take clippings from all finger and toe nails, along with a lock of hair; rise before sunrise on a Sunday; bore a hole in the first maiden ash encountered; place the nails and hair in the hole and seal it up. As the tree healed then so did the complaint.

Ash trees were believed to have other special properties, as Mrs Grieve tells us in her *Modern Herbal* of 1931:

> The Ash had the reputation of magically curing warts; each wart must be pricked with a new pin that has previously been thrust into the tree, the pins are withdrawn from the wart and then left in the tree, and the following charm is repeated: 'Ashen tree, ashen tree, /Pray buy these warts of me.'

Christina Hole in her *Traditions and Customs of Cheshire* (1937) notes that in the county the best way to erase warts was to 'steal a piece of bacon and push it under a piece of ash-bark. Excrescences would then appear on the tree; as they grew, the warts would vanish.' A variant of this comes from Hugh Pigott's article in *The Gentleman's Magazine* in 1867: 'Let the patient steal a piece of beef, and bury it in the ground; and then, as the beef decays, the warts will gradually die away.' Alternatively, 'Go to an ash-tree which has its "keys" upon it, cut the initial letters of both your Christian and surname on the bark; count the exact number of your warts, and cut as many notches in addition to the letters as you have warts; and then, as the bark grows up, your warts will go away.' It is always oddly fascinating to think that someone at some time had to try out these bizarre rituals. What on earth spawned these ideas, and how was the rate of success measured?

Not only did the ash have many unsubstantiated, even fanciful curative properties (by the standards of modern medicine), but it was also considered to have great protective powers, particularly against witchcraft. Ash walking sticks were supposed to be a protective amulet. Ash crooks and sticks used to drive cattle were supposed to protect them from evil influences. The Reverend John Lightfoot in his *Flora Scotica* of 1777 recalled:

> In some parts of the Highlands, a custom prevailed, at the birth of a child, for the nurse to put one end of a green ash stick into the fire, and while burning, to gather in a spoon the sap or juice which oozed out at the other end, and to administer this as the first spoonful of food to the newly born child. What the expected benefits to the child from so curious a custom may have been, it is impossible to say.

However, other writers who had observed the same custom suggested that this would provide the child with the strength of the ash tree as well as protection against all evil forces throughout its life. Richard Folkard in *Plant Lore, Legends and Lyrics* (1884) adds that mothers 'were admonished that the child should never be weaned while the [ash] trees were in blossom, or it would have grey hair'. Another reputed benefit from ash sap derived in this manner was that it could be administered into the ear as a cure for deafness. Clearly these tonics must have been used once the sap had cooled somewhat, although none of the accounts mention this proviso.

An old superstition long held in various parts of England is that if there should be a year in which no ash tree whatsoever bears fruits, ash keys, or 'locks and keys' (as they were often known), then some disaster would befall the royal family. The usual reference for this was that in 1648 this did actually occur and the following January saw the execution of King Charles I. The likelihood of this happening nationally was incredibly slender, but bearing in mind that many country people would not have travelled far in the seventeenth century so that, should this have happened in a localised area, it is easy to see how such a superstition might have evolved. A charming variant of this appears in Robert Forby's *Vocabulary of East Anglia* (1830): when the crop of ash-keys fails, 'many an old woman believes that, if she were the fortunate finder of a bunch, and could get introduced to the king, he would give her a great deal of money for it.' That, of course, before anything untoward befell him!

The ash has long been used for divination in matters of romance and marriage, most particularly with an ash leaf bearing an even number of leaflets – which, as anyone who looks diligently will attest, is hardly a rare occurrence (certainly not as unusual as four-leaved clover). John Symonds Udal in his *Dorsetshire Folklore* (1922) relates a typical version:

> The girl who wishes to devine who her future lover or husband is to be plucks an even ash leaf, and holding it in her hand, says: 'The even ash leaf in my hand, / The first I meet shall be my man.' Then putting it into her glove, adds: 'The even ash leaf in my glove, / The first I meet shall be my love.' And lastly, into her bosom, saying: 'The even ash leaf in my bosom, / The first I meet shall be my husband.

Roy Vickery in his *Dictionary of Plant Lore* records a variant of this divination rite:

> Starting at the bottom leaflet on the left-hand side and say:
>
> 'An even ash is in my hand
> The first I meet will be my man.
> If he don't speak and I don't speak,
> This even ash I will not keep.'

As each word is said, count a leaflet around the leaf until the rhyme is completed (this probably entails going round the leaf several times). When the rhyme's finished, continue by reciting the alphabet until the bottom right-hand leaf is reached. The letter given to this leaflet is the initial of your boyfriend.

Another variant from Northumberland runs thus:

> Even, even ash
> I pull thee off the tree:
> The first young man I do meet,
> My lover he shall be.

After which the leaf is put in the girl's shoe. Again, this time from Yorkshire, where the maid wishing to dream of her future husband puts an even ash leaf under her pillow:

> Even-ash, even-ash I pluck thee,
> This night my own true love to see;
> Neither in his rick nor in his rare,
> But in the clothes he does every day wear.

These rhymes appear to be quite universal, with many minor regional variations, although it inevitably seems to be the girl seeking her man rather than the other way around. In Oxfordshire an ash leaf with nine leaflets is preferred to the even ash.

ASH MYTH, MAGIC AND SUPERSTITION

A Cornish rhyme that is supposed to court good fortune, more in hope rather than expectation runs:

> Even ash, I do thee pluck,
> Hoping thus to meet good luck;
> If no good luck I get from thee
> I shall wish thee in that tree.

While another, rather strange incantation, perhaps for good fortune at court, appears in *Flowers and Flower Lore* by the Reverend Hilderic Friend in 1884:

> With a four-leaved clover a double-leaved ash and a green-topped seave
> You may go before the queen's daughter without asking leave.

Quite how this originated and what, apart from some sense of privilege, it is supposed to signify is something of a mystery. 'Seave' is an archaic name for a rush.

Ash has many associations with good fortune. Donald Watts in his *Dictionary of Plant Lore* (2007) gathers together several propitious traditions associated with ash when it comes to protection from evil:

> Branches of it were wreathed around a cow's horns, and round a cradle too. English mothers rigged little hammocks to ash trees, where their children might sleep while field work was going on, believing that the wood and leaves were a sure protection against dangerous animals and spirits. A bunch of the leaves guarded any bed from harm, and a house that was surrounded by an ash grove would always be secure.

Planting an ash tree to commemorate the birth of a child is supposed to auger a long and healthy life. It doesn't say what happens to the person if something untoward happens to the tree, but it is widely considered bad luck to break a branch from an ash. An adage gleaned from *The Transactions of the Highlands and Agricultural Society of Scotland*:

> 'May your footfall be by the root of an ash,' is a North Country proverb, signifying 'May you get a firm footing,' and is given as a God-speed to travellers, and is derived from the property possessed by ash roots of drying and draining the adjacent soil when merely damp.

Although all is not luck and good health with the ash, for like many plants it has a darker side. Ash is known as a lightning tree and caution is best taken when sheltering from the storm.

> Avoid the ash
> It courts the flash.

There may be some truth in this as the ash is our tallest native tree, and undoubtedly this couplet would have been in common parlance long before the introduction of species such as giant redwoods – now famed for having their tops blown out by lightning strike. Even so, many authorities believe that of all our native trees it is the oak that is most likely to be struck. A singularly unpleasant association from Lincolnshire is recorded in Britten and Holland's *A Dictionary of English Plant-names* (1886), whereby, 'If a man takes a newly cut "esh-plant" not thicker than his thumb, he may lawfully beat his wife with it [esh being a regional name for ash].'

How the weather-watch aspect of the ash has evolved and become so universally accepted, even though the outcome is never in any doubt, is a complete mystery.

> Oak before ash we're in for a splash,
> Ash before oak we're in for a soak.

Or, more succinctly, 'Oak choke, ash splash.' And, from Kent, 'Oak smoke, ash squash.'

Certainly the ash is probably more demanding of water, so if it was in leaf first that might reflect a particularly wet spring, but in reality leaf burst is all about temperatures and sunlight, and nobody can recall a year when ash trees were in leaf before the oaks, so maybe it is just simple country optimism – we'd prefer a warm, dry spring to a soggy one; although these couplets are usually thought to predict the summer weather.

Another, somewhat misaligned adoption of the ash springs from Ash Wednesday in the Christian calendar. In 1959 the folklorists Iona and Peter Opie recorded a tradition from Crowborough in Sussex, where 'children pick a black-budded twig of ash and put it in their pocket on this day'. Anyone who forgot to do this was liable to have their feet trodden on by the other children up until midday. Roy Vickery's researches confirmed this when he spoke to someone in 1991 who had lived in Crowborough as a child. They still remembered the tradition from their schooldays and how once, when the teacher had confiscated their ash twig that they were fiddling about with, all the other children tried to stamp on their feet as they struggled back to their desk. Fortunately the child had another bit of twig to ward off potential stampings at playtime. Another version that Vickery recounts is from someone who was a child in Heston, Middlesex in the 1930s. They were obliged to carry an ash twig for, if challenged, and one could not be presented, they risked getting a kick. The twigs had to be jettisoned by noon and there was still a vivid memory of how they 'risked the wrath of the teacher by rushing to an open window to throw out our twigs as soon as the midday dinner bell rang'.

In the dead of winter another ash tradition comes into play which has at its heart the spirit of rebirth in the midst of death and the chasing away of all evils. The lighting of bonfires at this time of year has its roots in the pagan celebration of the winter solstice Yule or Yuletide. The Yule log is one manifestation, whereby a huge log, usually of oak, but sometimes ash or even fruit wood, was hauled into the house to be kept alight throughout the twelve days of the Christmas festivities, with a small, charred remnant of the log being held safely in the home, to bring good luck, until the following Christmas when it would be used to kindle the new Yule log. Sadly, this tradition has been largely abandoned in today's celebrations, reduced merely to the symbolic chocolate-covered representations.

The ashen faggot was a particular variation of the Yule log theme at this time of year, either lit on new Christmas Eve or old Christmas Eve (5 January), in the past most commonly observed in Devon and Somerset. The faggot was a bundle of green ash poles bound together with withies, strips of ash or hazel bands, and sometimes these faggots were of prodigious size – maybe 8 or 9 feet long – so that they had to be fed slowly into the great open fireplaces a little at a time. Sometimes chains were required to stop the bundle from falling apart. With the advent of smaller fireplaces

BELOW:
'Ash', a soft ground etching by Charles Kennion, after drawings by his father Edward Kennion, 1820.

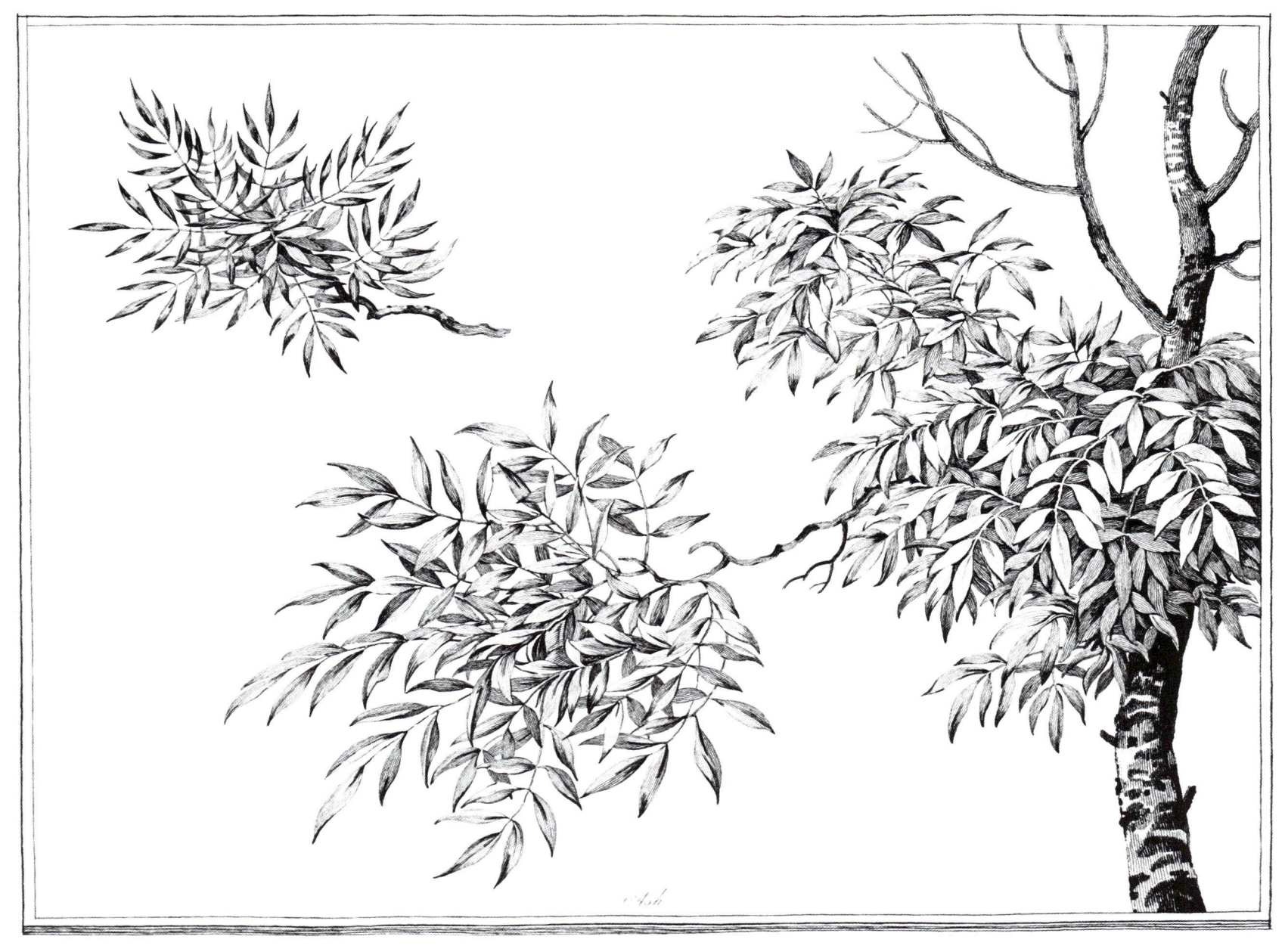

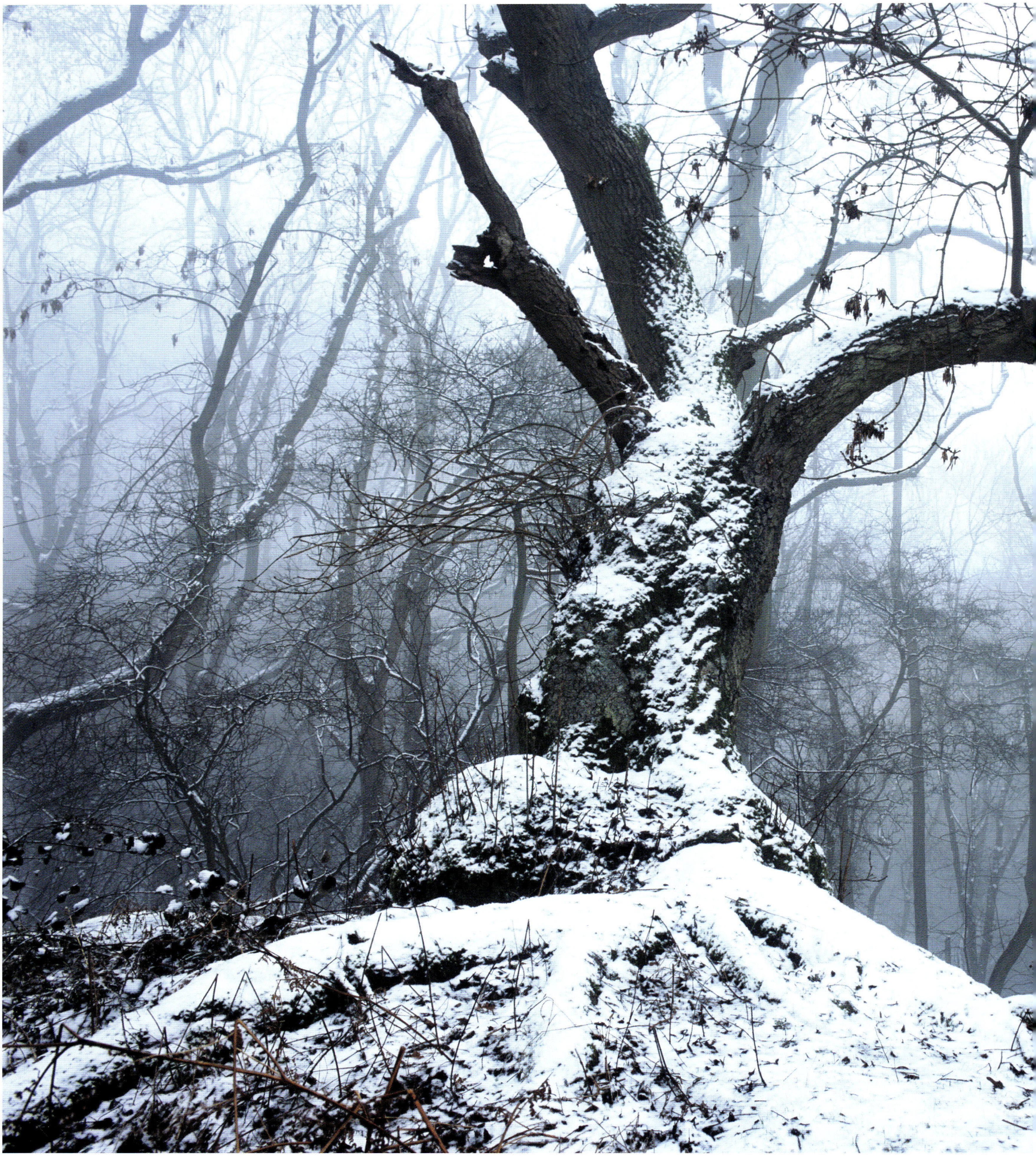

in more recent times the bundles have shrunk accordingly, sometimes only being a foot or two in length, but in the few public houses and homes where the custom is still observed, much jollity and consumption of drink is partaken as each withy bursts in the flames.

The custom is recorded in an issue of the *Birmingham Evening Despatch* from 1902:

> The faggot consists of green ashwood, cut lengthways, and neatly fastened into a bundle with withy bands. At eight o'clock in the evening this is placed on the fire with much ceremony, when the family and invited guests are gathered round the inglenook. The flames lick round the bundle, and when the first green withy holding the faggots bursts, glasses are raised and emptied to 'A Merry Christmas.' The breaking of each bond is a signal for a fresh toast. Legend accounts for this custom by the story that a fire of ashwood warmed the stable at Bethlehem, while local tradition tells of a greenwood fire kindled by Alfred the Great during his lonely wanderings in Somerset.

The Christian association quietly slides into view, displacing the pagan significance.

Charles Henry Poole, in his *Customs, Superstitions and Legends of the County of Somerset* (1877), says:

> The faggot is composed of ashen sticks, hooped round with bands of the same tree, nine in number [again the importance of the pagan ninefold]. Every time the bands crack by reason of the heat of the fire, all present are supposed to drink liberally of cider or egg-hot, a mixture of cider, eggs, &c. The reason why ash is selected in preference to any other timber is, that tradition assigns it as the wood with which Our Lady kindled a fire in order to wash her new-born Son.

Yet again a Christian interpretation has been invoked to neutralise any pagan symbolism. Another late-nineteenth-century account finds further fuel for the Christian story:

> A variation of this tradition given in some parts of West Somerset is that the Blessed Virgin being cold and suffering from the scanty shelter of the stable, St Joseph collected a bundle of sticks to make a

LEFT:
Ash grips the mist-clad ramparts of the Iron Age hillfort on Midsummer Hill at the southern end of the Malvern Hills.
It is quite possible that myths and superstitions associated with trees stretch back more than two thousand years when this hilltop was a thriving community.

ASH MYTH, MAGIC AND SUPERSTITION 117

BELOW:
'Cutting the Ashen Fagots in Devonshire', wood engraving from *'The Illustrated London News'*, 23 December 1854.

fire, but selected ash twigs in preference to others because he knew they were the only green ones that would burn.

W. G. Willis Watson, in his *Calendar of Customs, Superstitions, Weather-Lore, Popular Sayings and Important Events connected with the County of Somerset* (1920), states that in much the same way as a remnant of the Yule log is preserved for a year, 'in many farm-houses the last end of the ash stick which remains unburnt is kept to light next year's faggot with; and it is frequently placed in the cow stall to bring good luck in rearing calves through the year.'

Several other illuminating accounts are to be found in Willis Watson's book. A Miss Alice King, writing in 1891, says:

> And now the most important West Country custom, indispensable on Christmas Eve in every properly constituted West Country farm-house, is at hand. The door of the kitchen is opened wide, and the oldest labourer on the farm walks majestically in, carrying a huge ashen faggot on his shoulders. No West Country farmer would have any good luck throughout the coming year if the ashen faggot was not duly burned in his house on Christmas Eve. The faggot – which is a goodly load of wood, such as might be a respectable burden for a Spanish mule crossing the Sierras – is set on fire with much pomp and circumstance in the broad hearth...

On the subject of divination, Mr F. T. Elworthy, writing in *The Evil Eye* in 1895, avers:

> It is supposed that misfortune will certainly fall on the house where the burning is not kept up, while, on the other hand, its due performance is believed to lead to many benefits. The faggot must be bound with three or more 'binds' or withies, and one or other of these is chosen by the young people. The bind which first bursts in the fire shows that whoever chose it will be the first to be married. Hence, at the breaking of each

CUTTING THE ASHEN FAGOTS IN DEVONSHIRE.

118 ASH MYTH, MAGIC AND SUPERSTITION

LEFT:
The monstrous burry bole of the Purslow Ash in Shropshire conjures up images of mythical beasts.

bind the cider cup goes round to pledge the healths first of the lucky ones and afterwards of 'our noble selves,' &c.

While an extract from a late-nineteenth-century edition of the *Somerset Archaeological Society's Proceedings* proffers a slightly different suggestion for the use of ash in the faggot:

> A custom prevails at Taunton down to the present time of holding a ball, in the cold season of the year, called the Ashen Faggot Ball, in memory of the delight which King Alfred's men, coming up cold and hungry to the rendezvous (at Brixton Deveril, previous to the battle of Ethandune) all through the night, felt at finding that the ash-trees, common to the neighbourhood, would burn with ease, though green. This was a novelty to them, coming mostly from Somersetshire, where there is little wood but the elm, which burns with difficulty even when dry.

An extract from an early poem paints a vivid picture of the festivities:

> Thy welcome Eve, loved Christmas, now arrived,
> The parish bells their tuneful peals resound,
> And mirth and gladness every breast pervade.
> The ponderous Ashen-faggot, from the yard,
> The jolly farmer to his crowded hall
> Conveys with speed; where, on the rising flames
> (Already fed with store of massy brands),
> It blazes soon; nine bandages it bears,
> And, as they each disjoin (so custom wills),
> A mighty jug of sparkling cider's brought
> With brandy mixt, to elevate the guests.

One of the oddest superstitions associated with ash, conveyed by Folkard, is that 'in Northumberland, there is a belief that if the first parings of an infant's nails are buried under an Ash, the child will turn out a "top singer".' And in William Cobbett's *The Woodlands* (1825), this strange passage appears in his description of ash fruits and seeds:

> If you be curious, and have a mind to see a tree in embryo, take an Ash seed, put it into a little water lukewarm, and there let it remain for three or four days. Take it out: take a sharp knife, split the seed longways down the middle, and there you will see, standing as upright as a dart, an Ash tree, with leaves, trunk, and stem; that is to say, the head of the root: and all this you will see with the naked eye, as clearly as you ever saw an Ash tree growing in a field or meadow.

I have tried this but with little success. The challenge is out there!

OPPOSITE:
The impressive weeping ash at Chatsworth House.

The Weeping Ash

The weeping form of the common ash, *Fraxinus excelsior* 'Pendula', is a tree most usually found in parks and gardens, although there was also a Victorian penchant for planting them in cemeteries, its weeping form reflecting the sadness of loss. Since the tree is derived from a chance sport, it will not grow true to type from seed, and must be grafted on to a common ash stock, the union often defined by large unsightly swellings.

J. C. Loudon in his *Arboretum et Fruticetum Britannicum* describes the origins of the first tree.

> This singular and beautiful variety was discovered, about the middle of the last century, in a field belonging to the vicar of Gamlingay, near Wimpole in Cambridgeshire. Professor Martyn, in his edition of Millar's Dictionary, published in 1807, says that he recollects it for nearly forty years as a very fine pendulous-branched tree.

In 1835 Loudon asked a Mr James Dall, late gardener to the Earl of Hardwicke at Wimpole, to visit the tree and report back. It was in poor physical shape, according to Mr Dall, but had now been incorporated into the vicarage garden. Research by the Reverend Mr Hepworth, the present incumbent, had established that the tree was remembered as an already mature specimen by the parish clerk in his boyhood, during the 1730s, thus quite possibly taking its origins back to the seventeenth century.

The only way to reproduce the tree was by grafting scions from the mother tree, but Loudon was uncertain about how long cuttings had been taken, although he notes the presence of several local specimens of around 50 years of age, as well as many more throughout England, France, Germany and even America, where to this day weeping ash appears to be a popular choice in parks and gardens. Although such unusual sports may arise more than once, there is still a strong possibility that every single weeping ash in the world can be traced back to that one Cambridgeshire tree.

Probably one of the oldest, finest, even celebrity-status weeping ash trees came to the fore almost 200 years ago. William Cavendish, 6th Duke of Devonshire, had spotted a large mature tree in Derby and decided that this was exactly what was required for a specific location outside his home at Chatsworth House in Derbyshire. The epic task of transporting the tree to Chatsworth has been preserved in a news snippet from the *Derbyshire Courier* newspaper of 17 April 1830:

> This tree was purchased by His Grace from Messrs Wilson, and was removed from the gardens in the Kedleston Road, Derby (where it had been an ornament upwards of forty years), under the superintendence of the proprietors and Mr Paxton, upon a machine constructed by Messrs Strutt, of Belper. This was a carriage improved from Stewart's principal, and lent for the purpose to His Grace; and though the tree, with the earth attached, weighed nearly eight tons, it arrived at its destination in eighteen hours, the distance being 28 miles; and, contrary to expectation, it was able to pass through the different tollbars, with one exception, without displacing them. The greatest difficulty occurred at the Milford tollbar; but this by the skill and exertion of Mr Anthony Strutt, was considerably lessened. The gates and wall at the entrance to Chatsworth Park were, however, obliged to be taken down, and the branches of some trees in the park lopped off. His Grace met the tree at the entrance to the Park; and was much

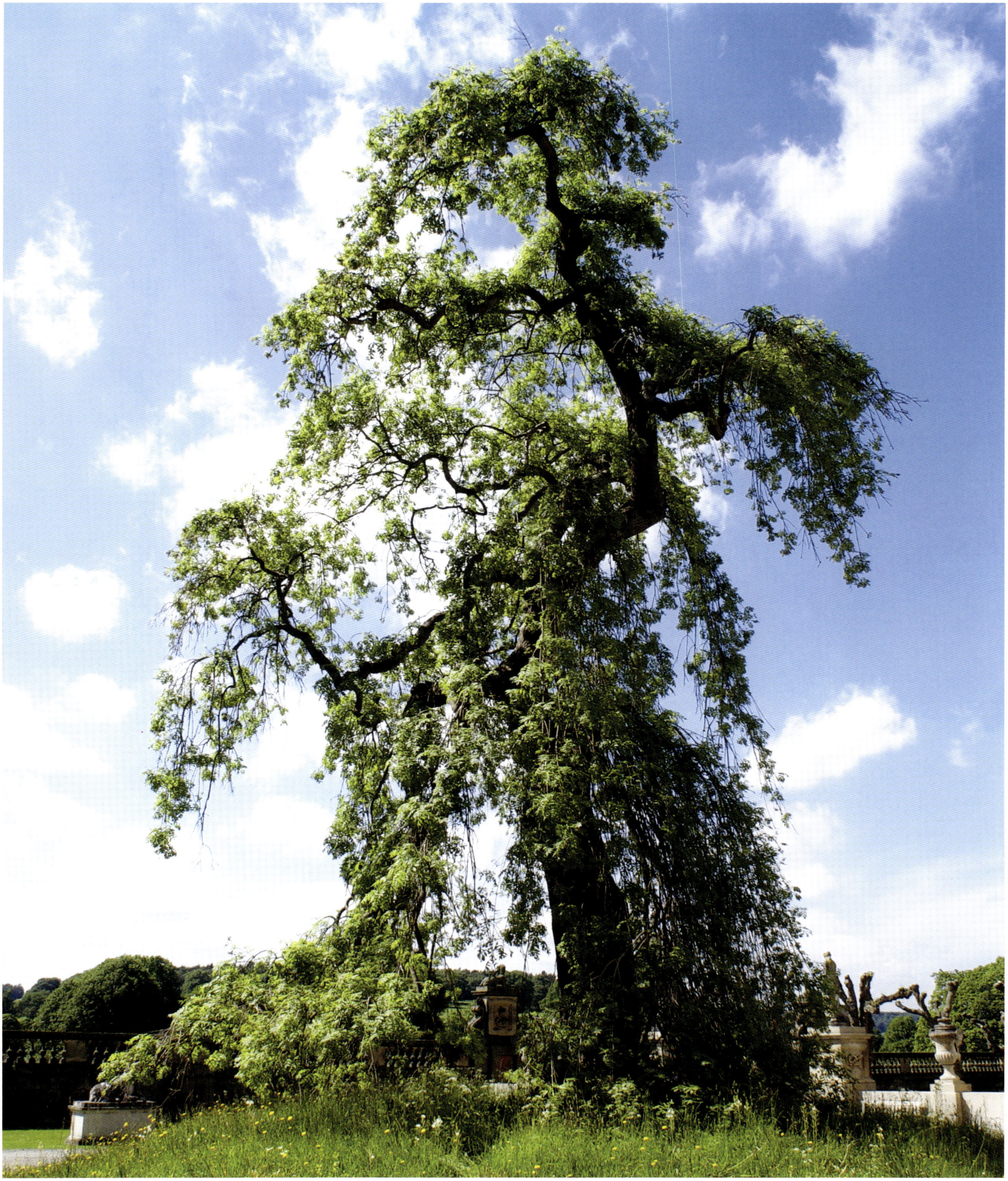

BELOW:
The Cowpen Ash, engraving from 'Arboretum et Fruticetum Britannicum', by J.C. Loudon, 1838.

OPPOSITE:
Weeping ash at Elvaston Castle, a photogravure from 'The Trees of Great Britain and Ireland', by Elwes and Henry, 1909.

gratified by its safe arrival. The undertaking was commenced on Wednesday, the 8th of April, and completed on the Saturday following.

The tree still stands where it came to rest almost 200 years ago, in the quadrangle at the south-west corner of the house. Accounts of its age when it was transplanted vary slightly, from 40 to upwards of 50 years, and from the contemporary account of its journey to Chatsworth it must have been a substantial tree. That it survived such upheaval is truly remarkable. The Reverend C. A. Johns in *The Forest Trees of Britain* (1847) states: 'In the first year after its transportation it sent out shoots twelve inches long.' Could this tree have been grown from a cutting taken from the original weeping ash, that sport first recognised in a Cambridgeshire field around 1750? If the Chatsworth tree is about 230–240 years old then it is eminently feasible. Of the thousands of visitors who file past this old ash tree every year to gain admittance to Chatsworth, one suspects that very few of them have the slightest inkling of the natural treasure they pass by.

The Reverend Johns briefly remarks on another interesting example spotted at a London tavern. 'A curious Weeping Ash is to be seen in the garden of the Vernon Arms, New Road, London. It is trained by trellis work, at a height of 7 feet from the ground over fourteen tables and twenty-eight benches, covering a space 36 feet long by 21 feet wide.' Recent research shows that the Lord Vernon Arms was at 188, Pentonville Road (part of what would then have been known as New Road), but no longer exists along with the remarkable weeping ash.

James Grigor, in his *The Eastern Arboretum, or Register of Remarkable Trees, Seats, Gardens, &c. in the County of Norfolk* (1841), wrote enthusiastically about the weeping ash:

> Norfolk ranks very high for specimens of the weeping plant (Fraxinus excelsior 'Pendula'), a variety of the common tree, originated about the middle of the last century, in the grounds of Gamlingay, near Wimpole, in the adjoining county of Cambridge. At the residence of C. Turner, Esq., Pottergate Street, Norwich, there is an elegant tree of it growing on the lawn in front of the house, an object which is noted by many on account of the singularity of its appearance. For the richness of its verdure and the regularity of its spray, which falls gracefully around it on all sides, we fancy it is not surpassed in this county. It was planted by the proprietor twenty-three years ago: it has now a stem 2 feet 6 inches in circumference, and is about 16 feet high. At 10 feet from the ground, the first tier of branches commence to descend; and, what is rather unusual, it is furnished with a loftier canopy, 6 feet above the other, from a stem which must have arisen, we presume, from the original stock. In the course of a few years, this addition to the usual character of the variety will considerably enhance the beauty of this object, by lessening its simple domical shape, and imparting to it more of the clustering, tree-like form.

And Grigor doesn't spare the plaudits in his account of the truly remarkable North Runcton weeping ash in Norfolk:

> North Runcton, the seat of Daniel Gurney, Esq., is one of those exceedingly elegant places, which, although not

122 THE WEEPING ASH

abounding in large trees, is remarkable for the neatness and propriety which prevail throughout … The finest tree here is a weeping ash, which is a tree indeed. It is unquestionably the finest specimen of the kind we ever beheld; and the only regret is, that the graft was not inserted on a stock 60 or 70 feet from the ground. It grows near to a pond, the tips of its branches reaching to the surface of the water, where of course its growth is stopped in that direction: the circumference of the space over which the branches extend is 18 yards; and it is altogether one of the most singular and striking objects of the tree kind in the county.

In his *Arboretum* Loudon notes two other occurrences of unusual ashes with very similar characteristics that had been brought to his attention by correspondents. A tree dubbed the Cowpen Ash was reported by a Mr Sydney, of Cowpen near Morpeth, who provided accompanying sketches, for he had located three very similar examples as well as several accounts of more such trees, and stated that, 'These trees have long attracted my attention, from the gracefulness of their appearance, and from their dissimilitude to the other ash trees in this neighbourhood.' Mr Sydney sent graft material to Loudon, which in turn was sent on to the Fulham Nursery. What later transpired we know not.

Another variation was the Kincairney Ash, growing on the estate of Mungo Murray, Esq., in Kincairney, near Dunkeld, that had 'a spray alternately pendulous, and rigidly upright, and thus forms a tree of fantastic shape'. Apparently the Perth nurseries of Dickson & Turnbull had propagated the tree and in 1838 had 'plants of it for sale'. The house at Kincairney still exists, but there is little chance that the tree survives as it was reported in *The Transactions of the Highland and Agricultural Society of Scotland* in 1880 that 'its chief branch has this year been broken off, from its having suffered last winter from the frost and superincumbent weight of snow.'

Probably one of the most remarkable weeping ash trees was recorded by Elwes and Henry in 1905 growing in the gardens of Elvaston Castle, Derbyshire, and they figured it in a fine plate in their *Trees of Great Britain and Ireland*. It had been measured as 98 feet high (although Elwes thought it closer to 90 feet), bearing branches that swept down 60–70 feet. It had been top grafted at 80 feet

ABOVE:
The weeping ash at North Runcton in Norfolk, an engraving from 'The Eastern Arboretum' by James Grigor, 1841.

BELOW:
A postcard from 1917 shows the Aberford Ash in Yorkshire.

on to a common ash in 1848 by Mr Barron, the head gardener. A most unusual procedure, as the grafts are usually a lot lower down and it would have been a deed of some daring at such a heady height. Another large specimen, some 50 feet high, was also seen in the gardens, which had apparently been grafted at the same time, although the wild stock had overtaken the weeping crown.

A strange confusion of dates occurs in the account of the larger tree as *The Gardener's Magazine* of 1839 recalls a tour of the gardens and notes an impressive 'weeping ash grafting on a common ash at 80 ft from the ground', but also mentioning Mr Barron as the head gardener.

To chance on old photographs or postcards of trees that have remained unknown to a wider audience up to the present day sometimes reveals some truly magnificent forgotten gems. One such postcard, dated 1917, features the Aberford Ash – a tree of some magnitude with a multitude of weeping boughs that appear to have been trained on to a wrought-iron, encircling framework of arched hoops. A smartly dressed gentleman (Mr Brown, the owner, maybe?) stands beyond. Local historian Brian Hull did a little delving into Aberford history and uncovered a newspaper cutting that mentioned the tree. Taken from the *Leeds Mercury*, 2 June 1880, there is an account of a group of naturalists visiting the nearby Parlington Estate,

124 THE WEEPING ASH

ABOVE:
The weeping form of the tree has long been associated with churchyard situations.

afterwards moving on to meet a Mr Brown, of Bridge House, Aberford (Saturday last – 26 May 1880). They were invited into the grounds of the house where members were shown a large drooping ash, '… the branches of which are trained over iron supports to a distance of about 28 yards from the stem, and form fine avenues, attracted much attention, and a visit to the adjacent maze concluded a very enjoyable excursion'. Brian Hull discovered a photograph of the tree taken in the 1980s and managed to contact the present owners of Bridge House who reported that the old tree had survived right up until a couple of years ago.

Several remarkable weeping ashes may still be found on large country estates today. An impressive specimen grows right next to the grand house at Bedgebury Manor in Sussex. This splendid old tree is reckoned to be the biggest in Britain, with a girth of a little over 4 metres, and has also dropped a couple of branches which have layered themselves. Its age is unknown, and due to the house having been empty for a few years great gouts of ivy have overtaken the canopy and dense layers of long grass and weeds beneath are also causing the tree to struggle, but new owners of the Estate are engaged in extensive renovation of both the house and gardens. What aroused most concern during a visit in the summer of 2017 was the possible infection with ash dieback. To lose such a nationally important tree would be very sad.

Another fine specimen resides in the centre of a lawn next to Seaton Delaval Hall in Northumberland. A few years ago one branch collapsed and fell to the ground, but has stayed

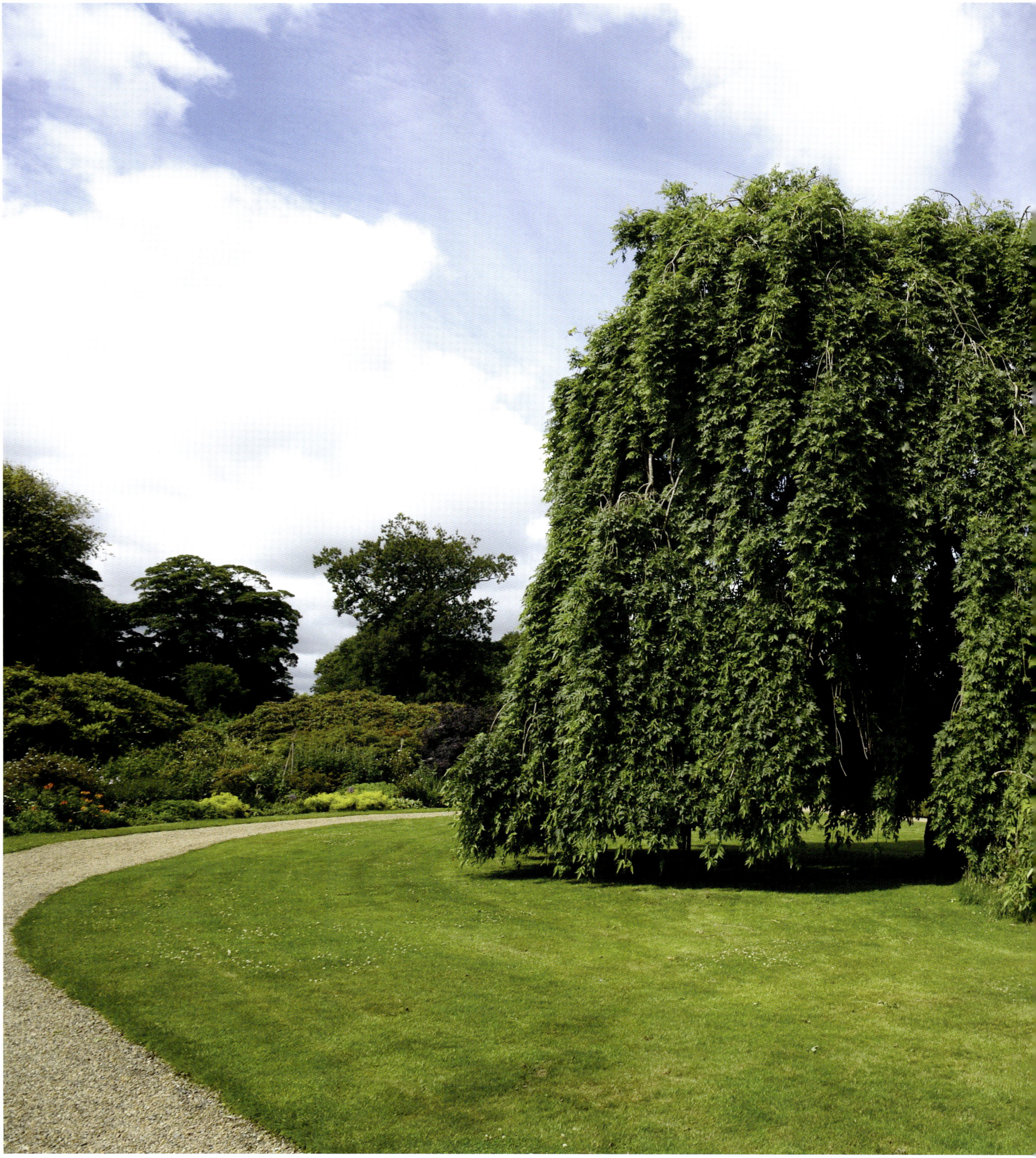

LEFT:
The splendid weeping ash at the National Trust's Seaton Delaval Hall in Northumberland.

BELOW:
Underneath the Seaton Delaval Weeping Ash.

BELOW RIGHT:
Unsightly graft union on a tree in London Road Cemetery, Coventry.

OPPOSITE:
Another plate from James Grigor's 'Eastern Aboretum' (see page 122 for his appreciation of this tree).

attached to the tree, skilfully propped by the gardening staff and remains very much alive. There has been a long-running belief that the tree is now almost 300 years old, perpetuated by the late Lord Hastings, the previous owner of the property. This would make it almost certainly a cutting from the original Wimpole sport. However, some very thorough research by Justine James, operations manager at Seaton Delaval, hinted at what may be a more accurate dating of the tree. It transpires that it appears on Ordnance Survey maps for 1855, 1897 and 1933, yet does not appear on landscape plans for the gardens dating from 1781 and 1808. It was also said that mention of the tree was made in early family correspondence, but no evidence of this has been traced. Hence, in reality, the oldest it could be is a little over 200 years. Perhaps the well-documented story of the discovery of the original tree led to the assumption that this one was contemporaneous. In the greater scheme of things none of this really matters, but it does show how easily assumptions and hearsay become hard fact. An extremely rare variant of the weeping ash is the Wentworth weeping ash (*Fraxinus excelsior* 'Pendula Wentworthii') – with a fine, tall example growing near Highgate Ponds on Hampstead Heath in north London. Since no graft line is visible it is thought that it may be a sport. The reason for the appellation 'Wentworth' is somewhat shrouded in mystery, but the nineteenth century dendrologist Karl Koch thought that the name was a corruption of 'Hepworth', the name of the vicar of Gamlingay who discovered the first weeping ash in the eighteenth century, suggesting that the tree was named as a tribute to the cleric. *Champion Trees of Britain and Ireland* (2003) edited by Dr Owen Johnson reports another large specimen growing at Lindridge Park in Devon.

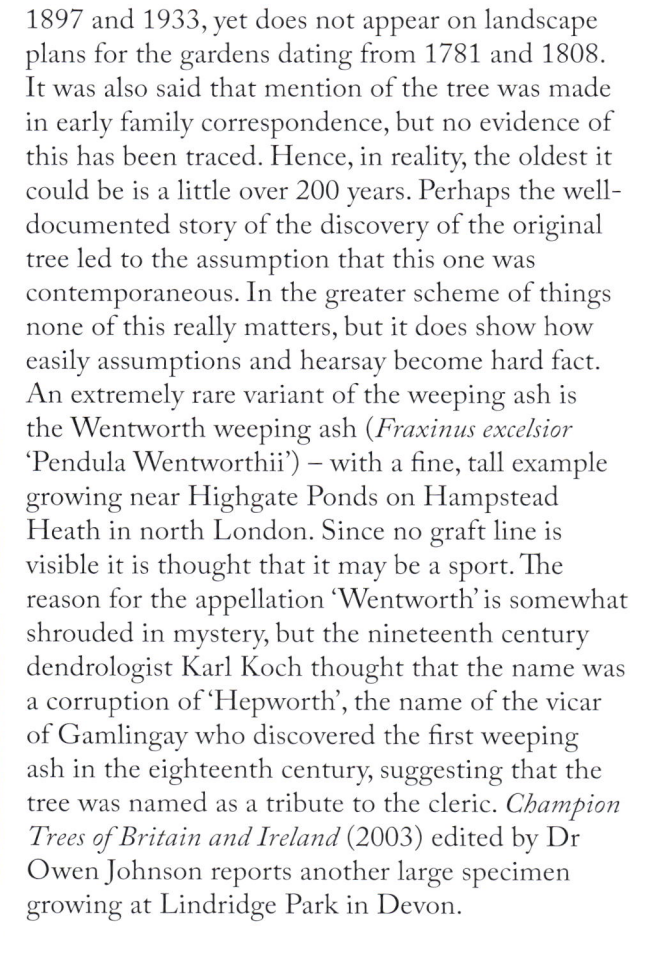

128 THE WEEPING ASH

*Weeping Ash
at
E Turner's Esq.
Pottergate Street House
NORWICH.*

THE WEEPING ASH

BELOW:
James, Duke of Monmouth, from an original by Sir Peter Lely. Engraving by E. Daniell from The Diary of John Evelyn, 1879 edition.

Remarkable Ash Trees

The ash tree, probably due to its much shorter lifespan than the iconic oak, has never attracted quite as many famous associations with celebrities, royalty, or events of a historical, cultural or even quirky nature. The ash very seldom attains the gigantic proportions of the very oldest oaks, with the kind of boughs that might hide a fleeing king or a highwayman waiting to pounce, or those huge hollow boles that have provided cock pens, homes or rooms in which to party. An ancient ash would usually be a tree over 300 years old, but with oaks it's over 600 years. Even so, a careful trawl through the works of various tree writers and historians of the last two centuries unearths a few remarkable and sometimes strange associations with ash trees. Inevitably the majority of these historical ashes are long gone, but there are still a few monumental trees located in various parts of Britain that have gained notice either for their exceptional size or their very characterful forms, and inevitably these are huge old pollards or ancient coppice stools.

The Monmouth Ash

The Monmouth Ash became an unwitting witness and memorial to a brief and bloody episode in the late-seventeenth-century struggle for supremacy on the British throne. When James II ascended on the death of his elder brother Charles II on 6 February 1685 there were some Protestants who resented this Roman Catholic monarch and looked for ways to depose him. One such was James Scott, 1st Duke of Monmouth, an illegitimate son of Charles, who claimed the throne as his own. Knowing that he had many sympathisers in the West Country, he planned to enter the country from Holland, gather forces and march on London. On 11 June 1685 the Duke of Monmouth, pretender to the throne, landed on the beach at Lyme Regis with some eighty-two followers (including a young Daniel Defoe, who would later write *Robinson Crusoe*). Marching north, they gathered support until they met the forces of James II led by John Churchill (later Duke of Marlborough) at Sedgemoor in Somerset on the 6th of July. After Monmouth's army was defeated, with some 2,000 rebels slain, he took flight across country with Lord Grey and three other companions. They headed towards Dorset, intending to take a boat from Poole back to Holland. At Woodyates in North Devon the group split up, leaving their exhausted horses. Monmouth, disguised as a shepherd, made for open country near Horton, but was spotted climbing over a hedge by one Amy Farrant who lived close by. A search was mounted and at sunrise a militiaman called Parkin found what appeared to be a pile of old clothes in a ditch beneath an ash tree. A bedraggled Duke of Monmouth was hauled forth and it is said he had nothing upon him but some raw peas and a badge of the Order of the Garter given to him by his father, Charles II. John Evelyn recorded the capture in his diary, having been told that Monmouth, with a £5,000 bounty on his head,

> was found by Lord Lumley [the nobleman in charge gets the credit rather than the militiaman, although the bounty was apparently distributed among the militia] in a dry ditch cover'd with fern-brakes, but without sword, pistol, or any weapon, and so might have pass'd for some countryman, his beard being grown so long and so grey as hardly to be known, had not his George [Order of the Garter] discover'd him, which was found in his pocket. 'Tis said he trembl'd exceedingly all over, not able to speake.

Undoubtedly Monmouth knew that the road to the scaffold inevitably lay ahead. Ever since, this place has been known as Monmouth's Ash, although the original tree, which for many years was propped

130 REMARKABLE ASH TREES

up with poles, succumbed before the end of the nineteenth century. Monmouth was later beheaded on Tower Hill on the 15th of July. The infamous 'Bloody Assizes' of Judge Jeffreys would later execute more than 300 of Monmouth's supporters and sentence a further 800 to transportation to the West Indies.

An interesting footnote claims that Daniel Defoe, while he hid in a churchyard after the Battle of Sedgemoor, discovered the name Robinson Crusoe on a gravestone.

Historical Ashes in Scotland

William Gilpin published the first edition of his *Remarks on Forest Scenery* in 1791 and provided a succession of illuminating portraits of great individual trees in Britain as well as Europe, but sadly his inventory does not include any ash trees. In 1834 a new and revised edition of Gilpin's book was published, and edited by Sir T. Dick Lauder, a Scotsman, who obviously felt it incumbent upon him to add some historical examples of renowned Scottish trees, with ash significantly included among these new entries.

Lauder talks of a remarkable ash tree near the house of Bonhill in Dunbartonshire which, at about 4 feet above ground, had a circumference of 34 feet 1 inch. From the description, it appears to have been an outgrown pollard with three huge branches, the main body of the tree having long ago become hollow.

> Many years ago, the tree being hollowed and opened on one side, the opening was formed into a door, and the rotten part of the tree scooped out. In this way a small room, 9 feet 1 inch in diameter, was formed within the trunk. Its roof is conical, and 11 feet high. It is floored, and surrounded with a hexagonal bench, on which eighteen people can sit, with a table in the middle; and above the door there are five small leaden windows. Though the tree has decayed in the heart, it has continued to live in the bark, and to form a great deal of new wood. The whole trunk, which is a vast mass, is thickly covered with fresh vigorous branches.

Lauder goes on to mention 'a noble ash, one of the most magnificent trees as to form we ever beheld, which grows at Earlsmill, near Tarnawa Castle, the seat of the Earl of Moray, in Morayshire'.

This tree measures above 17 feet in girth at 3 feet from the ground, but it spreads out so much below, that its measurement would be much greater if taken lower down. There is a small hole at the root of it, large enough to admit one man at a time, and on creeping into it, the cavity is found to be so great as to allow three people to stand upright in it at the same moment. The interior has been in this state during the memory of the oldest persons; and yet, until an accident in July, 1824, nothing could be more grand than its head, which was formed of three enormous limbs variously subdivided in bold sweeping lines. The foliage though appearing late, was, and indeed still is, abundant and beautiful. But some days

BELOW:
The Monmouth Ash, an engraving from 'British Forests and Forest Trees', 1853.

RIGHT:
The Earlsmill Ash from an etching by Kidd in Lauder's edition of William Gilpin's 'Remarks on Forest Scenery', 1834.

before the 23rd July, 1824, its great southern limb was broken down by a high wind, and even though the ruin thus created was sufficiently deplorable, yet it was strikingly sublime.

He provides a fine engraving of the tree, which appears to be unblemished by the storm, so obviously taken from a drawing prior to 1824. A few years later, in 1838, J.C. Loudon in his *Arboretum et Fruticetum Britannicum* also presents a fine engraving of the tree taken from a sketch by a Mr J. Steven, a drawing-master from Elgin (again made before the loss of the huge bough). Loudon solicited information on important trees from his many contacts on the great estates and in the gardening world and, most probably, through the subscribers to his *Gardener's Magazine* which he had launched in 1826. Substantial lists of the finest examples of all tree species (almost certainly the most extensive ever collected) grace the pages of the *Arboretum*. Many trees are entered with their measurements and details of their planting dates; a very useful guide when comparing growth rates. There appears to have been a particular wealth of fine ash trees in Scotland at that time.

Another huge ash of note in the churchyard of Kilmalie, in Lochaber, is recorded by Lauder:

long considered as the largest and most remarkable tree in the Highlands. It was held in reverence by Lochiel, and his numerous kindred and clan, for many generations, which probably hastened its destruction; for in the year 1746, it was burnt by the brutal soldiery to the ground.

Some years afterwards the remains at ground level were measured, revealing a circumference of 58 feet. 'A person present who had been well acquainted with the tree, described it as being of vast bulk, but not tall, as it divided into three great arms at about 8 feet from the ground,' Lauder noted. This certainly sounds like another giant outgrown pollard.

Bonnie Prince Charlie's Ash

Lauder describes several other impressive ash trees in Scotland – most of which would seem to have been ancient pollards, and all of which are now long gone. However, he did neglect to mention another ash with a very sombre link to the dark days of 1746, and most particularly to the bloody conflict at Culloden, near Inverness, on the 16th of April. 'Prince Charlie's Ash Tree' was featured on an Edwardian postcard by the Aberdeen photographic company established by George

132 REMARKABLE ASH TREES

Washington Wilson, as part of its Highland Series. It was supposed to mark the vantage point from which Bonnie Prince Charlie commanded his men at the Battle of Culloden – the last ever pitched battle fought on British soil, at which Prince Charles Edward Stuart and his Jacobite army were defeated by the forces of the Hanoverian King George II led by William Augustus, Duke of Cumberland. This fierce engagement was concluded in less than an hour, with almost a thousand Jacobites killed and many more wounded, and marked the end of any hopes that the Jacobites had of a Stuart restoration to the British throne. The slender form of the ash tree on the postcard suggests that it either grew very slowly over the intervening 150 years, from being a relatively small tree in 1746, or that it might even be a replacement for the original tree (a phenomenon repeated elsewhere – most famously with the Boscobel Oak in Shropshire). A relatively modern colour postcard from 1967 shows the tree looking much as it did around 1900, but the chance that it had survived into the twenty-first century seemed unlikely. Contact was made with Jon Wartnaby, a member of the National Trust for Scotland Learning Team at the Culloden Battlefield, who promised to take a walk across to Balvraid Farm, where the tree had stood. Low and behold, he found it! A forgotten Heritage Tree rediscovered. The ash had survived, although not in its entirety. Jon suspects that it had been struck by lightning at some time, reducing its height by at least 50 per cent, but in doing so creating a naturally occurring pollard, and thus probably helping to prolong the tree's life. In Jon's opinion this would have been an unlikely place from which to command a battle plan as the battlefield is over a rising piece of ground and hence out of sight, about a mile away. Perhaps the Prince used the farm as a base and had outriders bringing in reports and despatching orders. We will never know for sure, but for the tree to have attracted its appellation one assumes that it must have been a very poignant symbol to many a Scot with Jacobite leanings; loyalties that lingered on into the nineteenth century, when the old photograph would have been taken, and even into the twentieth century when the colour postcard was published.

A visit in February 2018 revealed a tree that appears to have been scrapping with the elements for a very long time, but so far just about winning. The shape of the lower bole with its very slight

LEFT:
An Edwardian postcard of Prince Charlie's Ash Tree on Culloden Moor, from a photograph by George Washington Wilson of Aberdeen.

BELOW:
The same tree today, with its top blown out, but still very much alive.

BELOW:
'Gorget Tree at Applegirth Churchyard', a drawing by Mrs. Strickland, published by the Anastatic Drawing Society, 1858.

curve, and the unmistakeable juxtaposition with the old stone barn and farmhouse, confirm it as the self-same tree as the one on the early-twentieth-century postcard. Some day, one day, it may well fall, at which point it will be fascinating to discover exactly how old it really is.

Dool Trees and the Jougs

Scotland was known in the distant past for various unsavoury uses of trees. Dool or dule trees (the name derives from an old Scots word meaning sorrowful or mournful) were used as gibbets, and two extant examples, both sycamores, exist at Leith Hall in Aberdeenshire and Blairquhan in Ayrshire. Close to the laird's homestead, these would have exhibited the corpses of miscreants as a warning to other local inhabitants to behave. Others would appear to have been ash trees; witness the account by Robert Hutchison of Carlowrie, in *The Transactions of the Highland and Agricultural Society of Scotland* (1880), recalling an ash tree with a gruesome past:

> The old ash at the ferry over the Tay, near the church of Logierait, Perthshire, in July 1770 measured 16 feet in girth at 4 feet from the ground. It was then a healthy well-shaped tree about 70 feet high, and was well known in the country by the name of the 'Ash Tree of the Boat of Logierait'. It still continues to live on and thrive. The lower part of the trunk is quite a shell, and has been formed into a summer-house or arbour, capable of containing a considerable number of people. Popular tradition ascribes the great size of this tree to the richness of the soil around it, from the fact of its having been the 'dool tree' of the district, on which caitiffs and robbers were formerly executed, and their bodies left hanging on

the tree till they dropped and lay around unburied! The present circumference of this tree is, at 1 foot from the ground, 40 feet 4 inches, and at 6 feet up it is 29 feet 7 inches.

Joug trees were another dark association with hardened criminals, or perhaps just the wayward or less fortunate. Wrongdoers would be shackled to them and often pelted with rotten fruit and vegetables (much like the stocks in England). Hutchison elaborates:

> An old ash, of historical celebrity, still stands in a waning state in the south-west corner of the churchyard of the parish of Moulin, near Pitlochry village. In olden times culprits were chained to this tree, while they were awaiting their doom (generally final) at the hands of the Council of Lairds, who were the administrators of justice in the Highlands in mediaeval times. These were the same executioners of justice who used the ash tree at the ferry of Logierait as their gibbet for that district. What their preference for ash was, both prior to and for the execution of their victims, does not appear, but probably there existed in these superstitious times, some association of doleful nature with this tree.

The Moulin joug tree survived until 2007 before being declared unsafe by the local council and hastily felled … rather too hastily, many local inhabitants felt, as nobody in the village was consulted!

Another, similar example emerges from the unlikely source of the 1858 annual collection of artwork published by the Anastatic Drawing Society. A splendid lithograph from a drawing by a Mrs Strickland shows 'The Gorget Tree and Jougs, Applegirth Church-yard, Dumfriesshire' (this should be Applegarth.) The following narrative accompanies the print:

> This venerable Ash is believed to be 300 years old. It is 19 feet in girth at the foot, and 16 4 feet from the ground. To it were attached the Jougs, which were found imbedded in the trunk when a branch was torn away during a heavy gale of wind in 1850. A small woodcut of these Jougs is given by Mr Wilson in the Archaeology and Prehistoric Annals of Scotland, p. 691, with the following description, - 'The Jougs, which consist of an iron collar attached by a chain to a pillar or tree, form the corresponding Scottish judicial implement to the English stocks, applied however, not to the legs or arms, but to the neck. A fine old pair of Jougs, the property of Sir William Jardine, of Applegirth, Bart., were found imbedded in a venerable ash tree recently blown down at the Church-yard gate, Applegirth. The Jougs were completely imbedded in the trunk of the tree, while the chain and staple hung down within the decayed and hollow core.'

These ash trees may have fallen and gone, leaving only the accounts of their grim roles, but in the village of Balfron, in Stirlingshire, the Clachan Oak, thought to be around 500 years old, its mighty bole still bound with two iron hoops, is a potent reminder of this brutal mode of punishment.

Wiggin's Tree

Dastardly deeds seem to have captured the public imagination for hundreds of years and there appears to be no shortage of such events with arboreal associations. J. H. Wilks, in his *Trees of the British Isles in History & Legend* (1985), relates the gruesome story of Wiggin's Tree, gleaned from the *Salopian Journal*, Vol. 19, No. 984:

> On Wednesday, 26th November, 1812, between six and seven o'clock in the evening, Mr Wiggin, a miller from Ardington, about 2 miles from Bridgnorth, was murdered between that place and his own house. He was returning from Wolverhampton Market and was met by a footpad about a mile from his home. It is supposed that on his making a stout resistance, the villain drew a pistol and shot him; the ball passing through in a direct line just below his heart. It seems that the assassin was alarmed by Wiggin's cries for he made off without taking any property, which consisted of between £50 and £60 in notes. It is conjectured that, after being shot, the unfortunate man pursued his murderer for about a hundred yards, but fell exhausted. Someone from a local turnpike house heard his cries and helped him to the house, but Wiggin expired within a short time.

RIGHT:
*'The Great Ash at Woburn Park',
a lithograph from 'Sylva Britannica',
folio edition of 1826, by Jacob
George Strutt.*

Although a bounty of £200 stood for many years on the head of the murderer, his identity was never discovered. Wiggin's Tree was an ash, cut down for road-widening purposes in 1957. However, right up to that time a story persisted that the area around the tree was haunted by the ghost of Wiggin, and it was said that on the anniversary of his murder a red, blood-like stain, in the shape of a cross, would appear around a hole in the tree bark.

Cury Great-Tree

The Reverend C. A. Johns rolls out another story of violent deeds in his *Forest Trees of Britain* (1847).

> In the parish of Cury, about 6 miles from the Lizard point, in Cornwall, stands a very fine Ash, known by the name of 'Cury Great-Tree' … it is worthy of notice as being the largest Forest-tree in the extreme southern promontory of England, and for the veneration in which it is held by the inhabitants of the surrounding district.

The tree measured 27 feet in girth and had a canopy 70 feet wide maintained by six huge, spreading limbs. However, it would seem that all was not well with the tree and, as Johns noted, 'In the spring of 1843, during a violent storm, a large limb of this tree fell with a terrific crash, to the imminent danger of some persons who were at the time passing in a carriage.' The tree was notorious as a rendezvous for smugglers and Johns recounts a gruesome tale of foul deeds which harked back to the 1750s when a large ship was wrecked between Lizard Point and Kynance Cove. Great rivalry existed between the various local communities as to who had the rights to seize booty from such maritime disasters. On this occasion the men of Wendron had a head start, and soon the men of Breage and Germoe caught wind of the rewards to be had, but being late they decided to ambush the returning Wendron men near the great ash as they returned heavily laden with loot. Sure enough, writes Johns,

> a furious battle ensued, might on either side being the only test of right, and several men were killed. But what principally distinguishes this fray from many others of the same character is, that a woman who was interested for one of the parties, having deliberately pulled off

136 REMARKABLE ASH TREES

LEFT:
'The Great Ash at Carnock', an etching from the later 1830 edition of 'Sylva Britannica', with much smaller reproductions utilising the original sketches.

Great Ash at Carnock.

one of her stockings and placed a large stone in it, mounted a hedge closely adjoining the scene of conflict, and with this unusual but murderous weapon actually beat out the brains of a man of the adverse faction.

In conclusion Johns remarks that, 'Now, happily, a better spirit prevails in Cornwall.' He conjectures that the tourist resting beneath the shade of the great old ash would 'scarcely be brought to believe that so dark a deed as that above described was perpetrated on the spot where he is sitting and almost within the memory of living men'. Again, sadly, this tree is long departed and no image of it appears to exist, which is strange given its notoriety.

The Ashes of Sylva Britannica

From 1822–6 the artist Jacob George Strutt toured England and Scotland gathering drawings for his masterwork *Sylva Britannica*: *Or Portraits of Forest Trees Distinguished for their Antiquity, Magnitude of Beauty*. The magnificent folio edition was initially published in parts, but it drew such a favourable response from an eager public that he was pressed to produce a smaller-format edition of the work, which might be affordable to a wider audience. This was accomplished in 1830. Of the fifty subjects chosen by Strutt only two were ash trees, and they appear to have had no particular anecdotal associations – they were simply very impressive specimens. Whether patronage of the aristocracy and the accommodation and entertainment on their estates lavished on the roving artist influenced his choices of trees to sketch must be left to conjecture.

Strutt made a beautiful drawing of the Great Ash at Woburn, in the park of His Grace the Duke of Bedford, recording it as 'an extraordinary specimen of the size which this tree will attain in favourable situations'. He faithfully records its dimensions – 90 feet high, 23 feet 6 inches in girth at ground level, 15 feet 3 inches at 3 feet above ground and a canopy 113 feet in diameter. He also calculates 872 cubic feet of timber and then proceeds in lyrical mode:

> It is in mountain scenery that the ash appears to peculiar advantage; waving its slender branches over some precipice which just affords it soil sufficient for its footing, or springing between crevices of

REMARKABLE ASH TREES

BELOW:
An Edwardian postcard shows a gathering of Winchelsea folk beneath the original Wesley Ash.

rock, a happy emblem of the hardy spirit which will not be subdued by fortune's scantiness. It is likewise a lovely object by the side of some crystal stream, in which it views its elegant pendant foliage, bending, Narcissus-like, over its own charms.

In Scotland Strutt figured the mighty, spreading ash tree on the estate at Carnock, Stirlingshire. Again he records its exceptional dimensions in great detail when he made his drawing in July 1825 – 90 feet high, 31-feet girth at ground level, 19 feet 3 inches at 5 feet from the ground, spreading to 21 feet 6 inches at 9 feet from the ground. Just above this the tree branched into three mighty stems and he estimates the whole to contain the very precise 679 cubic feet of timber. He begins, 'This beautifully luxuriant tree almost embraces the venerable mansion near which it stands. It is the property of Sir Michael Shaw Stewart, and is supposed to be the largest in Scotland, even when measured at the smallest part of the trunk.' It was reputed to have been planted in 1596 by Sir Thomas Nicholson of Carnock, who was then Lord Advocate of Scotland in the reign of James VI. 'It is at the present period in full vigour and beauty, combining airy grace in the lightness of its foliage and the playful ramifications of its smaller branches, with solidity and strength in its silvery stems and principal arms,' Strutt writes. The form of the tree indicates that it was possibly pollarded long before his visit, something that would have helped an ash such as this to have achieved a remarkable size in 230 years, while keeping it in good heart.

Neither of these trees appear to have had any particular claim to fame other than their magnitude, and today they are admired as the only two ashes chosen by Strutt for his landmark publication – the first to feature a comprehensive collection of illustrations of some of England and Scotland's greatest trees. Both are long gone, but in 1909 Elwes and Henry do mention the Carnock tree, only to report that they had received reports that it had died and been broken up around 1870.

The Wesley Ash

Although the vast majority of historical ash trees have died long ago, a few still have a foothold in the twenty-first century. The Wesley Ash at

138 REMARKABLE ASH TREES

Winchelsea in Sussex may not have the honour of being the original tree beneath which John Wesley preached his last open-air sermon on 7 October 1790, but it can claim to be a direct descendant. When Wesley first visited Winchelsea in 1771 he is reputed to have preached from beneath the great ash tree just outside the west wall of St Thomas's churchyard. He came to Winchelsea again in 1789 and preached in the village's new chapel, but for his final visit in 1790 the chapel proved too small for the assembled congregation and, since he was barred from the parish church, he once again took to the open auditorium afforded around the ash tree, standing on a large oak table to address the substantial crowd. The event is recorded in Wesley's journal: 'I stood under a large tree and called to most of the inhabitants of the town, "the kingdom of heaven is at hand: repent and believe in the Gospel." It seemed as if all that heard were, at the present, almost persuaded to be Christians.' Winchelsea's community website notes: 'The French Protestant immigrants, who were numerous in Winchelsea after the weaving industry was established there in 1761, would have found Wesley's teaching akin to that of their own church.'

The original Wesley Ash survived until 1927 when the tree, much reduced and weakened thanks to the unwelcome attentions of souvenir hunters (a not uncommon story with famous trees), was felled by a gale. Fortunately, cuttings were taken from the old tree and the current representative was planted in the same spot in 1931. However, due to the unwelcome progress of ash dieback, now particularly widespread in the South East, the community is once again having to think of taking cuttings to preserve the unbroken lineage back to the eighteenth century. A visit to the current Wesley Ash in July 2017 revealed it to be in good health, having had some remedial work, including a crown reduction, done in 2013 due to the presence of hairy bracket fungus (*Inonotus hispidus*), often associated with the onset of white rot.

Ash Arbour at Heanton Satchville

In recent years we have become accustomed to artists, gardeners and garden artists working trees into living sculptures, commonly with willow. It is easy to weave into all manner of structures and the instant the ends are pushed into the earth the cut wands spring back into life. Historically, most garden sculptures arose during the intermittent vogues for topiary, notably using yew or box, but changes in garden fashion were just as likely to destroy such caprices as create them.

In a few instances it appears that live trees were used to create structures by weaving them together and grafting them into desired forms and patterns, and such techniques were set forth in some detail by a correspondent (W. P.) to John Claudius Loudon's periodical *The Gardener's Magazine* in April 1841.

> To form an arbour, plant a weeping ash, the stem of which should be several feet high, in any convenient spot; at the distance of 4 or 5 feet from it, according

LEFT:
The present manifestation of the Wesley Ash, planted in 1931.

BELOW:
A Francis Frith postcard from around 1900, shows the original tree in fine fettle.

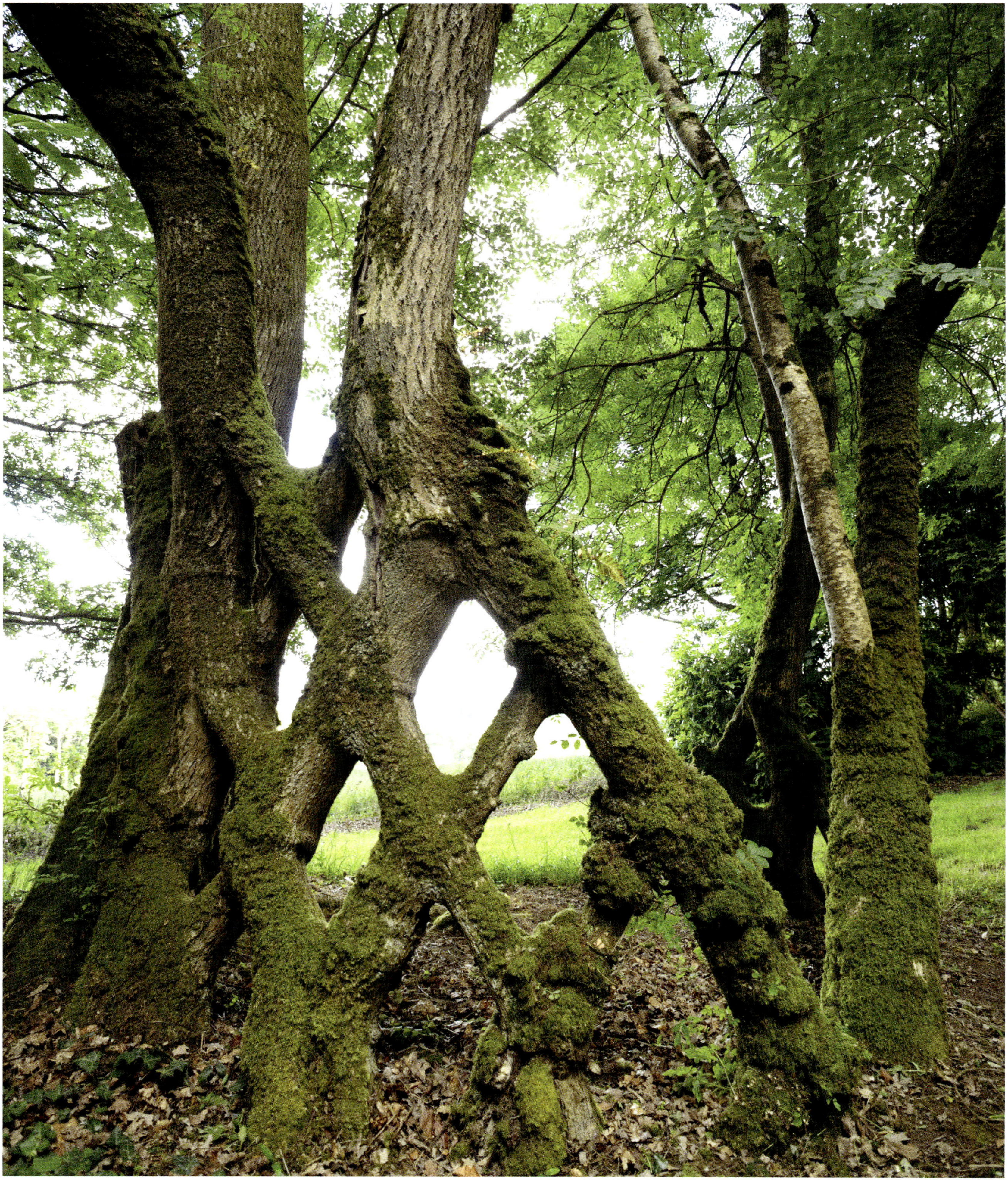

to the size you wish to have the arbour, plant some of the common ash, at 6 or 8 inches' distance from each other, leaving a space of 3 ft for the entrance; with every alternate plant slanting in an opposite direction. By being brought together, they will now be found to form diamond-shaped openings, at the intersections a small piece of bark must be removed from each stem, and the stems bound together, and clayed in the same manner as for grafting: as the trees grow, they can be inarched to the pendulous branches of the weeping ash. This will be found to form a very strong living arbour; and by the same means a very strong and ornamental fence might be formed in a short time. I have no doubt other trees will answer the same purpose, but the ash is the only one I have tried.

If many such garden features were actually created during this period then, sadly, few remain in evidence today. However, one notable exception has remained tucked away on a very private estate at Heanton Satchville in Devon. Situated in the Cottage Walk shrubbery, poised at the edge of the formal gardens, is a remarkable little arbour constructed from woven ash trees precisely in the manner espoused by W. P. – a sheltered viewpoint where Charles Rodolph, the 19th Lord Clinton, and his wife Elizabeth might have sat enjoying the distant view towards Dartmoor in the mid nineteenth century.

Loudon paid a visit to Heanton Satchville during his West Country tour of 1843 and was delighted to see that 'there is a living arbour formed of ash trees, in the manner recommended in our volume for 1841, p. 312, which has succeeded admirably'. From Loudon's observation one must assume that the success of the project was clearly discernible from the trees having already fused together at the graft points, suggesting that they must have been planted at least a couple of years prior to his visit. Conjecture leads us to imagine Lord Clinton's head gardener, the Scot, John Cato, leafing through his copy of *The Gardener's Magazine* in 1841 and being inspired to put the account he read into practice.

In 1909 Henry John Elwes wrote in the monolithic *The Trees of Great Britain and Ireland* of a recent visit to Heanton Satchville, where he 'saw it [weeping ash] trained in combination with a trellis of living ashes which were planted all round the central weeping tree, and had their stems woven together when young so as to form the walls of the arbour; but in the course of time this had become ragged …' This reaffirms that the 1841 instructions were carried out to the letter. Of course today there is no sign of the weeping tree and almost certainly other sections of the woven 'wall' have succumbed; add to this the obliteration of the original distant view of Dartmoor by a large tract of woodland, and yet the original sense of the feature, some 180 years on, is somehow still very much alive.

The Hardy Ash

Tucked snugly between the busy Pancras Road and the main railway line out of St Pancras station is one of north London's lesser-known green spaces: the sylvan environs of St Pancras Old Church, a religious site that is believed by some to date back to the fourth century, although there is little evidence to support this. A more reliable estimate of the church's origins would be pre-Norman, based largely on the fact that the original cemetery seems to have been of sub-circular form, typical of many Saxon burial grounds.

Until the mid nineteenth century, St Pancras was north London's principal burial ground, although by 1855 it had become so seriously overcrowded that burials ceased and a new cemetery was opened in east Finchley. With the cessation of burials, it was probably a much easier process for the Midland Railway Company to push a bill through Parliament in 1862 to acquire a large bite out of the cemetery land for its railway lines from the north into a brand-new terminus at St Pancras. Not only did the MRC have to contend with the cemetery, but it also had to negotiate the Regent's Canal to the north, the Fleet River to the east, a large gasworks and the impoverished communities

OPPOSITE:
The ash arbour in the gardens at Heanton Satchville in Devon.

BELOW:
Exhumations underway in Old St. Pancras churchyard, a wood engraving from 'The Illustrated London News', 1866.

REMARKABLE ASH TREES

OPPOSITE AND BELOW:
The Hardy Ash in Old St. Pancras churchyard. Each gravestone was carefully numbered in the 1860s with the intention that they would meet up with the reinterred bodies at a new burial site, but clearly this never happened.

of Agar Town and Somerstown. Power and influence prevailed, land was acquired and many families were displaced by 1868.

During the mid 1860s the future author and poet Thomas Hardy was a student architect working for Arthur Blomfield and was delegated the less-than-enviable task of overseeing the respectful exhumations from the part of the burial ground that was to be relinquished to the railway. While the human remains were transported to other burial grounds, scores of gravestones remained at St Pancras. It is said that Hardy organised their arrangement in the circular mound that surrounds an old ash tree to this day. Roman numerals carved into the tops of these stones must have been a guide allocating them to the appropriate remains in some new location, but the stones never left.

The tree has now become celebrated as the Hardy Ash, but looking at its size today it would seem slightly optimistic to think it is actually 150 years old, although it has undeniably been somewhat hampered by the tight collar of memorials around its base. The most likely explanation for this feature is that the stones were placed before the tree sprang up from a chance seed that had lodged deep beneath the central hollow, and ash being ash it was very quickly irrepressible.

It is generally thought that Hardy's 1882 poem 'The Levelled Churchyard' was inspired by his labours at St Pancras some twenty years previously:

> O Passenger, pray list and catch
> Our sighs and piteous groans
> Half stifled in this jumbled patch
> Of wretched memorial stones!
>
> We late-lamented, resting here,
> Are mixed to human jam,
> And each to each exclaims in fear,
> 'I know not which I am!'

142 REMARKABLE ASH TREES

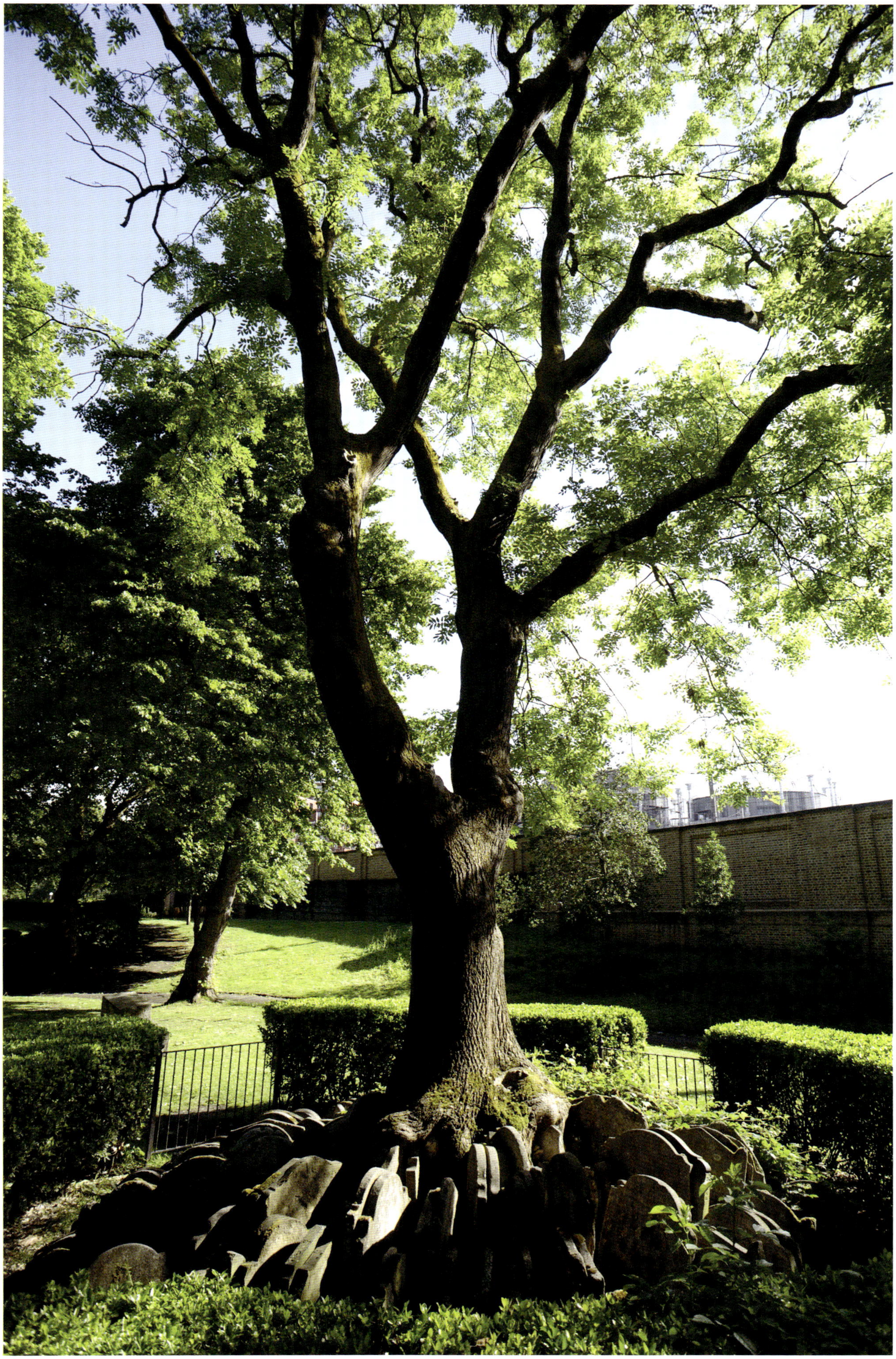

RIGHT:
The Clapton Court Ash in Somerset is one of the largest and oldest ash trees in Britain.
Some estimates consider it to be as much as 500 years old.

REMARKABLE ASH TREES 145

BELOW:
The massive burry old bole of the Clapton Court Ash is wreathed in epicormic shoots.

The Clapton Court Ash

The Clapton Court Ash is arguably the largest ash tree growing in Britain today, with a girth of about 9 metres, although several other ancient ashes vie for the record and are roughly of the same circumference. With such trees it is very difficult to be exact with measurements, as their boles are almost always very heavily burred, and different people on separate days will undoubtedly obtain dimensions that slightly vary.

This giant, shaggy old beast of a tree squats squarely in the parkland adjoining the gardens of Clapton Court, near Crewkerne in Somerset, and was once pollarded on a regular basis, over several centuries, when deer or livestock roamed around it, but that regime must have been abandoned at least a hundred years ago. Its incredibly gnarled, burry bole is the result of years and years of nibbling, chewing and rubbing by livestock, causing the tree to produce successive layers of scar tissue to patch up the damage and protect itself. Age is very difficult to assess, as the tree is hollow, but a wide-ranging estimation of 200–500 years has been suggested.

It seems strange that until about thirty years ago nobody had recorded or remarked upon this very special tree. It would have already been an impressive specimen in Victorian times, yet no mention of it is found. Even Elwes and Henry, in their exhaustive survey in the Edwardian era, knew nothing of it. Ash rarely attains such great size and antiquity as the patriarch oak or the mystical yew, and famous associations and anecdotes are uncommon, so it wasn't until Thomas Pakenham featured the tree in his Meetings with Remarkable Trees in 1996 that anyone in the wider world knew of its existence.

To the owners it is very much a treasured member of the family and there was some concern in 2017 when a suggestion of ash dieback loomed large. Fortunately, analysis of leaf samples drew a negative result, but the cause of the withered foliage was still unexplained. Close scrutiny of the tree over coming years will be critical, as losing such an important ash specimen would be a national tragedy. At present nobody really knows quite how tolerant such ancient ashes will be to the disease and, more importantly, whether anything can be done to protect them. If specific fungicides can be proven to combat ash dieback, here is a prime candidate for treatment.

The Scottish Giants

In Scotland, particularly impressive individual ash trees are currently few and far between, with only three examples recorded in The Heritage Trees of Scotland in 2006. The Tinnis Ash on the Bowhill Estate, near Selkirk, is merely the slowly crumbling remains of a once massive pollard, believed to have been about 10 metres in girth. When it was photographed about fifteen years ago three large fragments remained, but recent storms have seen the collapse of this last vestige. The Glen Lyon Ash in Perthshire is considered to be Scotland's oldest ash tree, as well as the largest, with a girth of 6.4 metres. Apparently the tree was once 30 metres high, but latterly was cut back to about 4 metres; almost certainly the reason it has managed to survive so long, with current estimates being 300–400 years. A visit in February 2018 found the tree to be seemingly still in very good shape, with plenty of evidence of young growth. Its hollow interior has long been a handy shelter for sheep and they also appear to like gnawing at the knobbly roots, but it's a reasonable guess that this has been happening for eons and the old tree can shrug off such abuse. In 2006 perhaps the most impressive ash was a huge outgrown pollard in the grounds of Gordon Castle, near Fochabers, Moray. With an outstanding girth of 7.79 metres and a height of 28.5 metres, this was the indisputable

Scottish champion. However, on 4 December 2013 gales gusting to 100 mph were the death knell for this grand old tree, thought to have been around 270 years old. Because it was hollow it was almost certainly the leverage of its giant, extended boughs above the deteriorating bole that proved its downfall. In 1838 Loudon mentions an ash 'in Banffshire, at Gordon Castle, 82 ft high, the diameter of the trunk 5 ft, and of the head 60ft'. After about a hundred years an ash could certainly have achieved these sort of dimensions, so it might well have been the very same tree.

LEFT:
The Glen Lyon Ash near Aberfeldy in Perthshire is Scotland's largest ash tree, and even the gnawing of sheep around its base cannot trouble it.

RIGHT:
The gargantuan Moccas Park Ash in Herefordshire.

The Moccas Park Ash

Challenging the Clapton Court Ash for national champion is the Moccas Park Ash in Herefordshire. The deer park at Moccas has long been renowned for its remarkable assemblage of ancient oaks – both maiden and pollard trees – but amid this oak-laden landscape the real stand-out tree has to be a stupendous outgrown ash pollard. Yet again the bole is very knobbly and difficult to measure precisely, but almost 9 metres is about right.

J. C. Loudon refers to a different ash of note, now long gone, growing at Moccas in 1838 as

> an ash growing on the edge of a dingle, with immensely large roots, running on the surface of the ground for 50 ft and upwards down the steep side of the dingle, has a clear trunk of 30 ft, which at 15 ft from the ground, is 7 ft in diameter; the contents of this trunk, and of three large limbs, make 1003 ft.

Talley Abbey Ash

Somewhat off the beaten track in the Welsh countryside, the ruins of Talley Abbey, a monastery of the Premonstratensian order founded in 1185, are set in the peaceful Cothi Valley, about 7 miles north of Llandeilo in Carmarthenshire. It was just another religious house to succumb in the massive inventory of cultural vandalism in the name of religious intolerance at the Dissolution of the Monasteries by Henry VIII. Although seldom bombarded with tourists, most of them will saunter through this romantic ruin, a monument safely in the hands of Cadw, with little inkling that there is a superb green monument only a few hundred metres away to the east, along a public footpath.

The Talley Abbey Ash, a stupendous maiden tree, towers above an old hedgerow that has grown to a prodigious size. Access for making accurate measurements of the tree's girth is difficult, as you have to battle with closely confining (and very prickly) hawthorns, a wire fence and a dense sheath of ivy. Working carefully around the many knobbles and undulations, the girth at chest height seems to be about 7.6 metres, making it the largest maiden ash tree in Wales. It is actually a twin-stemmed tree, which could mean that the lower part, where measurements are taken, is two stems fused together, technically limiting its claim to be the largest single-stemmed ash, and yet it would

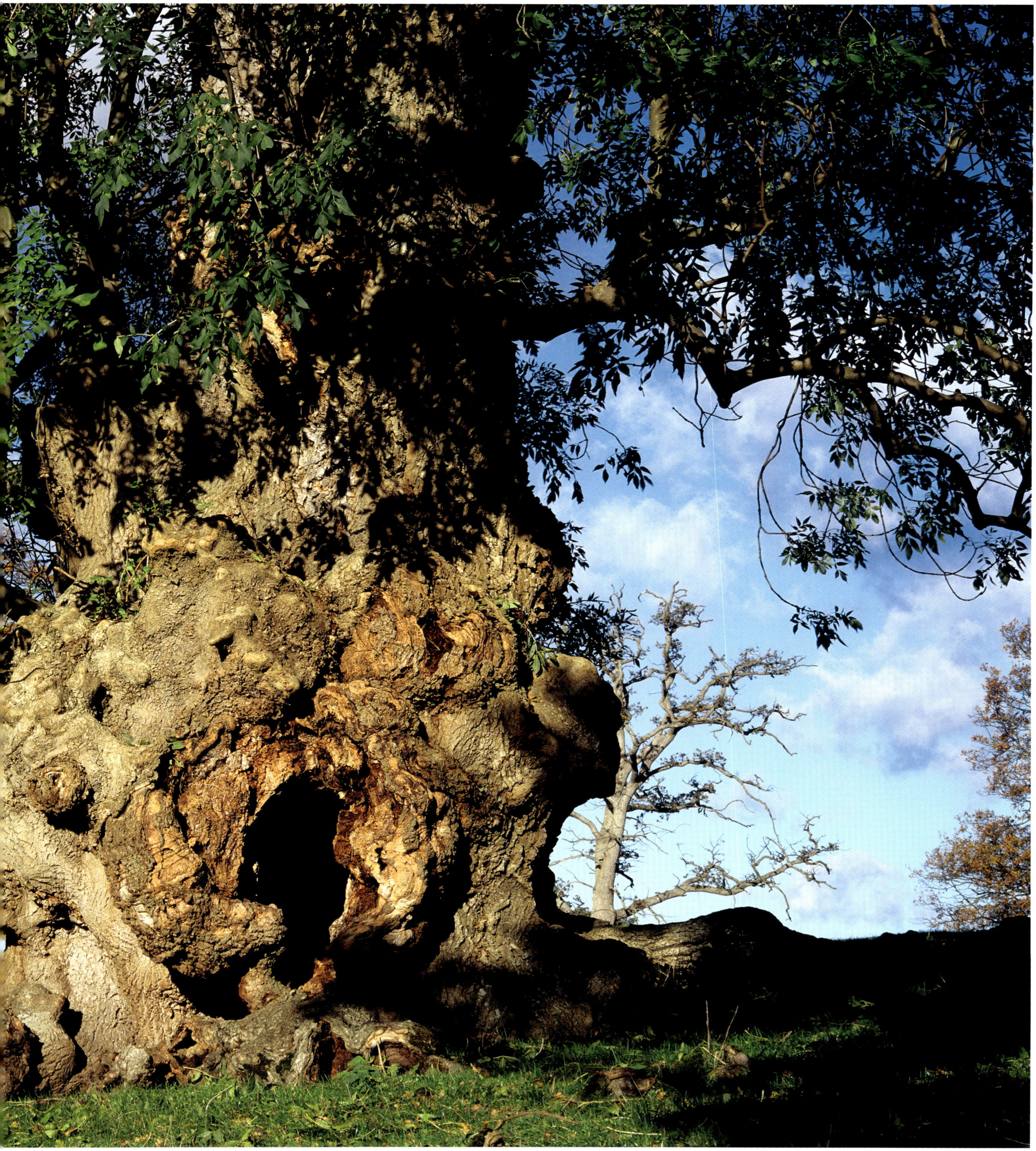

RIGHT:
The Talley Abbey Ash in Carmarthenshire is the largest maiden ash in Wales.

LEFT:
The huge knobbly base of the Talley Abbey Ash.

BELOW:
The Ystrad Meurig Ash, a hollow shell but full of life.

seem a little pedantic to rob this great tree of its champion mantle. Trying to gauge the age of such a large ash is problematic, as there are relatively few similar-sized trees with which to make comparisons. However, an estimate of 250–300 years may not be far off the mark.

Ystrad Meurig Ash

Moving from the statuesque to the bizarre leads to a paradoxical ash tree that almost defies belief – aged and rotten to the point where most of the tree has disappeared, yet still displaying a vibrant renewal of life. In the little village of Ystrad Meurig in Ceredigion grows a tree that seems to have survived in a most unusual form.

First inspection from the roadside reveals a bole that appears to have a very broad base with numerous branches of fairly recent growth ascending vertically, giving every appearance of being a coppice stool. However, once around the other side, the sprawling, buttressed base of the tree forms a giant ring around a great void where the centre of the tree once grew. This gives the impression that it may once have been a maiden, or perhaps a pollard, which has rotted away inside while the live sapwood around the outer edge has continued to carry the tree onward and upward. The girth measures almost 7 metres around – outstanding dimensions for any ash and perhaps comparable with the Talley Abbey tree for age.

The vitality of the sapwood is indisputable, its new growth enfolding the dead carcass of the inner tree, and a healthy crop of poles shooting skyward, so that one can only assume that regular lopping has been the secret of this tree's longevity (although the farmer who owns it can't remember when it was last cut). Inside the central cavity strange and slightly spooky anthropomorphic beasts and faces can be detected in the rotting hardwood.

RIGHT:
The weird interior of the Ystrad Meurig Ash.

The Cumbrian Giants

Cumbria is a county well known for its landscapes richly endowed with ash trees, but there are a few truly exceptional specimens usually tucked away on the more remote byways, sometimes only a stone's throw from a main road, and all of them are guaranteed to take the breath away. I am particularly grateful to Maurice Pankhurst from The National Trust for showing me the last two of these trees that he discovered on his travels.

On the eastern edge of the Lake District, in an old pasture below the A6 near Forest Hall, sits a handsome, moss-decked pollard with a girth of a little over 7 metres. Hollow, but extremely healthy, it is one of several other pollards in the same field, so quite possibly a remnant of wood pasture.

Another great ash that would be so easy to hurtle past with barely a second glance, although it is partially hidden by the hedge, squats right next to the A5092 near Penny Bridge, at the southern end of the Lake District. A huge split pollard of expansive, yawning form, it appears to be tearing itself apart in slow motion, but the regeneration in a photograph taken in 2013 shows how powerful the life force still remains (see page 86).

To find the two other remarkable ashes requires a giant leap to the north-west corner of the Lake District. The Lorton Ash grows next to a very minor road in Lorton Vale and is a pollard of immense proportions, but also of very beautiful form. The question of whether or not to repollard arises, as it may be that cutting back will keep this great tree viable for a lot longer, and yet it does seem to be in perfect equilibrium at present. There is also a very strong case for leaving well alone with many of these ancient trees. Another special aspect of this tree is that it bears many different lichens, one of which, *Lobaria virens*, is only known at two other sites in Cumbria.

Probably the most stupendous of all these Cumbria ashes is the Loweswater Ash – an ancient pollard of gargantuan proportions hidden away on the edge of private woodland and close to the long-abandoned remains of a sizeable farmstead, indicating that this was once very much a working

BELOW:
The Lorton Ash in Cumbria.

REMARKABLE ASH TREES

154 REMARKABLE ASH TREES

LEFT:
Maurice Pankhurst inside the massive bole of the Loweswater Ash in Cumbria illustrates the impressive proportions of this ancient tree.

REMARKABLE ASH TREES 155

RIGHT:
The Forest Hall Ash in Cumbria, quite possibly part of an old wood pasture.

tree. Its shambolic, tortured bole is a profusion of mossy protuberances and deep, dark holes – a rugged circle of life surrounding a huge hollow chasm within. Awesome is a greatly overused word, but this tree really does deserve that appellation.

Monster Cornish Coppice Stool

Oliver Rackham may have identified ash coppice stools in Suffolk that he believed could be a thousand years old, but far away in Cornwall a coppice stool to rival these was recently discovered on the edge of a public woodland park at Tregoniggie, on the outskirts of Falmouth. Almost lost in the undergrowth and shrouded by ivy, it was only after volunteers cleared round the tree that they discovered the true nature of the mammoth hidden within, with its mightily impressive girth of 13.7 metres. Since the tree lies along an old boundary bank, there is a likelihood that it was once laid into a hedge, but now it is just a splendid agglomeration of about a dozen stems.

LEFT:
An exceptionally large coppice stool along an old boundary bank in Tregoniggie Park, Falmouth, Cornwall.

BELOW:
An Edwardian Postcard of the 'Rock' Ash at Llanbeder-y-Cennin, Conwy.

The Rock Ash

Some strange trees, not just ash, became instant celebrities during the postcard era, most particularly during the heyday of the genre between 1900 and 1920. Everything the photographers could possibly think of to turn a quick buck became fair game. The tourist market was insatiable and even for local communications, at a time when people often used postcards in much the same way as we use WhatsApp or Twitter today you could invite someone to visit, send the postcard in the morning, they received it the same afternoon and, hey presto, they arrived in time for tea.

Local landmark postcards were the perfect medium for chatty invites and family news. Exactly why the Rock Ash at Llanbedr-y-Cennin, in Conwy, was notable other than for its strange position atop a huge boulder is still a mystery, and the postcards are fairly rare today, so perhaps not a huge print run. However, the presence of the Salem Chapel in the background might lead one to think that this natural pulpit may once have been used for outdoor sermons. After all, many of Wesley's followers would have preached in the great outdoors, in much the same way as their inspirational leader. Sadly we will never know because the tree has

The "Rock" Ash, Llanbedr.

REMARKABLE ASH TREES

RIGHT:
Another rock ash in Upper Wharfedale, North Yorkshire.

gone, as has the rock it grew on, from the field below the chapel.

In the upper reaches of Wharfedale in Yorkshire, a little above the village of Kettlewell, another rock ash balances precariously on top of a huge limestone boulder. It's a large tree without matching the size of the Welsh example, but when trees grow in such difficult circumstances growth rates can be surprisingly slow, so that this tree, which under normal circumstances might be considered to be twenty or thirty years old, could in fact be four or five times that age. At present there is no known cultural significance to this strange ash, but there is something rather refreshing about the fact that the farmer who owns it thinks it special enough to let it continue to flourish on its own little natural pulpit.

The Wall Ash of Ty-uchaf

One of the strangest ash trees, growing in a form that one is challenged to place in any specific category, is to be found hidden away along a remote, ancient green lane high above the farmstead of Ty-uchaf in the Usk Valley.

Its most likely formation is as a long-forgotten hedgerow tree that had two large lateral boughs laid horizontally, but a very long time ago. A century or more later, and the two great ash arms now have the benefit of support from a dry-stone wall beneath them, but whether this is a wall that replaced a hedge or vice versa is a bit of a conundrum. The tree is beautifully propped and braced against the worst the weather can do up on the hills and it measures about 8 metres from one end to the other. Such a sprawling old tree as this is extremely difficult to age, but up on the hilltops where growth rates will undoubtedly be much slower it could easily be 200 years old, maybe considerably older.

Weird Ashes

And finally into the realm of the truly bizarre and the ash trees growing in the very oddest of locations and presenting some of the weirdest forms.

There is an ash 'mask' hidden within the depths of a Herefordshire wood and I fear for its future. Clearly this tree is something special, unique, haunting, unexplainable. Is it my overactive imagination that turns such phenomena into beasts or other-worldly beings? This tree has changed almost imperceptibly over the thirty years I have known it, gathering a little more moss and the odd sprig of fern during that time, as it has become an old and familiar friend on a regular walk. Many of the ash trees that surround it are nearing what foresters would usually consider maturity and would therefore make plans for an impending date for felling. I fervently hope that this tree is spared; that just maybe the chainsaw crew will see the character in the tree, perhaps be amused, or maybe

ABOVE:
The out-stretched 'arms' of the Ty-uchaf Ash rest along an old stone wall above the Usk Valley.

REMARKABLE ASH TREES 159

BELOW LEFT:
Autumnal ash inside a barn above Wharfedale.

BELOW RIGHT:
Strange gravestone-devouring ash in the General Cemetery in Nottingham.

OPPOSITE:
Uncanny ash 'mask' in Brockhampton Woods, Herefordshire.

a little disturbed or reluctant to proceed for some unspoken superstitious reason. We will see …

High on a hillside back in Wharfedale an ash-tree denizen commands a remote, roofless barn. Exactly how and why this tree was ever allowed to reach maturity is a mystery; one assumes that when the roof fell in the farmer had no further use for the barn, but it does make a unique landscape feature.

And finally, an ash tree that came as a by-product of some forgotten Google search. It has long been known that the weeping ash was a popular choice for the nineteenth-century landscapers of cemeteries – the weeping ramification speaks for itself. One of the weeping ashes in Nottingham's General Cemetery, which was probably coeval with the adjacent gravestone from the 1860s, had grown round the memorial, enveloping it in the folds of its encroaching bole, and slowly demolishing the memory of John Smith Thorpe and his three little children. The online photo that I found showed a seemingly healthy, upright tree, but by the time I arrived in early 2018 it had been wind thrown and the fallen carcass revealed that extensive decay inside the main trunk had led to its collapse. Perhaps all is not lost, though, and the tree's own offspring, the vigorously shooting poles from the old stump, might be permitted to be the resurrection.

160 REMARKABLE ASH TREES

REMARKABLE ASH TREES **161**

BELOW:
Bacterial ash canker in a woodland ash tree.

Growing on Ash

In much the same way as all other trees, ash plays a central role as a host to many species of lichens, mosses, liverworts, ferns and fungi. These in turn will have an associated range of invertebrates that are dependant upon them. The invertebrates will in turn attract birdlife and so the realm of the ash takes its place in the chain of life in the wide variety of habitats in which it occurs. In the wake of ash dieback the hope must be that most of these interdependent organisms will be able to adapt to new host tree species, maintaining their presence rather than becoming extinct.

Bacterial Ash Canker

A very commonly observed phenomenon to be seen on the bole and branches of ash is bacterial ash canker (*Pseudomonas savastanoi pv. fraxini*), which gives the appearance of the tree having exploded from within, leaving jagged, irregular, blackened craters and scars with necrotic tissue seemingly bubbling out around the wounds. Depending on the level of infection, there may be only one or two such episodes on the odd branch or in some cases the whole tree is riddled with it. Infection enters the tree at wound points, through the lenticels (raised pores in the bark) or via the feeding sites of a twig miner called *Prays fraxinella*. It is also thought that ash bark beetles, which normally only bore into the bark of dying or cut ash boughs, may be a vector for the canker. Although the cambium is destroyed by these wounds, the trees, somewhat surprisingly, still retain the ability to get water and nutrients up and past these sites to the crown. In this way, even badly infected trees, which appear to have almost been ring-barked by the infection, seem to have the capacity to stay alive despite the damage. Another risk is that such wounds will provide the points of entry for secondary infections, including harmful invertebrates and fungi.

Fungi

The popular image of fungi on trees is that of large mushroom-like fruiting bodies either crowded in great colonies around the base of the tree, impressive bracket species exuding from trunks and large boughs or those fungi that invade and thrive on fallen dead wood. These are only the tip of the iceberg – the organism's vast network of mycelia spreading far beyond, and often into the surrounding soil. However, there are other fungi, the mycorrhizal species, which exist exclusively in the soil and are so minute that most are barely visible to the naked eye. The phenomenal scale of these fungi, the vast networks which their mycelia create, and their indispensable benefit to almost all plants, not just trees, is something of which very few people are aware.

The mycorrhiza is actually the name for the symbiotic relationship between fungi and plant roots. The benefit to the fungus is principally the ready access to carbohydrates, such as glucose and sucrose, manufactured by the plant through photosynthesis and translocated down to the root system. Benefits to the plant include enhanced absorption of water, nutrients and minerals, particularly gleaning of phosphate or converting organic nitrogen into inorganic nitrogen, as well as aiding resistance to pests, diseases and improving resistance to drought. There are hundreds of different species of these fungi, many still unidentified by science, with many being specifically associated with individual plant species. The fungi can be either ectomycorrhizal, where the fungi form hyphal sheathes around the plant roots without intracellular invasion, or endomycorrhizal, where hyphae actually enter the plant root cells to exchange nutrients, as is the case with the ash tree, where the relationship is termed a vesicular-arbuscular mycorrhiza.

While it is claimed that mycorrhizal fungi can improve resistance to soil-borne pathogens that might threaten trees, it would be interesting to speculate on whether they can have any effect against the fungal pathogen of ash dieback. It has already been widely observed that young ash trees, newly planted out, are particularly susceptible to ash dieback and undoubtedly they have no existing mycorrhizal fungi around their roots, having been transplanted, often bare-root, from a nursery bed. Planting sites are frequently in environments such as green fields where the appropriate mycorrhizal species for the tree will be absent. If trees are planted on reclaimed agricultural land, the prognosis for success is even bleaker, as long histories of deep ploughing and excessive use of fertilisers, pesticides and fungicides will have completely destroyed the natural balances in the soil, including mycorrhizal fungi. The failure or poor quality of many of the trees in newly planted woods has been put down to the almost total lack of mycorrhizal activity. This extends not just to the trees, but also to the ground flora and shrub layer. Even though this concern is now largely irrelevant with regard to ash, as it will not be planted for some time to come, the principle is most appropriate when applied to tree planting in general. Mycorrhizal fungi have taken hundreds, if not thousands, of years to build up their mutually beneficial networks, particularly in ancient woodlands. We lose such rich habitat at our peril!

BELOW:
King Alfred's Cakes (Daldinia concentrica) are one of the most familiar fungi on dead and dying ash wood.

CLOCKWISE FROM TOP LEFT:
Polyporus squamosus.
Auricularia aricula-judae.
Inonotus hispidus.
Perreniporia fraxinea.

The Fungal Records Database of the British Isles lists sixty-eight species of fungi that have some degree of association with the ash and states that eleven are obligate, nineteen are highly dependent and the other thirty-eight are only partially dependent on the tree. These records do not offer a great deal of information on subterranean fungi, but the general understanding seems to be that there are few if any that are ash specific.

One of the most readily identifiable, and widely distributed, fungi is the dark brown, maturing to black, globular King Alfred's Cakes (*Daldinia concentrica*), a wood-rotting fungus highly dependent on dead and dying ash wood. One species of beetle, *Cryptophagus ruficornis*, is specifically associated with this fungus, so in the wake of ash dieback, when all ash dead wood has rotted down and gone, it could be the last call for this beetle. A strange phenomenon has been observed with this fungus, illustrating a remarkable drive to reproduce. Place it in a drawer in the dark and it will continue to fire off spores, regular as clockwork, every twelve hours. Another interesting aside is its historical use as a method of transporting fire from one place to another (as publicised by Ray Mears in his television survival programmes). Take one of these fungi that have been in the fire, wrap it up, and it will remain as a glowing ember for many hours. To strike a new fire, simply place under some furze-like tinder, blow gently, and the fire returns. One wonders how many thousands of years ago this very useful quality was discovered.

Some of the more dramatic fungi found on ash are the complete antithesis of the microscopic, underground symbiotic species. These are killers! And not to be taken lightly – they will rot and destabilise trees as they do their dastardly deeds within. *Perenniporia fraxinea* may sound as if it could be specific to ash trees, but it is not, being fairly widespread on several other host species. In its initial incarnation it appears as creamy, knobbly folds exuding from crevices in the lower bole of trees and will eventually become large brackets,

LEFT:
Honey fungus may well take hold of trees in decline from ash dieback, inevitably hastening their demise.

BELOW:
Many of the ash flowers are invaded by the cauliflower gall mite, changing ash keys into galls.

occasionally almost a metre wide. It will cause white or soft rot that leads to the wood becoming brittle. The shaggy polypore (*Inonotus hispidus*) is frequently found on ash, as well as several other broadleaf species, particularly planes, and is identified by its distinctive hairy, red-brown upper surface. It usually invades the tree through either cut stems or natural breaks and causes white rot. Another bracket fungus of ill omen is *Polyporus squamosus,* commonly called dryad's saddle or pheasant's back mushroom, which also causes white rot. More often found on dead elm or maples, it has many potential hosts including ash. That universally reviled fungus, honey fungus (*Armillaria*) – not one, but about ten closely related species – will, in most cases, be the death knell for the trees it invades. It has been suggested that trees struggling to survive against the onslaught of ash dieback will become infinitely more susceptible to honey fungus, in turn hastening their decline, death and decomposition.

Galls

A vast array of strange and often beautiful little galls are to be found on most of our native trees and probably the most readily recognised will be the oak apples and marble galls commonly associated with oaks. All of these bizarre mutant forms are the result of cellular ingress by tiny insects – flies, wasps or mites – laying their eggs in the tissue of the host tree. A weird reaction then occurs, causing the tree to produce the mutated cells which form the protective structures and food sources for the emerging larvae. When these insects finally mature, they will bore out of the gall and leave the browning husks of their juvenile homes behind them. How the various individual galls are formed is still something of a mystery.

GROWING ON ASH 165

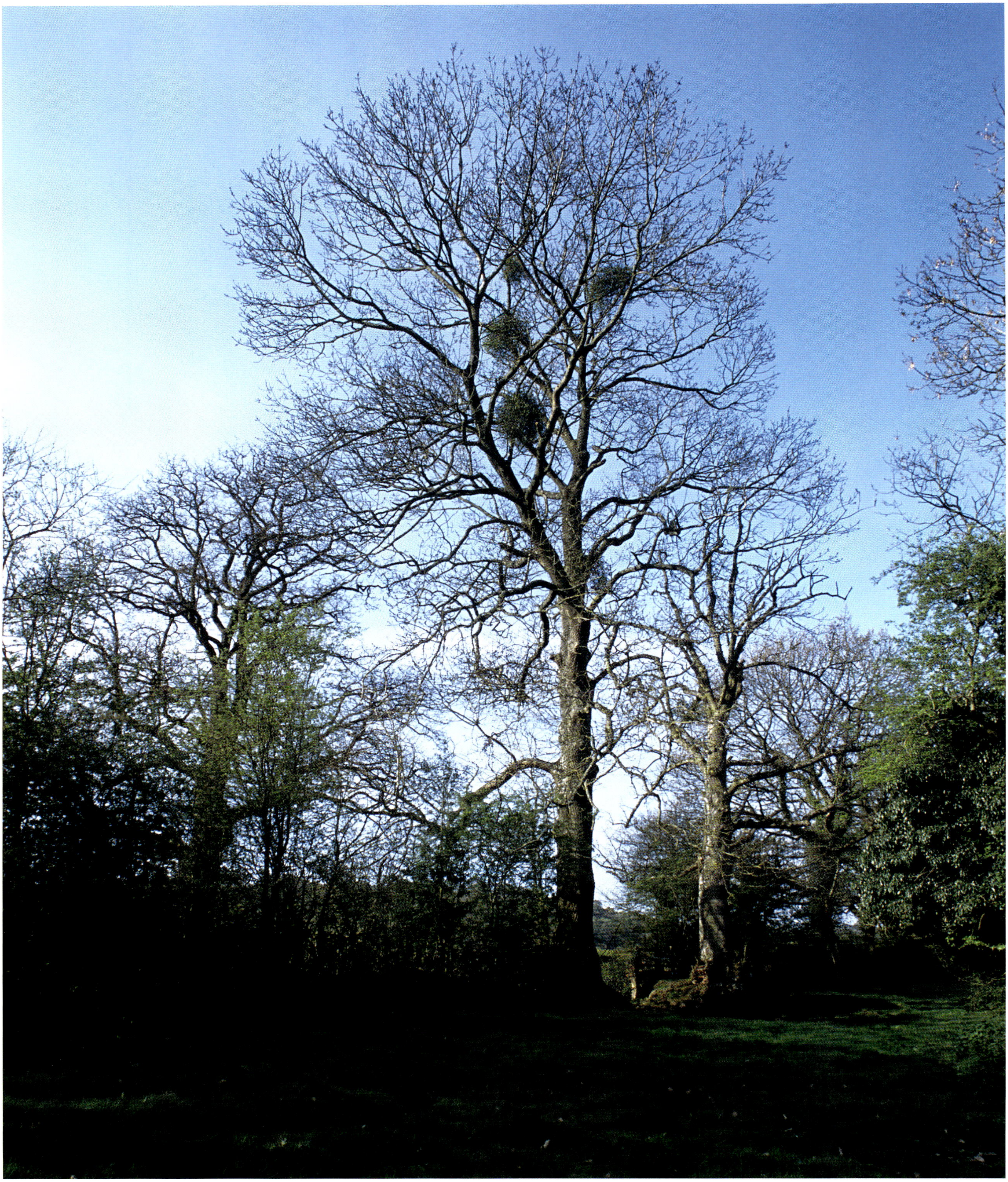

Ash does not seem to host many of these gall-producing insects, but one that may be found in varying concentrations from one year to another is the aptly named cauliflower gall caused by the cauliflower gall mite (*Eriophyes fraxinivorus*). These minuscule mites, barely 0.5 millimetres in length, lay eggs in the flower cells of the ash and a rough, irregular encrustation, much like a tiny cauliflower, is the result. They can occur in large clumps around the site of the male flowers or, on female trees, when the fruits begin to form, instead of the slender, twisted samara a gall is produced. It is initially green, maturing to brown and finally turning black. The developing mites will live off the sap of the tree. The galls may occur singly or in large bundles, and can remain on the tree for up to two years, although their frequency is sporadic and does not seem seriously to threaten the overall fecundity of the ash population.

G. Clarke Nuttall, in his *Trees and How They Grow* (1913), describes minute galls to be found in the U-shaped rachis of ash leaves caused by the gall-gnat *Diplosis botularia*, which lays its eggs in the channel. He notes: 'The insect has some power of stimulating cells of the leaf, with the result that they increase in number and form cushions which rise up on either hand and almost cover it in. Later, when the time comes for the gall-gnat to depart, the enclosing walls shrink and gape apart.'

Mistletoe

The principal host species for mistletoe in the UK are apple and hawthorn, closely followed by common lime, hybrid black poplars and willows. Native oaks are the rarest hosts of mistletoe, with less than a dozen examples known countrywide, and most of these were first recorded during the nineteenth century. It's remarkable that these oaks have been bearing mistletoe continuously for over 150 years. Ash always appears on the list of host trees, but mistletoe-bearing trees seem to be rather uncommon.

When David Griffith, a fellow tree enthusiast, reported that he'd discovered several clumps of mistletoe on a large ash tree and, bizarrely, this tree was right next to a mistletoe oak, it came as something of a surprise. Was this purely by chance or was there some kind of synergy at play? Could mycorrhizal interaction be influential – affecting some chemical balance between the trees that increases susceptibility to colonisation by mistletoe? This seems highly unlikely, and the potential benefits from a semi-parasitic plant to either tree appear obscure; however, the two trees are certainly close enough to be in subterranean interconnectivity. Mistletoe expert Jonathan Briggs suggests that susceptibility to mistletoe in the tree species on which it seldom appears may have a link to the genetic strain of the host species. It would be interesting to look for some genetic commonality between mistletoe-bearing ashes. Observations of large amounts of mistletoe also identifies genetic variations within the species, typically in leaf colour or size, so perhaps there is some genetic preference in the mistletoe for certain tree species. A recent arrival in my garden was the unusual occurrence of mistletoe on a plum tree – a plant with notably large leaves, 10 centimetres long and 3 centimetres wide, and unlike any other mistletoe on the surrounding apple trees. In respect to ash it would seem unlikely that the genetic preference comes from the mistletoe, for with so many ash trees available to colonise, it would be strange that more ash mistletoe isn't evident.

With the realisation that mistletoe really does occur on ash trees after all, David and I began scrutinising the ashes we passed on a regular basis, and slowly but surely we managed to log about twenty examples in the space of six months – one in a small roadside tree that I pass on an almost daily basis. How could I not have noticed it before! Then the sightings dried up; so it would appear that we had been observing something very unusual, although not as rare as mistletoe on oak. Maybe we just need to travel further afield to find more, but it does seem very strange that many of the Herefordshire orchards, with apple trees that are positively inundated with mistletoe, are frequently surrounded by ash trees in the

OPPOSITE AND ABOVE:
The unusual occurrence of mistletoe in ash trees.

BELOW LEFT:
Typical mottled patterns created by crustose lichens, principally Lecidella elaeochroma, on the smooth bark of young ash trees.

BELOW RIGHT UPPER:
Ramalina fastigiata.

BELOW RIGHT LOWER:
Mainly Lecanora argentata, with some Lecidella elaeochroma.

The lichens on this page and the opposite are all associated with poorer air quality, often with higher levels of ammonia gas.

hedgerows, yet none of them bear a single clump of mistletoe. Since so many authorities stretching back to the nineteenth century list ash as a known host species, one has to wonder if that is because it was commoner on this tree in the past and something has changed to make it scarcer.

Lichens

Most people looking at lichens for the first time might assume that they are one simple organism, but they are in fact the result of a symbiotic relationship between two organisms: a fungus, described as a mycobiont, and a photosynthetic partner known as a photobiont, which may be either a green alga or a cyanobacterium. In a nutshell, the mycobiont provides a stable location and the facility for the photobiont to expand its range, while the mycobiont benefits from the photosynthesis of the photobiont which produces sugar alcohols from green algae, or glucose if from a cyanobacterium. These latter organisms can also capture and fix nitrogen compounds from the atmosphere which benefit the fungus. Sometimes both an alga and a cyanobacterium may be found in the same lichen.

The fruiting bodies observed on fungi almost always represent a very small part of the whole organism, with an extensive mycelium network remaining unseen below the ground. With lichens this is different, as the lichenised fungi will account for about 80 per cent of the whole organism, most of which remains visible. In a similar manner to non-lichenised fungi, the fruiting bodies are always tiny when compared to the rest of the organism; in this case the thallus (lichen body).

With lichens that appear on trees there are two principal driving forces which ordain what grows in certain locations. The acidity of the substrate, in this case tree bark, is very important for individual lichen species and those which cleave to ash seek the base-rich bark: ash typically with a pH between 5.2 and 6.6. Levels of pollution are the other major factor that inhibits or promotes lichen colonisation or, in the case of existing colonies, survival or extinction. In the past, excessive levels of sulphur

168 GROWING ON ASH

dioxide in urban and industrialised areas have proved problematic for lichens. The knock-on effect of this harmful air pollution was the formation of acid rain that could carry the effects long distances, typically falling on tree bark and making it much too acidic for many lichens. Fortunately these emission levels have been reduced in recent years, which has seen a resurgence of some species in areas from which they had been lost. A few lichens such as *Lecanora conizaeoides* have proven to be remarkably tolerant of sulphur dioxide and are generally most evident in built-up environments. However, despite stricter emissions legislation, road vehicles still churn out huge amounts of nitrogen oxide. Farming practice over the last fifty years has also affected the ranges of many lichens. Some lichens can thrive in nutrient-poor environments, but modern farming uses large quantities of artificial fertilisers and intensive procedures such as battery-farmed poultry and egg production. This produces high levels of ammonia gas in the atmosphere. Add the cars to the chickens and you have harmful levels of nitric acid. Some lichens can manage this chemistry at moderate levels, typically *Physcia* and *Xanthoria* species, but others succumb until eventually, in some places, all that is left is a crust of green algae.

Another factor that will influence lichen occurrence is climate – for example, the wetter, warmer conditions of the west coast of Britain and its associated woodlands suit species such as the *Lobarion* community, most typically found on oak and birch, but they will also grow on ash which is just within their favoured acidity range. Levels of light and shade, as well as different textures of bark, all exert influence too.

The British Lichen Society firmly believes that the effects of ash dieback could be severely detrimental to lichens throughout Britain, citing the fact that many species that were once typically associated with elm trees, prior to the Dutch elm disease epidemic of the 1970s and 80s, found refuge on ash because of the similar acidic balance of its bark. The BLS database holds 31,000 records of lichens on ash trees, made up of 582 taxa (more than a quarter of the British lichen flora). Of these

BELOW RIGHT:
The beauty of tiny lichen colonies is epitomised by this Parmelia sulcata.

BELOW LEFT UPPER:
Ramalina farinacea.

BELOW FAR LEFT:
Xanthoria parietina, a very successful species often covering whole trees and making them glow orange.

BELOW CENTRE:
When air pollution levels have become too toxic for lichens then green algae take over. In this instance one of these species, Trentepohlia, contains an orange pigment.

170 GROWING ON ASH

LEFT:
This remarkable old ash in the Dundonnell River valley is noted not only for this weird and inexplicable burr, but also because this single tree hosts thirty-three different species of lichen.

GROWING ON ASH

ABOVE LEFT:
Lobaria pulmonaria on a towering ash above Ganllwyd, Gwynedd.

ABOVE RIGHT UPPER:
Peltigera membranacea at Ganllwyd.

ABOVE RIGHT LOWER:
Lobaria amplissima in the Dundonnell River valley, in Wester Ross.

The lichens on this page and the opposite are usually associated with clean air and wetter climatic conditions.

220 are nationally rare or nationally scarce and 84 have a conservation status of near-threatened or above. It may be that some of the erstwhile elm- and currently ash-dependent species will have to move their allegiance to the sycamore, the next best alternative host.

Examining lichens on ash, or for that matter on any tree, launches one into a whole new world of remarkable organisms which, particularly when studied under the magnifying glass, open up a ravishing new mini-panorama of colours and forms that can so easily be overlooked. The field is convoluted and complex and even the experts will admit that there is still much to be learned.

Mosses, Liverworts and Ferns

Bryophytes, which include mosses (*Musci*) and liverworts (*Hepaticae*), in much the same way as lichens, particularly favour different types of habitat on each individual species of tree on which they are found; from the relatively smooth bark of young trees through to the gnarled, deeply fissured bark on old ash coppice stools and pollards. Oliver Rackham considers the best places to see these organisms in profusion are the Atlantic hazel woods on the west coast of Scotland and Ireland. He proffers three of the species most specifically associated with ash, as well as maple, in lowland England as *Isothesium alopecuroides*, *Homalia trichomanoides* and *Neckera complanata*. There are 58 bryophytes associated with ash although none are solely associated with the tree. Differentiating one lichen from another is tricky, but accurate identification of individual bryophytes is probably even more challenging, particularly without the aid of a strong magnifying glass. Most bryophytes on ash will be superficially observed as a verdant green carpet covering the base of the bole and often reaching up to a metre above ground level. The first reaction may be that this 'carpet' only consists of a single species, but close examination may well find several different mosses growing together. Rackham mentions the phenomenon of green 'socks' of moss on the bases of young, suppressed ash trees in unthinned plantations and it is a commonly observed feature of these woods, particularly on heavy clays where there is plentiful moisture retention in the upper levels of the soil. Perhaps the moss, which itself will encourage moisture retention around the base of the tree, as well as the stress on developing root systems, partially caused by limited crown space in trees far too closely grown, will lead to an increased risk of basal rot and, ultimately, the failure of the tree.

Epiphytic species other than lichens and bryophytes are typically ferns, although there are some wild flowers that will readily colonise moss-clad trees with loamy substrates in nooks and crannies. It is not uncommon to find wood sorrel or herb robert springing from mossy boles. Probably the most often-found fern is common polypody, which will readily grow on the mossy boughs of veteran and ancient ash trees, typically in the Atlantic oak woods where the occasional ash has infiltrated.

Strange Growths

There are a few examples of quite strange bulges, burrs or excrescences which grow on ash trees that are difficult to explain. Knobbly forms at the base of trees are most commonly caused by the unwelcome attention of herbivores that chew the bark, and this phenomenon is simply the tree repairing itself. Some of the burrs or burls that form further up the bole and are out of reach of marauding animals are a little more puzzling. It could be a reaction from the tree to some previous tissue invasion by an insect – the sort of thing that sets up the formation of galls – or perhaps a viral infection (see page 165), or simply damage caused when caught by other wind-thrown trees or boughs. There seems to be no hard and fast opinion, but the contents of these can often be very beautiful and are keenly sought by woodturners and for slicing into veneers. The outcome is always a complete lottery as sometimes they are full of tiny voids.

William Gilpin in *Remarks on Forest Scenery* (1794) mentions a different kind of ash malformation:

> Another curiosity in the ash, which is likewise of the picturesque kind, is a sort of excrescence, which is sometimes found on a leading branch, called a wreathed fascia. The fasciated branch is twisted, and curled in a very beautiful form; which form it probably takes, as Dr Plot supposes, from too quick an ascent of the sap: or as other naturalists imagine, from the puncture of some insect in the tender twig, which diverts the sap from its usual channel, and makes the branch monstrous. I have a fasciated branch of ash, found in the woods of Beaulieu in new-forest, which is most elegantly twisted in the form of a crozier.

An extreme example of this weird malformation was discovered in Gloucestershire by Elwes and

ABOVE LEFT:
Peltigera horizontalis at Watendlath, Cumbria, with spore-producing discs in evidence.

ABOVE CENTRE:
Lobaria virens on the Lorton Ash, in Cumbria, one of only three known locations for this species in the county.

ABOVE RIGHT:
Pertusaria albescans var. corallina in Borrowdale.

CLOCKWISE FROM TOP LEFT:
Common tamarisk-moss (Thuidium tamariscinum).

Flat-leaved scalewort (Radula complanata), being killed by something fungal, with forked veilwort (Metzgeria furcata) above.

Lesser yoke-moss (Zygodon conoideus) and Dilated scalewort (Frullania dilatata).

The great scented liverwort (Conocephalum conicum).

Common feather-moss (Kindbergia praelonga).

174 GROWING ON ASH

Henry and illustrated in their *Trees of Great Britain and Ireland*. Elwes noted: 'A curious malformation occurs in a tree growing close to Cirencester, on the east side of the Tetbury road nearly opposite The Kennels. The remarkable growths on its branches, specimens of which were sent to Kew, were found to contain numerous examples of *Hylesinus fraxini* [the ash bark beetle].'

Aerial Trees

It is not uncommon for a variety of other trees to gain purchase among the upper branches of ash trees. These aerial trees have arisen either from seed blown into some declivity or, more often, from berries dropped by birds. Old pollards, where there are likely to be areas of rotted-down detritus in the middle of the crowns, are favourite anchorages for these opportunist trees, but occasionally they may simply have grown in the fork of two large branches. Sometimes these aerial trees can attain quite impressive proportions and it is something of a mystery how they manage to get enough sustenance to keep them alive. The presumption is that somehow the aerial tree has developed a root system determined enough to find its way down through the main bole of its host to reach the ground for water and nutrients, and yet inspection does not always prove conclusive, as the whole process is hidden inside the host tree. Aerial trees most often noted include rowans, hollies and elders, but the odd yew and sycamore have also been spotted. One has to wonder, with the great fecundity of the ash, whether rogue ash keys have blown into hollows of large ash trees setting up aerial trees, but due to them looking identical this would be very hard to disseminate.

A colourful account from the eighteenth century, where ash infiltrated a willow, comes from Gilpin's *Remarks on Forest Scenery*:

> It is not uncommon for the seeds of trees, and particularly of the ash, to seize on some faulty part of a neighbouring trunk, and there strike root. Dr Plot [in his Natural History of Oxfordshire] speaks of a piece of vegetable violence of this kind, which is rather extraordinary. 'An ash-key rooting itself on a decayed willow; and finding, as it increased, a deficiency of nourishment in the mother-plant, it began to insinuate its fibres by degrees through the trunk of the willow into the earth. There receiving an additional recruit, it began to thrive, and expand itself to such a size, that it burst the willow in pieces, which fell away from it on every side; and what was before the root of the ash, being now exposed to the air, became the solid trunk of a vigorous tree.'

Exactly how many years these processes take to occur would make a fascinating study – by using time-lapse photography over thirty or forty years, for example. Such a process can still be readily observed in numerous examples of rowans growing inside alders in the ancient wood pasture of Geltsdale in the far north-east corner of Cumbria, with the exposed roots, once the mother tree has burst apart, putting on bark and morphing into trunks. We simply do not know how long these things take – it could be a hundred years or more! Sadly, Dr Plot in his eighteenth-century account does not supply a timeline.

BELOW:
A dense colony of mosses on one of the ancient pollards in Watendlath, Cumbria, including: tamarisk scalewort, mouse-tail moss, broom forkmoss and a couple of sprigs of common polypody fern.

BELOW:
Bizarre phenomenon in the boughs of an ash near Cirencester, recorded by Elwes and Henry in their 'Trees of Great Britain and Ireland', 1909.

RIGHT:
A bulbous burr on a Derbyshire ash tree has probably taken many years to grow to this size, but the reason for its occurrence is obscure.

OPPOSITE:
A large aerial rowan tree has thrived in the fork of this substantial ash tree in Borrowdale. Exactly how its root system has managed to draw water and nutrients is a mystery.

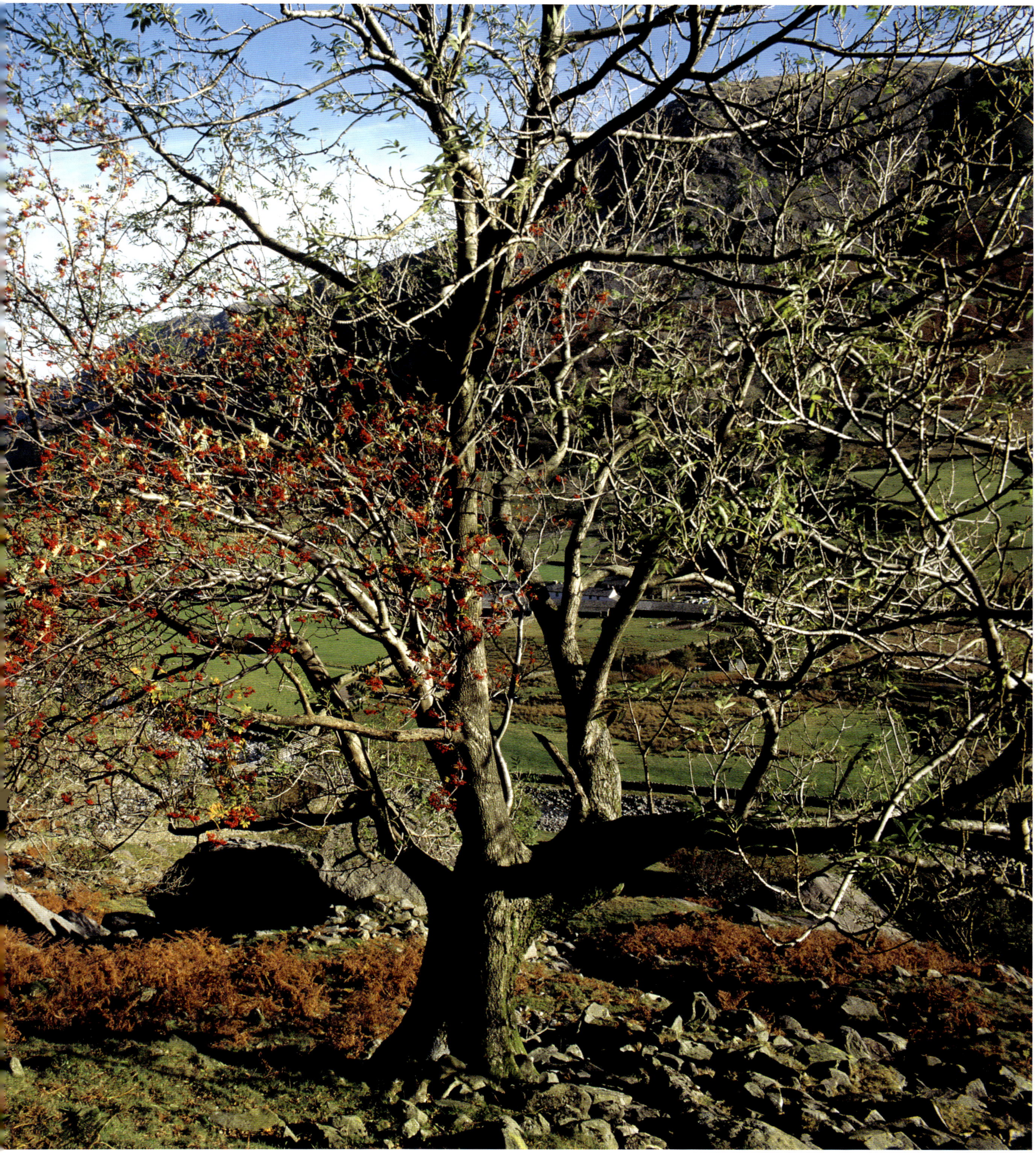

OPPOSITE:
Ash dieback has devasted the woods at Ashwellthorpe in Norfolk.

Ash Dieback

Ash dieback, the grim reaper of ash trees, has been sweeping across Britain culling relentlessly since 2012, but almost certainly for many years prior to this, perhaps since early this century. The dying back of ash trees had been observed for over a decade before the current epidemic, but probably due to the subtlety of the disease declaration in pole-stage, mature and ancient ash trees, and insufficient numbers and concentrations of victims, nobody had made a concerted effort to identify exactly what was leading to the decline. Often it was presumed that it was simply age-related (maiden ash trees usually go into decline after about 120–130 years) or down to conditions such as severe drought – a factor that would have been very likely in decades since the 1950s – root damage in agricultural environments, pigeon damage or any other unidentified pests.

The dying back of hedgerow ash trees in particular has been observed since the 1960s, long before the arrival of the disease, and was thought to be the effects of ash bud moth (*Prays fraxinella*), possibly in conjunction with root damage and a lowered water table caused by ditch clearance. Again, similar declines in the 1970s were put down to lowered water tables as a result of climatic variation.

Recently, close inspection of trees infected by ash dieback reveals the distinctive symptoms: initially, leaves with many brown or black spots where spores have landed and entered the tree's vascular system: then completely brown, and eventually blackened and withered, leaves which hang down; browned dead and dying shoots; and large portions of the crown that have completely died. The supposedly classic symptoms of diamond-shaped lesions around side shoots, long narrow cankers along stems and the purplish colouring of diseased tissue are not always obviously apparent. The disease is caused by the fungal pathogen *Hymenoscyphus fraxineus* (syn. *Hymenoscyphus pseudoalbidus*), originally described and named *Chalara fraxinea* in 2006. If there is any confusion here – blame the taxonomists! Initial misidentification of the fungus first arose because it looked exactly like another, less harmful fungus called *Hymenoscyphus albidus* (hence the *pseudoalbidus* appellation) which has co-existed with ash, harmlessly, for at least eighty years (and probably a lot longer). To keep it simple, ash dieback is still commonly referred to, even in scientific and arboricultural circles, as *Chalara*.

In the Far East ash species appear to be able to co-exist with *Hymenoscyphus fraxineus*. Is this because the fungus is less aggressive or because the trees have evolved to cope with it, or both? As the fungus has spread its range around the world, something in the relationship has changed so that by the time it arrived in Eastern Europe the tolerance of ash trees to the fungus no longer existed. The trees were mostly different ash species and the few that were the same would undoubtedly have been genetically different, but perhaps the fungus had also mutated in some subtle way.

Trees become infected when the windborne fungal spores land on leaves, damaging them with the toxic chemical viridiol and, as its effect intensifies, carrying the viridiol further into the tree, constricting and killing the vascular tissue so that the tree cannot draw nutrients and water to the tips of the crown. The reproductive phase of the fungus occurs on the fallen leaves and may be observed as tiny, pale buff, cup-shaped fruiting bodies, only 2–3 millimetres across, growing on the separated leaf rachis (mid-rib). The countless thousands of microscopic ascospores released by these minute 'mushrooms' between June and September are then able to reinfect other areas of the host tree or other trees close by, but could

ASH DIEBACK

CLOCKWISE FROM TOP LEFT:
Signs of ash dieback:

Typical view of an ailing hedgerow tree with thinning crown and 'pom-pom' effect clumps of leaves.

Dead brown leaves at the ends of boughs which will eventually turn black.

The classic diamond lesions of ash dieback, but not commonly observed.

More typical signs are necroses such as this on young infected stems.

180 ASH DIEBACK

also be carried by birds, mammals or humans, or borne on the wind over significant distances. Early conjecture that spores had blown in from mainland Europe was initially heralded as the source of the disease, but later considered to be unlikely, as some authorities believed that travelling long distances at altitude would soon desiccate them and they would inevitably lose their viability. In the light of more recent studies, overlaying the genetic profiles of the fungus found in East Anglia (the supposed blow-in zone) with those of woods in the Midlands and South Wales planted with diseased stock imported from Northern Europe, there is a high degree of commonality, suggesting that the source of all the fungi was from similar parts of Europe. Opinion is still divided about whether the disease was principally introduced by wind blow or nursery-stock importation.

The symptoms of ash dieback may easily be seen on young trees – it would seem that saplings and both pollard and coppice regrowth are particularly susceptible. However, with older, larger specimens it is much harder to view what is occurring in the crown, but from a distance the trees soon begin to show the cumulative effect of infection. When a large, healthy ash tree is in full leaf it should be quite difficult to see much daylight when looking through the crown. As ash dieback takes hold, the foliage becomes thinner, the leaves smaller, sometimes yellowing prematurely in summer, and the branch tips begin to die off, with leaf growth pulling back to the last healthy zone below the diseased areas, often creating lots of small bunches or 'pom-poms' of leafy growth as the ailing tree pushes out more and more leaves from its lateral buds in a bid to survive. The rate at which the trees die is quite variable, but research and observations carried out by Gary Battell, tree officer with Suffolk County Council, seems to indicate that between 10 and 20 per cent of the original crown per annum is about average, although clearly as the disease progresses percentage loss per annum increases exponentially. This means that a large mature ash tree can be lost in about five to ten years, confirmed by the numerous dead hulks of ashes now to be seen in East Anglia, Kent and Sussex, where ash dieback began its trail of destruction at least ten and quite possibly twenty years ago.

Of all the ash species it seems that common ash is one of the most susceptible to attack and once infected the majority will eventually die, although a small percentage may have a degree of tolerance that will allow them to survive, perhaps even rally and recover. One form of the native ash, the weeping ash (see page 120), is particularly susceptible to ash dieback and this may relate to the clonal nature of many of these trees, which must be grafted from existing trees, the majority of which are probably descendants of the original single sport. This may also indicate a genetic vulnerability to ash dieback.

After several years of research into potential tolerance to ash dieback, maybe even resistance, an indication of low susceptibility was eventually linked to three genetic markers following the genome sequencing of a highly tolerant Danish ash tree (known as Clone 35), and comparisons made with an ash of high susceptibility. Hopes were raised in early 2016 at Ashwellthorpe Wood in Norfolk, where ash dieback was first identified in existing woodland, rather than among nursery stock, back in 2012. A single tree (named 'Betty' by the research team) in the middle of an infected and dying population, with a promising genetic profile, seemed to have remained unaffected. As of late 2017 the tree survives, but now shows typical signs of ash dieback. Exactly what degree of tolerance it will exhibit remains to be seen. However, widespread studies have revealed that there is a much greater genetic diversity among British ash trees compared to the rest of Europe and, most particularly, ash trees in Denmark, where such a heavy toll was exacted on the population with a loss of 90 percent of the trees. Studies of trees in clonal seed orchards, test-bed nurseries and in the wild will attempt to identify the most promising trees for future breeding programmes.

Research is ongoing into potential efficacy of fungicides to treat diseased trees, but the practicalities of administering these to all but a small percentage of trees would be extremely difficult, and would probably have to be repeated on a regular basis. However, by way of protecting some of Britain's most important, arguably irreplaceable, individual, ancient and veteran trees it might prove invaluable.

Ash dieback was certainly prevalent in Eastern Europe as long ago as 1992, slowly progressing westwards ever since, so by now the majority of Europe (apart from Spain and Portugal) has been affected. After the first confirmation of the disease in the UK in 2012 in a Buckinghamshire nursery, among trees imported from the Netherlands, ash dieback was very soon identified at a widespread number of sites, principally in south-east England, leading to the realisation that it had probably already been in the country for many years. It was only because there wasn't a

ABOVE:
Apothecia or spore-bearing bodies of Hymenoscyphus fraxineus on the rachis of an ash leaf.

significant and widespread mortality among the ash population with a readily noticeable impact on the landscape that it took so long for the diagnosis to be recognised. The spread has continued unchecked and as of early 2017 over 40 per cent of 10-kilometre grid squares in the UK contain infected trees (this compares to only 7 per cent in 2012), but this is an average and the statistics for England, where ash dieback is evident to varying degrees in every county, are much higher at 57.6 per cent and in Wales at 52.5 per cent it is fast approaching similar levels to England.

There is still much debate as to how the disease has managed to spread so fast, and often into existing mature stands of ash with no apparent links to nursery stock, as typified by the outbreak at Ashwellthorpe. Various vectors have been suggested, such as the wind, migratory birds and the footwear, clothing or car tyres of people moving around the country after visiting infected areas, but all of these except wind blow have been discounted as making any great impact on spore transmission. Travelling around Britain, gathering the photographs for this book, it was noticeable in some of the most westerly parts, where ash dieback was a relatively recent arrival, how a high percentage of the infected trees appeared alongside or at least fairly close to the main roads, suggesting that the wind-tunnel effect might draw spores along them. The pace of the spread of ash dieback has been seen to be very variable from one year to another and this could be linked to prevailing climatic conditions, so that a warm, wet summer would possibly be more favourable for sporolation.

It has also been widely recorded that damp environments show higher levels of infection.

A new direction in potentially solving the ash dieback crisis emerged in 2016 when Dr Glynn Percival of Reading University carried out studies administering a product called Biochar to the soil around the base of ash trees in a test-bed plantation. Biochar is made by slowly charring waste wood biomass with a restricted oxygen supply, somewhat akin to charcoal production, but more highly refined. This creates a product with a microscopic honeycomb-like structure, well suited to beneficial soil micro-organisms such as mycorrhizal fungi, and aids drainage and aeration in the soil. Initially this was a field trial to assess the effects of Biochar on plant growth, but quite by chance some ash trees in the trial wood became infected with ash dieback, and remarkably none of those had been treated with Biochar. Dr Percival asserts that not only does Biochar enrich the soil, but that it also helps the tree's defence mechanisms, thus making it more resilient in the face of disease. The principle of using charcoal to promote plant health and growth has come down from native tribes in the Amazon some 1,500 years ago. Sadly, due to access to the trial beds having been terminated by a new owner, this research has ground to a shuddering halt. This is a great shame, as there just might have been a treatment that could have been used to save some of our ash trees. Again the logistics and costs of actually treating great numbers of trees this way would have been somewhat impractical, but the thought that we could have introduced this system to save a select band of our most important ancient and landmark ash trees might have been of great importance.

Without doubt we have ash dieback for the foreseeable future. Nobody can say for sure how many trees will succumb, but latest predictions suggest that 99 per cent could well die within the next 15–20 years. Whatever the outcome, the next threat to ash trees, gradually heading towards Britain from either the east (it is already in Russia) or perhaps hopping the Atlantic from America, is the dreaded emerald ash borer beetle (*Agrilus planipennis*). As I write, this pest has already been responsible for the demise of over 150 million ash trees in North America – more than the total number of large, mature ash trees we have in the whole of Britain. The tiny iridescent green beetle lays eggs in the ash bark and then the larvae burrow through the tree's phloem, their network of tunnels cutting off the flow of nutrients and water up the tree. It reputedly entered America in a shipment of Japanese car parts, the larvae presumably burrowed in the wooden pallets; a threat that nobody probably even considered in such an unrelated cargo. It doesn't have to be something as obvious as a shipment of plants, trees or timber to require a biohazard alert.

Stopping diseases reaching our plantlife is always going to be fraught with problems, both biological and economic. Winds blow spores and humans, animals and birdlife may inadvertently transport them; and beetles lay eggs and fly where they will. All these vectors are beyond anyone's control. However, the biohazards presented by international trade in plants most definitely are within our control. *Hymenoscyphus fraxineus* has never been listed as a regulated organism in the EC Plant Health Directive, which would stipulate action to prevent its spread. Too late in the day, emergency legislation in late 2012 put a ban on the importation of ash plants and seed from regions where the pathogen was known to be present. Thousands of imported nursery and recently planted trees were destroyed in a futile attempt to staunch the spread of ash dieback. It is imperative that Britain has the political will to implement rigorous constraints, if not a ban, on this type of trade. But that haunting phrase 'not good for business' rears its ugly head. The environmentalist George Monbiot sums it up succinctly, writing in the *Guardian* in June 2017:

> The entire live plant trade presents a threat. The freedom with which it can move plants and the soil in which they are rooted across borders is a classic example

BELOW:
Same view of a country lane one year apart shows the decline due to ash dieback in the principal tree. On the right hand side of the road young trees that were thriving a year previously are now reduced to dead sticks, showing that the progression of ash dieback is highly variable.

ASH DIEBACK

LEFT:
Asholt Woods in Kent, where ash dieback is making the woodlands look like the aftermath of the Dutch elm disease epidemic of fifty years ago.

BELOW:
Another view of Asholt Woods reveals skeletal ash trees among the other healthy woodland species.

of regulatory failure that has over the years spread hundreds of invasive species around the world. Unless there is a radical change of policy, the UK appears likely to repeat its grim experience with Dutch elm disease and ash dieback, but in this case potentially affecting far more species. What this threat appears to demand is a moratorium on the import of all live plants other than those grown through tissue culture (propagation in sterile conditions). This would require negotiation with the EU or (in future) the World Trade Organization. But while the government has long been happy to pursue a holy war in such forums on behalf of financiers and other favoured interests, it is not prepared to request concessions to serve the wider public good.

As someone who once offered my older daughter, Rowan, 1p for every ash seedling she could pull from the flowerbeds in our garden, and consequently had my wallet speedily emptied of several pounds, I have always been bemused and infuriated that we should need to grow our native tree species in mainland Europe (often with native seed shipped out for the purpose) and then import potentially infected saplings, along with tons of alien, potentially infected soil, back into Britain. It doesn't take the wit of a genius to prognosticate the likely outcomes. Growing our native trees in foreign lands and alien soils may be cheaper and seem to be more expedient in the short term, but the outcome when contending with imported diseases is highly detrimental to the indigenous nursery industry in the longer term and infinitely detrimental to the environment for the foreseeable future. Who knows how many generations will come and go before we see landscapes full of large elm trees again, and who knows if the effects of ash dieback will create similar landscape voids? The genie is most definitely out of the bottle with ash dieback, and although evidence does seem to suggest that the disease was partly imported and partly windblown into the UK, it would be marvellous to think we might be better prepared for any potential epidemics that threaten to arrive here in the future. With regard to ash, we know that emerald ash borer is en route so now is the time to strengthen and enforce our border biosecurity.

As ash dieback becomes more entrenched and increasing numbers of trees begin to fail, die and risk falling, there are going to be very difficult decisions, both practical and financial, to be made by councils throughout Britain. With funding for almost everything in the public sector under severe pressure, one has to wonder where the billions will be found to make roads, railways, buildings and public spaces safe from dangerous ash trees. There is a danger here too of potentially losing ash trees that may exhibit a tolerance to ash dieback – the 'throwing the baby out with the bathwater'

BELOW:
The tree in the foreground is struggling with the effects of ash dieback clearly evident. It is worthy of note that this tree also bears two clumps of mistletoe. Is that contributing to the loss of vigour? The next tree in the hedgerow shows early signs of ash dieback, while the third tree still looks reasonably healthy.

ABOVE:
In 2017 the omens were not good for this ancient pollard above a pasture near Putley in Herefordshire as the crown was exhibiting the early signs of ash dieback. A year later the tree does not appear to have declined any further.

syndrome. If a contractor agrees to fell diseased and potentially disease-prone trees along a highway, is there any way of making a decision to leave some and not others? The answer is probably not, as it is usually easier and cheaper for contractors to complete these jobs in one pass. Potential survivors are then lost to the gene pool of regenerative trees.

Prior to the onset of ash dieback, Forest Research published figures that stated 30,000 hedgerow trees needed to be planted each year just to maintain current levels. Obviously, with the high occurrence of ash trees in hedgerows and the expected levels of loss from ash dieback, there will need to be a concerted effort to establish even more hedge trees, so important for flood alleviation, counteracting soil erosion and providing wildlife corridors, not to mention their significant contribution to landscape character, often in areas of relatively low woodland density.

The practicalities of managing ash dieback in the woodland environment are simply to thin and dispose of any trees exhibiting symptoms and either to encourage or replant tree species that will accommodate many of the associated species of invertebrates and plantlife dependent upon ash. Oak, beech, hazel and sycamore will fill the bill for the vast majority. To perpetuate the ecosystem function that could be lost with the removal of ash, which would affect light levels in the woodland and structural changes in the soil due to loss of ash leaf litter, small-leaved lime and alder are recommended replacements. Unless woods are principally for amenity use, health and safety issues are less pressing than in non-woodland settings.

In private gardens, parks or anywhere that individual ash trees are highly valued features, the only way possibly to stave off the advance of the disease is to remove any dead or dying branches and twigs with clusters of drooping, blackened dead leaves as soon as possible, cutting back well beyond the obvious signs of necrosis. This is not to say that disease won't be in other parts of the tree without being obviously visible. Before any work of substance is contemplated the advice of a fully accredited and insured tree surgeon should be sought, and it is also well worth consulting the Forestry Commission and Tree

LEFT:
In 2017 this hedgerow ash would appear to have been entering the final throws of life although strangely a small tree next to it appeared to be unaffected.

BELOW:
One year on and quite remarkably this ash would appear to be bouncing back, but is it fighting ash dieback or is this resurgence down to something else? Reduced predation by pigeons? Less salt on the road in winter? Cessation of ploughing or use of agri-chemicals in the adjoining field? And if any of these factors were influential then why wasn't the smaller tree on the right similarly affected?

While ash dieback is undoubtedly killing trees there are still many other factors that affect tree health.

Council websites. When the leaves begin to fall, gathering them up and burning them will remove the potential location of the fungal fruiting bodies which produce the spores and spread the disease. Ultimately, the unpalatable truth is that if the tree has ash dieback the likelihood of saving it is extremely slender, but if it is a particularly special tree then maybe it's worth a shot.

A small ray of hope is slowly emerging among the ash stocks in Eastern Europe where a longer time frame for the disease has existed. A small percentage of ash trees that were stricken by ash dieback more than twenty years ago have begun to show signs of regeneration. Exactly how the trees have overcome the disease is not currently fully understood or whether, like the ebb and flow of elm trees afflicted by Dutch elm disease, they will enter into rolling cycles of regeneration and decline, controlled either by ongoing levels of tolerance or susceptibility to reinfection.
If the worst should happen, and eventually there are few if any ash trees left standing, then we need to think about what comes next. We know that nature abhors a vacuum and it is not very long before a patch of bare ground or a gap in a wood or a hedgerow is colonised by some opportunist species. Ironically, when Dutch elm disease wrought its worst and all the large elms tumbled, it was ash that filled those voids in many cases. The knee-jerk reaction might well be a rash of well-intentioned tree planting, but if lessons have been learned from the aftermath of national disasters, typically the Great Storm of 1987, then we should be well aware that natural regeneration will be the best way forward. If it has to be planting then careful study of the already successful species in any given habitat will offer direction and, wherever possible, using seed collected from local stock. Trees that choose their natural place in the landscape will usually thrive much better than the ones that humans impose upon it. This may mean that a large section of the British populace will have to overcome their aversion to the sycamore, the alien tree perceived by many as the over-successful interloper that sets seedlings as ubiquitously as the ash has been doing since time immemorial.

BELOW:
A romantic vision of the ash in a bucolic setting in this plate by William Delamotte, 1821.

The Inspirational Ash

Seeking evidence of inspiration from the ash tree in the realms of poets, writers and artists is not the simplest of tasks. Since time immemorial the British oak was that iconic tree that seemed to get the creative juices flowing. It resonated with the pride of a nation, the oak hulls of British men-of-war (John Evelyn's 'Wooden Walls') and the finest frames for the greatest buildings. Oak was sturdy, strong, resilient and reliable. Remarkable for its ability to last a thousand years, the tree was magnificent in its prime and romantic in hoary decline. Massive ancient oaks still honour kings, queens, statesmen and all manner of historic events. The poor ash tree will never compete with the oak for longevity, and seldom arrive at that rugged beauty so typical of great oaks in antiquity. How could the ash tree possibly match such stature?

William Gilpin in his *Remarks on Forest Scenery* (1791) had much to say about the various aesthetic attributes of all native trees, when most of his contemporaries were focused on the silvicultural and economical aspects, but his judgement on the ash is very much of a curate's egg. In its favour,

> … its chief beauty consists in the lightness of its whole appearance. Its branches at first keep close to the trunk, and form acute angles with it: but as they begin to lengthen, they generally take an easy sweep; and the looseness of the leaves corresponding with the lightness of the spray, the whole forms an elegant depending foliage. Nothing can have a better effect, than an old ash, hanging from the corner of a wood, and bringing off the heaviness of the other foliage, with its loose pendent branches.

It is best to stop at this point since the ash then proceeds to attract Gilpin's displeasure as he notes its ugliness in old age and its tendency to lose its leaves earlier than other trees.

The poets of the eighteenth and nineteenth centuries usually ascribe some picturesque, rocky gorge as the setting for the ash, typically Robert Southey (1774–1843) in 'Roderick':

> … Here amid the brook,
> Grey as the stone to which it clung, half root,
> Half trunk, the young Ash rises from the rock:
> And there the parent lifts its lofty head,
> And spreads its graceful boughs;
>   the passing wind
> With twinkling motion lifts the silent leaves,
> And shakes its rattling tufts.

This setting also creeps into many of the engraved and etched portraits of ash trees prepared for the various books on trees and forests, but as Oliver Rackham observed one seldom sees an accurate, unmistakeable image of an ash tree. Even the great John Constable's sketches of ashes could be interpreted as birches or tall, sinuous beeches. Rackham also notes the dearth of literary and poetic reference to the ash, reducing its appearance in the texts of Shakespeare, Wordsworth, Tennyson and Yeats to a mere statistic among the other tree species (unsurprisingly, oak at the top). Such prosaic analysis should in no way devalue the work of other writers.

While most poets find grace and beauty in the ash tree – after all, it is the Venus of the Woods – one or two have been moved by the commonly overlooked details of the tree's typical growth patterns and peculiarities. Sydney Dobell (1824–74) took an intimate interest in an ash tree, whether dying or at the onset of winter is difficult to ascertain, but his close observation and palpable connection is vividly revealed in his poem 'Dead-Maid's Pool':

> …Thou art wizen and white, ash-tree;
> Other trees have gone on,
> Have gathered and grown,
> Have burgeoned and borne:
> Thou hast wasted and worn.
>
> Thy knots are all eyes;
> Every knot a dumb eye,
> That has seen a sight
> And heard a cry …
>
> … Thou hast no shoots nor wands,
> All thy arms turn to the deep,
> All thy twigs are crooked,
> Twined and twisted,
> Fingered and fisted,
> Like one who had looked
> On wringing hands
> 'Till his hands were wrung in his sleep …
>
> … Ash-tree, ash-tree,
> That once wert so green!
> Ash-tree, ash-tree!
> What hast thou seen?

Who has not observed the strange unseeing eyes of the lost branch scars on the ash bole; ash with its uncanny ability to callus over these breaches due to urgent necessity, for allowing the ingress of water into a timber so unsuited for exposure to the outdoors would undoubtedly hasten its demise.

These scars, often raised into small protuberances along the trunk when healed over, hide strange little voids within, awaiting discovery when the tree is felled. The Herefordshire artist Jan Trewin was entranced by these intriguing anomalies, and moved to make miniature artworks from each of the unique forms she finds (see page 196).

BELOW:
This engraving from a German botanical book of the 1890s is one of the few images of an ash tree that is clearly defined with every single ash leaf rendered by the artist.

THE INSPIRATIONAL ASH 191

BELOW:
A winter ash on the Malvern Hills.

Various authors on countryside matters have rejoiced in the ash. In the late nineteenth-century Richard Jefferies, writes in his *Wildlife in a Southern County* of discovering a springtime ash copse:

> The green sprays momentarily pushed aside close immediately behind, shutting out the vision, and with it the thought of civilisation. These boughs are the gates of another world. Under trees and leaves – it is so, too, sometimes even in an avenue – where the direct rays of the sun do not penetrate, there is ever a subdued light; it is not shadow, but a light toned with green.

Writer and poet Edward Thomas (1878–1917) writes like a man permanently intoxicated by the natural world he senses all around him; a kind of naturalistic hyper-drive or ultra-sensitivity to the tiniest detail, where the barely noticeable or the commonplace becomes deeply significant. Many must have casually observed what Thomas saw, when he watched the autumn metamorphosis of an ash, but few could transpose those moments or that emotion so poignantly to the page:

> As the sun rose I watched a proud ash tree shedding its leaves after a night of frost. It let them go by threes and tens and twenties; very rarely, with little intervals, only one at a time; once or twice a hundred in one flight. Leaflet – for they fall by leaflets – and stalk twirled through the windless air as if they would have liked to fall not quite so rapidly as their companions to that brown and shining and oblivious carpet below. A gentle wind arose from the north and the leaves all went sloping in larger companies to the ground – falling, falling, whispering as they joined the fallen, they fell for a longer time than a poppy spends in opening and shedding its husk in June. But soon only two leaves were left vibrating. In a little while they also, both together, made the leap, twinkling for a short space and then shadowed and lastly bright and silent on the grass. Then the tree stood up entirely bereaved and without a voice, in the silver light of the morning that was still young, and wrote once more its grief in complicated scribble upon a sky of intolerably lustrous pearl.

Only a year before he died in 1917, Thomas wrote 'The Ash Grove', a poem that recalled a fleeting experience on one of his many wanderings long before: discovering a remote and abandoned ash wood in the hills, prompting a brief reverie, losing himself for a moment beneath the ash shade, enshrined with the trees, he appears wistfully euphoric. Thomas's first draft of the poem paints a more complete picture of that brief encounter than the truncated version that was published:

192 THE INSPIRATIONAL ASH

BELOW:
Autumnal ash tree after a storm, dramatically lit by evening sunlight.

THE INSPIRATIONAL ASH

BELOW:
A 'pheonix ash' in winter.

> In an ash grove among the mountains once,
>   I was glad
> Exceedingly, walking under the trees,
>   notwithstanding I had
> Nought that I knew to be glad of.
>   Bare and decayed,
> Their few leaves shaking in silence,
>   the trees were not sad
>
> Though half of them stood dead
>   & the living made
> Little more than the dead ones made of shade.
> If it led to a house the house was long since gone,
> But the ash grove welcomed me
>   & my feet delayed
>
> From where I saw the first of the
>   strong roots clasp the stone
> And I forgot myself & the past & future, on
> To where the last of the shadows fell & the blaze
> Of the sun returned, & outside I walked alone …

Thomas could cling to such sylvan recollections amid the death and despair of the trenches in France when, so it would appear, he found another ash grove that transported him back, but whether it was to an inner peace or melancholia or both:

> … And now an ash grove far
>   from those hills can bring
> The same tranquillity in
>   which I wander a ghost
> With a ghostly gladness …

And yet from his second stanza there is something uncannily prophetic when one considers, a century later, what is happening to the ash woods today; there will be time aplenty for ashen ghosts to haunt those lost groves.

John Fuller is one of today's poets whose oeuvre spreads to all points of the compass of human experience, but, like Thomas, he is frequently inspired by the natural world around him. Part of his life has been spent living in rural Wales where he has always kept a close eye on the minutiae of nature and the turning of the seasons around the homestead. He includes this brief cameo of an ashy metamorphosis in the depths of his poem 'The Grey and the Green':

194 THE INSPIRATIONAL ASH

… But most regret in this last winter
The passing of an ancient ash
Which air, that changed location at
Unlikely speed, disturbed and flattened
With an unheard crash.

But now, although it leans upon
One hinge of bark, new leafage shoots
From stumps the guilty wind has healed.
It dipped its elbows in the field
And there established roots.

If only our unrooted lives
When felled could simply change direction
And all our tall assumptions both
Be trimmed and find amazing growth,
A perfect resurrection!

The tree has found a way of walking
Not as our childhood stories told us
Through sudden supernatural strength
But through first tumbling its full length
Then growing from its shoulders …

Such 'phoenix trees', as they have become known in recent times, are constant reminders of the incredible innate drive to survive that trees have locked within them; simply waiting for their opportunity after disaster has struck. What seems certain to be a departure in the wake of a storm turns into a new arrival, striking out into new territory, and with some trees this can keep happening time after time. Black mulberries, for example, are past masters at this, tumbling their way across many a formal lawn to create mini-woodlands. Ash will do it, but the risk is that because the fallen wood can rot so quickly the tree needs to put down roots where the fallen boughs dig into the earth as soon as possible. Alternatively, some phoenix trees may survive on the few original live roots that have been left in the ground after the fall.

The crossover between what might be termed artistic endeavours and true commercial crafts and industries is sometimes blurred. Functional items can often exhibit great beauty as well as innovation in form and design, and vice versa. Once upon a time such crafts as turnery, rake-making, cleft hurdle-making, chair-making and coopering were all important suppliers to buoyant markets. In the course of the twentieth century most of that changed, due to mechanisation and new manufacturing materials, so that although a handful of skilled artisans do still make a living from these crafts, now a great many people have taken them up either as a small part of a whole range of other products they offer or purely at an amateur or enthusiast level.

Typically, this might be found among a great many woodturners, where only a small proportion will actually earn anything like a living wage from their labours, but among professionals and amateurs alike, many people are producing some truly stunning pieces of work, and using a huge variety of different timbers from home and abroad. Some may consider the purest form of this to be the ancient tradition of pole-lathe turning, a skill that had almost disappeared until fairly recently, but over the last three decades increasing numbers of green woodworkers have decided to learn the art of using a pole-lathe. Turners who wish to use exotic hardwoods or seasoned native hardwoods must employ the range of powered lathes, using dedicated tools and different techniques. It was the phenomenal range of different things that have historically been made, as well as those that are still made out of ash, that inspired one man to embark on an epic journey with a single tree.

BELOW:
'The Wheelwright' (1939) by Stanley Anderson (1884 - 1966). He was a gifted artist who was inspired to create a monumental collection of people engaged in a wide variety of English country crafts, making a series of beautiful engravings over a period of 20 years, from 1933 onwards. While not specifically influenced by ash as such, he was moved by many of the people who used it (see also page 91).

HAPPY THE MAN WHOSE WISH AND CARE
A FEW PATERNAL ACRES BOUND,
CONTENT TO BREATHE HIS NATIVE AIR
IN HIS OWN GROUND.
POPE

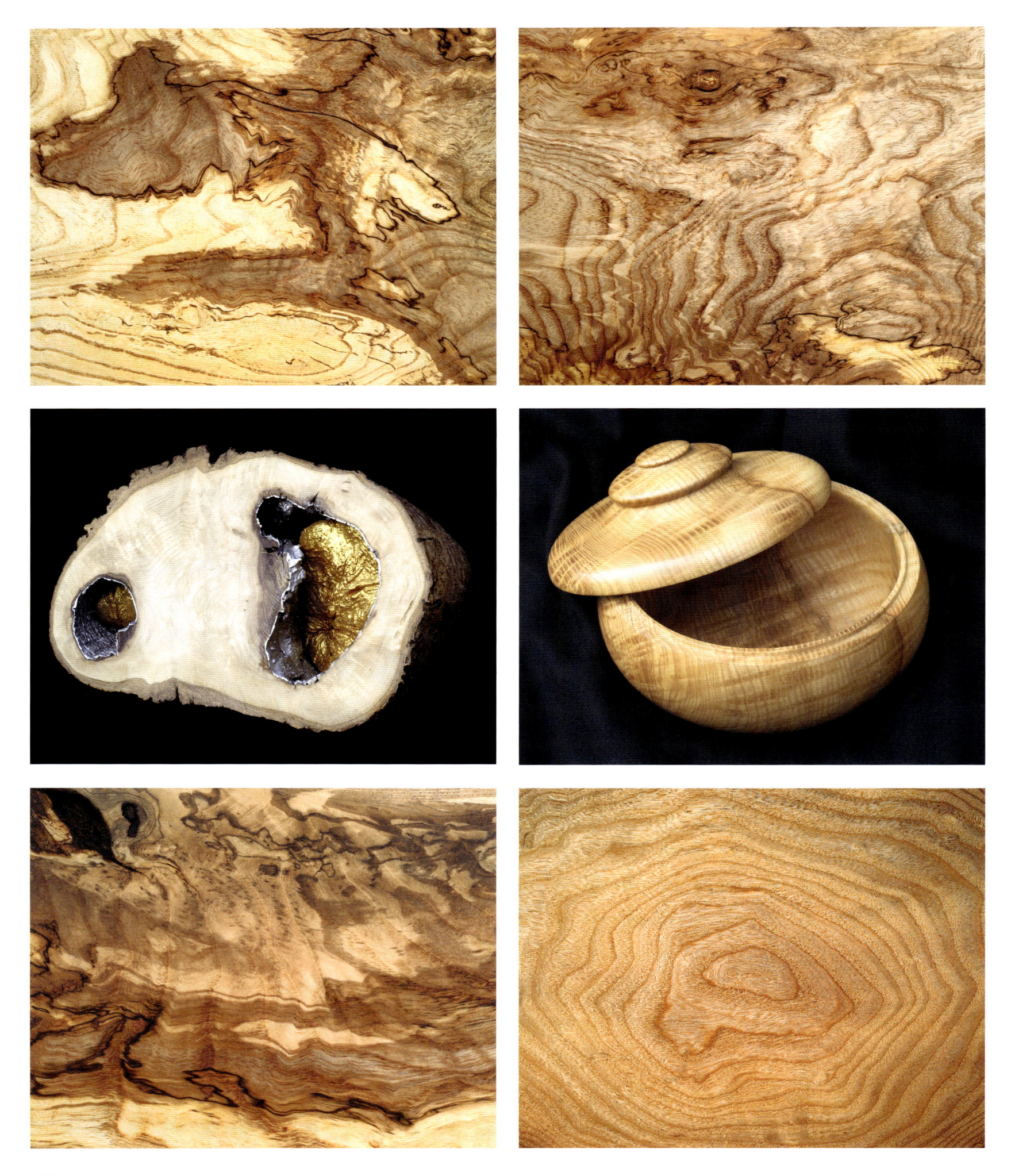

196 THE INSPIRATIONAL ASH

The Man Who Made Things Out of Trees

Several years ago, while writer Rob Penn was working in the community woodland near his home beneath the Black Mountains, in the Welsh borders, he began to think in greater depth about the ash trees he was felling and coppicing on a regular basis. It was the ubiquity of ash, not just in his part of the world, but throughout the land, combined with the thought that almost everyone has some sort of connection to the wood of the tree – a relationship that can be tracked back for centuries if not millennia. This relationship may have been more intimate – indeed, more crucial – in the days when we made spears for hunting or weapons of war, or when there was a universal necessity for fuel wood, but Penn identified an astonishing catalogue of uses for ash wood, many of which have been consigned to history, but, remarkably, many that are still very much alive in the twenty-first century. Spurred on with the knowledge that the deadly fungal pathogen of ash dieback is very likely to eradicate the vast majority of ash trees, and with the germ of an idea, Penn began his search for a single mature maiden ash tree.

The plan was to select that perfect ash tree and to see how many different things it was possible to make out of it. A similar project with an oak, 'One Tree', was set up at Tatton Park in Cheshire back in 1998, and seventy artists and craftsmen were invited to make different things from this one tree; the results became a touring exhibition in 2001–2. However, nobody had ever attempted anything along these lines with ash. Two strands of research began. Most important was the identification and acquisition of a suitable ash tree; one that would provide all the specific types of timber that Penn needed for a whole array of very different products. Initially, with the sheer number of ash trees in his neighbourhood, he had thought this would be a simple task, but no matter who he talked to or where he roamed in his quest for the 'right' ash tree his goal continued to prove elusive for many months. The second strand was to identify as many different applications for the use of ash wood as possible, track down the manufacturers and craftsmen that used it, and then ask them if they would make something from the wood of his chosen tree.

ABOVE:
Rob Penn in Callow Hill Wood with his felled ash tree.

OPPOSITE:
Ash timber is often thought to be quite bland and uninteresting, but these examples contradict that assumption. The spectacular figuring in this dark timber is cut from the black heart of a log and traditionally know as 'Olive Ash' (the black lines or spalting are more oftern associated with beech wood). The example on the lower right is a crown cut section of a large burr which accentuates the annual rings.

The inside of a burr has been embellished by artist Jan Trewin into one of her 'Ash Treasures'.

The lidded bowl was turned by John Bennison from timber retrieved from a 160-year old tree felled in our garden twenty years ago.

THE INSPIRATIONAL ASH

RIGHT:
Rob Penn, author of 'The Man Who Made Things Out of Trees', with just a few of the 45 different items he had made from his ash tree. He holds a piece of the timber containing all 130 annual rings (half the diameter of the tree).

The sort of ash tree that Penn needed was one with a reasonable girth, around 200 centimetres, and a good straight butt of at least 6 or 7 metres, so that he could eventually cut enough boards of varying widths and thicknesses to suit all the different uses he had slowly accumulated on his wish list. If the trees were straight, then they had a fork (a common problem with ash) or they had grown too old and rot had set in. If they had the girth required, then they were always crooked. Finally he met with Mark Potter, director of a local forestry company, who understood the sort of tree that he was seeking. After checking over several woods they arrived at Callow Hill Wood, near Ewyas Harold, where Penn's elation at finally finding that right tree was palpable. The dimensions were right and it was a good straight tree, around 130 years old, and in the peak of condition.

Penn's odyssey had begun with his search for the 'right' tree, but one senses that after such a long and previously fruitless quest it was the felling of the tree that was the true birth of the project. It was felled at the tail end of winter, before the sap began to rise, so that moisture levels were relatively low. The felling and trimming and hauling of the butt from the edge of the wood to the roadside, followed by the milling of the boards at a local sawmill, took on a ritualistic significance, creating a bond that would drive him forward with his mission to extract the utmost from his chosen tree.

From the outset Penn quickly discovered that different craftsmen required different sorts of wood. Some, such as pole-lathe turners, wanted green wood to make bowls, while at the other end of the spectrum the wheelwright would season three-inch boards for at least four years (an inch per year plus one for luck) before considering using them for the felloes of wheels. Cabinet-makers required wood with a very low moisture content, so kiln drying was necessary. While the makers of fine furniture relished any interesting figuring in the wood, the tool-handle-makers and the arrow-

THE INSPIRATIONAL ASH

maker sought the straightest grain possible with absolutely no knots.

Penn cast his net both at home and abroad to get his ash used. Phill Gregson, Master Wheelwright, from Lancashire and John Lloyd of the South Wales tool-handle manufacturers A.S. Lloyd & Son were two extremely knowledgeable and amiable contacts and were keen to pass on their accumulated knowledge from four generations of their family businesses. Renowned woodturner Robin Wood made a nest of three ash bowls. Expert bowyer and arrow-maker Tom Mareschall showed Rob the deft art of making ashen arrows. Trips to Austria yielded a toboggan, America a baseball bat and Ireland a hurley. All told, Penn ended up with forty-five different items (some small things in multiples) and at the end of the project still had a good few logs left for his fire.

What seems to have made Penn's project so personally engrossing, and this comes over beautifully in his book, is his fascination with his chosen medium, a sort of fine-tuning to a level where all the senses are pricked and poised so that he appears to have acquired a distinct intimacy with his ash timber, which clearly intensifies as he reaps the pleasure of absorbing every last detail of all the different artisans' expertise and anecdote along with the exacting nature of the various creative and manufacturing processes. Somehow one feels that this was more about a very personal journey than constructing the bones of a book … and maybe it was, but thankfully we have the book too.

Ash Dome

And then, of course, there is David Nash, the celebrated sculptor and land artist – how could he not be included in any book about the ash tree. Even his name resonates with ashen association: Nash – 'place at the ash-tree', a combination of Old English *æsc* (ash) with Middle English *atten* (at the). It would seem as if what might be considered one of Nash's seminal works was predestined. *Ash Dome* is a living land artwork begun by Nash in 1977 when he planted twenty-two ash saplings in a 9-metre-wide circle in Caen-y-Coed, a remote tract of woodland a few miles from his home and

BELOW:
David Nash 'Ash Dome – Project Drawing, 2013' pastel on paper.

RIGHT:
Autumn light steals into Caen-y-Coed illuminating David Nash's 'Ash Dome'.

THE INSPIRATIONAL ASH 201

RIGHT:
David Nash's 'Ash Cube', high on the wall of his chapel gallery, was made using prunings from 'Ash Dome', and seems to me to be a representative vignette of 'Ash Dome' itself with the exuberance of nature making a break for freedom from the man-made constraints of the inorganic cubic form – the conflict of wills in miniature.

BELOW:
David Nash 'Ash Dome, 2013', charcoal on paper.

studio in Blaenau Ffestiniog, Snowdonia. It was the first occasion that he had made a piece of living art and at the time he was moved to do so because he was acutely aware of a world in political and ecological turmoil. The Cold War still loomed large and it appeared that we were hurtling towards ecological Armageddon. In an unstable world Nash felt the need to create something in the spirit of continuity and hope, something that might reach the twenty-first century, and something that would possibly outlive him (maybe all of us). Ironically and tragically, forty years down the road, all the old fears are with us once again, but with the added and unwelcome ingredient of ash dieback.

As Nash has often explained, he knew from the very start that *Ash Dome* would be a long-term, lifetime commitment, an act of faith, to be coaxed and tended into the foreseeable future. The initial inspiration evolved after studying the way skilled hedge-layers could cut and weave, bending their subjects to their will, and yet the unstoppable natural life forces in the hedge trees would eventually combat the forced prostration, throwing new stems straight up once more; a kind of nature versus human battle of wills. In his remarkable book Wildwood – A Journey Through Trees Roger Deakin had the pleasure of visiting and interviewing Nash, as well as paying a visit to *Ash Dome*, which clearly impressed. Deakin relates the various techniques that Nash had adopted to get his circle of ashes to do what he wanted, to tease them into the domed spiral he envisaged. This included much clambering about on ladders, pruning and grafting, cutting little nicks in the stems in order to get the bends he desired and then protecting the joints with binding, as well as using guy ropes to haul his free-spirited trees towards the middle of the *Dome*. As Deakin so rightly observes,

> As in any collaboration, the trees have their own ideas, and Nash must continually work his hedgerow skills to influence them as a sculptor, or choreographer. He admires and enjoys the sense of purpose in each tree, its stroppiness. Again it is a question of resistance, of arm-wrestling the muscular trees.

202 THE INSPIRATIONAL ASH

It all sounds like a battle royal, but it isn't, it is very much a relationship; and in the best relationships there is give and take from both parties. Deakin again: 'There is the strong sense of the serious business of play about working with trees like this. You bend them down, they spring back. You cut them down, they spring back again. You lay them down and they send new shoots growing straight up.' In this instance it may be true, but have a chat with any hedge-layer and ask him or her if their task feels like play, and one can easily guess the response.

Not only does Nash regularly visit and tend *Ash Dome*, but for over forty years he has made many drawings, paintings and photographs of the structure, so it must by now be one of the best-documented works of art in the land. Many of the sketches are made using charcoal, one of Nash's favourite mediums, creating very free, often quite abstract images, and Nash takes the prunings of the trees back to the studio to create other smaller works. I had seen many photographs of the *Dome* at different stages of its growth and in all seasons. I was intrigued and dearly wanted to visit to see for myself, but given the fame of the artwork I am not alone. Nash is understandably very cagey about letting the wider world know the exact location, and maybe that has helped to build the mystique around *Ash Dome*. What you cannot have becomes more eagerly desired. Many have quested, but few find their grail.

I corresponded with David Nash and explained my rationale for embarking on this ash monograph and he generously invited me to visit. Sadly, he wasn't available on the day I went up, but his assistant Nia Roberts kindly showed me around and took me to *Ash Dome*. Did expectation exceed realisation? Absolutely not! I found myself completely entranced. It was early September; we arrived in the afternoon and the sunlight was still high enough to find its way into the clearing where a platform in the wood, an arena, a stage had been cleared for the performance and the dancers had already started without us. The dynamism of *Ash Dome* is at once energising, but paradoxically there is this uncanny sense of it being frozen in time, freeze-framed in nature. I lay on my back in the very centre and gazed at the white wisps of cumulus lazily drifting eastwards beyond the breeze-stirred ash boughs, and was consumed by an overwhelming sense of tranquillity. *Ash Dome* engendered the same strong emotion I have had in the presence of a 3,000-year-old yew tree or even my trip of a lifetime when I wandered among the ancient bristlecone pines in the White Mountains of California. The effect is magnetic, hypnotic, and

BELOW:
Shadow patterns below 'Ash Dome'.

THE INSPIRATIONAL ASH 203

ABOVE:
Felling one of the ashes intended for the 'Ash to Ash' artwork by Ackroyd and Harvey, commissioned by The ASH Project.

tearing oneself away is extremely difficult. Would it have done the same for me on a wild and woolly winter's day? I think so, but who knows? I am sure that *Ash Dome* imparts something very personal, very different, to every person fortunate enough to visit.

Only one sad observation tempered my enjoyment, and that was discovering that a couple of the trees are exhibiting the symptoms of ash dieback. Could it be that the days of the *Dome* are numbered? Nash is philosophical about the future. Nature in all its guises will do what nature does and if that means the death of the ashes then so be it, but I am sure he had hoped that the *Dome* would at least outlive him. However, a delightful postscript to my visit came from Nia, as we had a coffee afterwards. She showed me a letter that had been sent to Nash by an ardent admirer of his work, a lady who had been searching the hills for years trying to find *Ash Dome* without success. Then, one day, quite by chance she happened upon it. Her joy was unconfined … and she promised to keep its secret.

Ash to Ash

At present the ash landscapes of Kent are being transformed out of all recognition as the ravages of ash dieback intensify. Woodlands begin to look like the aftermath of the Dutch elm disease epidemic of the 1970s, with stands of dead, skeletal ashes clattering in the wind, and individual trees in fields, hedgerows, roadsides, towns and cities are diseased and dying and becoming hazardous. What Kent, and neighbouring Sussex, are experiencing now is a gloomy preview for the rest of Britain in the coming years.

With this in view the Kent Downs Area of Outstanding Natural Beauty has launched The ASH Project. Through an ongoing series of events, including walks, talks and workshops, working with schools, compiling an ash archive – a collection of objects, artworks and poetry – and holding exhibitions, the plan is to raise awareness of the ash and its cultural significance in the Kent Downs, where it has long been the predominant broadleaf tree.

As part of these activities a monolithic artwork has been commissioned from the acclaimed artists Ackroyd & Harvey. Heather Ackroyd and Dan Harvey are renowned for their 'multi-disciplinary works that intersect art, activism, architecture, biology, ecology and history'. Both reveal formative connections with ash that helped to shape the ideals and direction of their current practice, but more specifically this new commission has obliged them to channel their broad-based knowledge of the ash tree and its multi-faceted influences on the British landscape and culture.

The Kent Downs AONB brief sought a large-scale ash-related artwork that could be prominently displayed in a publicly accessible location. After much research, including consultations with Rob Penn, Ackroyd & Harvey finally chose the ash arrow as the keynote for their intended artwork. Not only because ash was historically used to make vast quantities of arrows, principally for warfare, but also because the natural response of ash trees to ash dieback, whereby the tree's defence mechanisms cause it to produce copious quantities of epicormic shoots in a bid for survival, struck them as 'the ailing tree's final flourish, in which the tree appears to be arming itself with spears'.

Ackroyd & Harvey describe the proposed artwork, *Ash to Ash*, thus:

> The arrow is integral to our artwork, stripped of feather flight and steel head, it is impaled in its thousands into the monolith form of two ash trees. A monolith describes a pollarded tree, where major branches are truncated. One tree is stripped of bark, pale and smooth. The other tree is burnt dark ash. Both trees standing vertically, up to 10 metres high, have their natural forms extended by the extruding mass of arrow shafts. The arrow mass creates an aura, where natural light will add a shifting dimension of interplay between sunlight and shadow. The two forms with their truncated arm branches assume an anthropomorphic presence; they seem to mirror each other, yet one casts a dark shadow of loss. In Homer's epic *The Iliad*, Achilles' spear is made of ash and on his death became a talisman, which allowed entrance and exit to and from the Underworld.

Work is currently under way. Two ash trees have been selected for the piece, felled, trimmed and transported to the studio for preparation. Sadly, by the time this book went to press Ash to Ash was yet to be installed at the chosen location in the Kent Downs, but the accompanying computer-generated image provides an excellent impression of this imposing yet poignant homage to the ash tree.

ABOVE:
Heather Ackroyd and Dan Harvey at work on one of their trees, inserting some of the arrow shafts.

Due to the fact that the final artwork was not complete on 'Ash to Ash' by the time this book went to press, we present the CGI concept of the work (inset).

206 THE INSPIRATIONAL ASH

LEFT:
Lying on my back in the middle of 'Ash Dome'.

THE ASH PROJECT

Ash trees are the unsung heroes of many of our finest landscapes and as tree and timber it is intrinsic to our lives. Ash trees are common throughout Britain and they are home to an extraordinary ecology of life and cultural heritage. The tree is home to myriad species, it is known for its uses in both traditional and contemporary medicine, in legend it is the tree of life, Yggdrasil and it is a strong and flexible material which has made wheels, arrows, spoons, cars, aircraft and many, many more things.

We probably all know a place or person with 'ash' in their names. How many of us have climbed an ash tree as a child, played swords with its branches, sat in its gentle, dappled shade or warmed ourselves as it crackles on a pub fire?. What are we to do as we see this beautiful, elegant part of our natural and cultural heritage disappear before us?

The ASH Project asks how we might mark and celebrate ash trees before it is too late. The project combines a number of significant new artistic commissions with a wide ranging exhibition, walks, talks and workshops programme, an online archive and a plan for landscape restoration. Collaborating across conservation, scientific and artistic research we are developing an approach that will preserve memories of the tree in extraordinary and enduring ways for the generations who will live with the loss.

Ash is perhaps most closely associated with some of our most valued landscapes, the Areas of Outstanding Natural Beauty and National Parks. Places like the Cotswolds, Chilterns, Kent Downs, High Weald, Lake District, Dorset, Snowdonia and the White Peak area of the Peak District are, in part, defined by their relationship with the Ash tree.

As part of the work of The ASH Project, several of the Areas of Outstanding Natural Beauty joined with the Woodland Trust to fund and support the publication of 'Ash'. We see this magnificent book as part of the vital work to record and celebrate our Ash trees and their heritage before they are lost.

The Areas of Outstanding Natural Beauty (AONBs) which have contributed to the financing of this publication are: The Blackdown Hills, Chilterns, Dedham Vale, Dorset, East Devon, High Weald, Howardian Hills, Kent Downs, North Wessex Downs, Suffolk Coast & Heaths, Surrey Hills, Tamar Valley, Wye Valley and also the Bellhurst Trust.

The ASH Project is funded by the Heritage Lottery Fund, Arts Council England and Kent County Council it is led by the Kent Downs AONB.

We would also like to thank all of the AONB teams which gave support and advice to the preparation of this book.

WOODLAND TRUST

The Woodland Trust is the UK's largest woodland conservation charity and at the forefront of the fight to protect, plant and restore the country's woods and trees. That's why we are pleased to support Archie Miles' reverential book about the ash tree, a species that has been part of our landscape for thousands of years but which now faces an unprecedented threat to its survival.
The threat comes from a fungus responsible for a disease commonly known as ash dieback. It first came to our attention just a few years ago and since then it's been on the march! It is likely that we will lose millions of ash trees across the country as a result. But we've not given up.

In 2015 we joined like-minded organisations and individuals across the UK to share knowledge and expertise which might help protect UK trees from the growing number of pests and diseases. Called Observatree, the partnership relies on trained volunteer specialists to search for and record signs of tree disease, enabling a more cohesive approach to tree health within the UK. We also set up the UK-Sourced-and-Grown Assurance scheme which guarantees that the stock of companies registered on the scheme has been raised from UK-sourced seed and grown on in the UK for its entire lifespan. This is important because we believe the ash-dieback fungus was originally imported on infected saplings.

New scientific testing has also been searching for ash trees that could be more tolerant than others to ash dieback. So the hope is that with continued research we may eventually find a way of propagating trees resistant to the disease. But in the meantime, our familiar landscapes with ash trees at their heart are likely to change for ever.

Apart from the measures being taken to tackle the disease itself, there are other things we can do to manage the ash decline and mitigate the effects on the landscape. These include extensive re-planting to replace the affected trees with other native species to ensure we maintain our wildlife habitats and corridors. Wildlife needs lots of connections to move around; therefore it's not just ash trees in woodland we're concerned with, but also the roadside and hedgerow trees.

In future, it is essential that we make the broader landscape more resilient to disease and the potential effects of climate change. We are therefore working with other landowners and tree-related organisations, using joined-up thinking to implement changes on a landscape scale. Together we can do it.
Archie's book will remind us why the ash tree is so important and why we need to fight for its future.

To find out how you can support our work, visit woodlandtrust.org.uk/support-us.

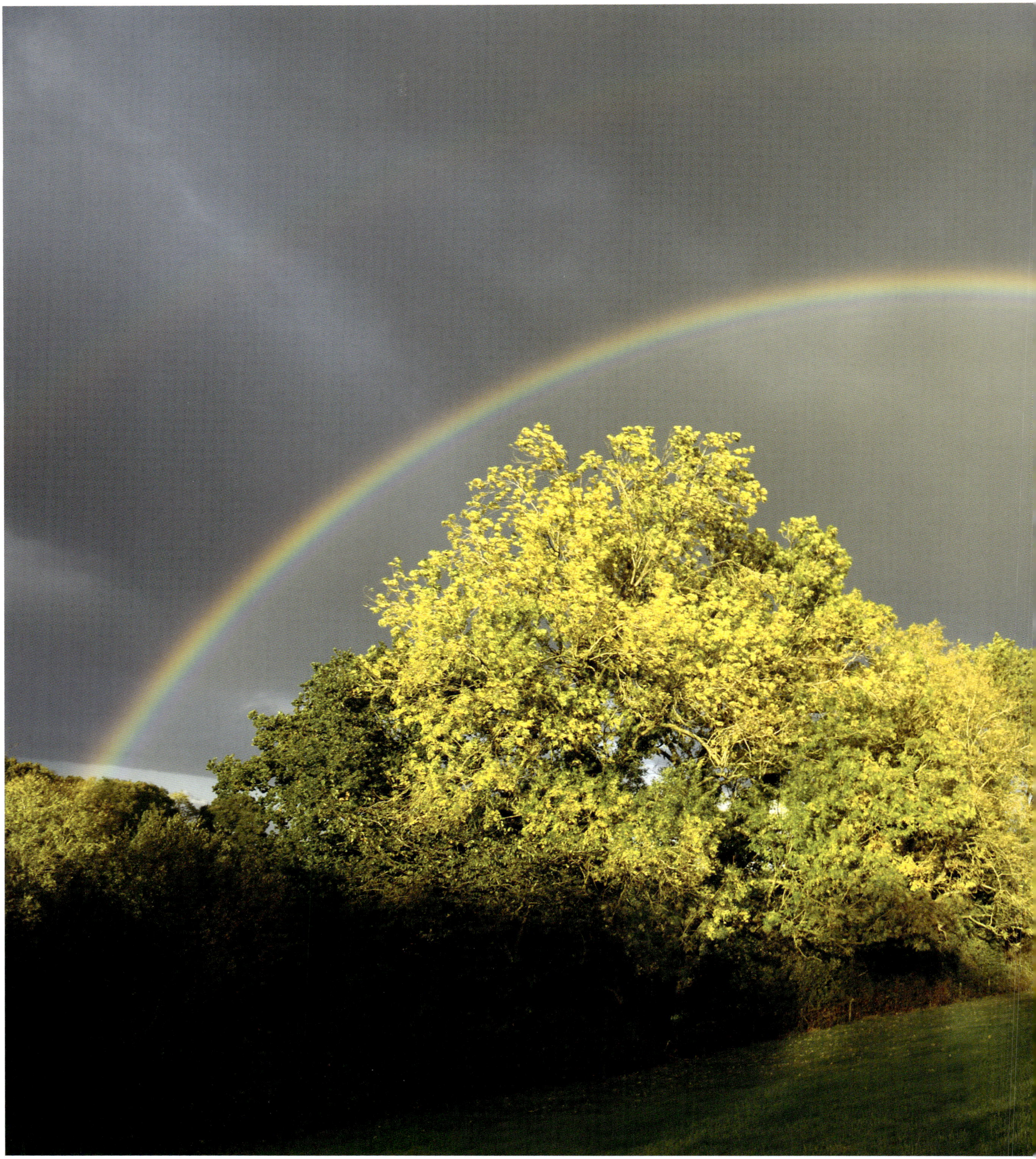

LEFT:
Autumn ash beneath a double rainbow.

Index

Page numbers in *italics* indicate illustrations.

A. S. Lloyd & Son, Bridgend 97, 98–9, *98*, *99*, 199
Abbott, Mike *94*, 95–6, *95*
Aberford Ash, Yorkshire 124–5, *124*
'Abhainn Ashik to Yr Onnen' (Ackroyd & Harvey) 40
Ackroyd, Heather 205
aerial trees 175, *176*
Agricultural Economics Research Institute, Oxford 86
Anastatic Drawing Society 134, *135*
Anderson, Stanley *195*
Arboretum et Fruticetum Britannicum (Loudon) 86, 101, 120, 123, 132
arrow-making 90
Art Workers' Guild 95
Ascham, Roger 90
ash
    arrival in Europe 17
    bark *25*, 27, 48, 102, *103*
    buds 18, *18*
    characteristics 14, 18
    cultivation 29, 46–52
    diseases and parasites 162–77, 178–89
    field layer 30–31
    flowers 19, *19*
    fruits 27–8, 103
    germination 27
    history 17–18
    in autumn *26*, 27, *193*
    in summer *17*
    in urban treescape 39, *39*
    in winter *16*, 18
    keys *19*, 27–8, 102, *103*, 112
    leaves 24–7, *25*, 102, *103*
    locations 30–31
    management 48–9, 80–81
    planting *see* cultivation
    raising *see* cultivation
    root system 20, 24, *27*, 29
    sap 102–3, 112
    seedlings 20, *20*, 49
    seeds 18, 28, 46, 49–50, 103, 119
    sexuality 19–20
    timber 48, 49, 50–52, *52*, *197*; *see also* uses
    uses 84–103
    woodlands 54–83
Ash (place name; Devon, Dorset, Kent, Somerset and Surrey) 40
Ash Arbour, Heanton Satchville 139–41, *141*
ash dieback 9–10, 29, 39, 51, 64, 80, 139, 146, 163, 165, 178–89, *178*, *180*, *182*, *183*, *185*, *186*, *187*, *188*, *189*
    resistance 181
    spread 181–2
    symptoms 181
    treatment 181, 182

'Ash Dome' project 199–204, *199*, *200*, *202*, *203*, *207*
'Ash Grove, The' (Thomas) 192–4
Ash Magna, Shropshire 43
Ash Parva, Shropshire 43
'Ash to Ash' project 204–5, *204*, *205*
Ash Wednesday 114
Ashbocking, Suffolk 40
Ashbourne, Derbyshire 40
Ashbrittle, Somerset 40
Ashby de la Zouch, Leicestershire 40
Ashe, Hampshire 40
Ashen, Essex 40
Ashford (Derbyshire, Devon, Kent and Surrey) 40
Ashkirk, Scottish Borders 43
Asholt Woods, Kent *185*, *186*
Ashreigney, Devon 40
Ashton Wood, Worcestershire 45
Ashwellthorpe, Norfolk *178*, 181, 182
Ashwellthorpe, Norfolk 40
Askham, Yorkshire 40
Askrigg, Yorkshire 40
Askwith, Yorkshire 40
Aspatria, Cumbria 43
Aubrey, John 102
Augustus, William, Duke of Cumberland 133

Balfron, Stirlingshire 135
Barkston Ash, North Yorkshire 43, 44–5, *44*
Battell, Gary 181
Bedgebury Manor, Sussex 125
Bettws Dingle, Wales *110*
Big Stoke Woods 62
billiard cues *97*
Biochar 182
Birks, H. J. B. 17
Birmingham Evening Despatch 117
Black Down, Somerset 61, *61*
Blomfield, Arthur 142
Bonhill, Dunbartonshire 131
Bonnie Prince Charlie's Ash 132–4, *133*
Borrowash, Derbyshire 43
Borrowdale, Cumbria *8*, 68–9, *69*
Boscobel Oak, Shropshire 133
bow-making 90
Bradfield Woods, Suffolk *52*, 82
Bridge House, Aberford 125
Britain at Work (Philpott) 94
Britain's Green Mantle (Tansley) 30
British Lichen Society 169
broadleaf trees 14
Brockhampton Woods, Herefordshire *14*, 159, *160*
Brow Gill Beck, High Birkwith 75

Brown, James 49
Broxash Wood, Herefordshire 83, *83*
bryophytes 172–3, *173*, *174*, *175*
    Broom forkmoss *175*
    Common feather-moss (*Kindbergia praelonga*) *174*
    Common tamarisk-moss (*Thuidium tamariscinum*) *174*
    Dilated scalewort (*Frullania dilatata*) *174*
    Flat-leaved scalewort (*Radula complanata*) *174*
    Great scented liverwort (*Conocephalum conicum*) *174*
    Homalia trichomanoides 172
    Isothesium alopecuroides 172
    Lesser yoke-moss (*Zygodon conoideus*) *174*
    Lobaria virens *173*
    Mouse-tail moss *175*
    Neckera complanata 172
    Peltigera horizontalis *173*
    Pertusaria albescans var. *corallina* *173*
    Tamarisk scalewort *175*
Buckinghamshire 94–5
Burnt Ash Road, Lewisham 45
Burren, Republic of Ireland 75
Burrington Combe, Somerset *12–13*, 61, *61*
burrs 173, *176*

Calendar of Customs, Superstitions, Weather-Lore, Popular Sayings and Important Events connected with the County of Somerset (Watson) 118
Callow Hill Wood, Herefordshire *197*, 198
Cambridgeshire 80–82, 120, 122
Campsea Ashe, Suffolk 43–4
Carlyle, Thomas 106
Carmarthenshire 148–51
Carnock, Stirlingshire, Great Ash *137*, 138
Cato, John 141
Cavendish, William, 6th Duke of Devonshire 120
Ceredigion 151
chair-making 94–6
Chalara see ash dieback
Champion Trees of Britain and Ireland (Johnson) 128
Charles I, king of England 112
Charles II, king of England 130
Chatsworth House, Derbyshire 120–21, *120*
Cheddar bedstraw 60
Cheddar Gorge, Somerset 60, *60*, 62
Cheddar pink 60
Cheshire 197
Christianity 106, 109, 114, 117–18
Christmas 115–19
Churchill, John, 1st Duke of Marlborough 130
Cirencester, Gloucestershire 173–4, *176*
Clachan Oak 135
Clapton Court Ash, Somerset *144*, 146, *146*
Clissett, Philip *94*, 95–6

212

Clissett Wood Trust 95–6
coach-building 92–3, *92*
Cobbett, William 30, 46–8, 119
Cobham Park, Kent *50*
Colt Park Wood, Ribblesdale 75, *75*
Colwell, David 96, *96*
Complete Herbal, The (Culpeper) 102
Congreve, Celia 100
Constable, John 191
Conwy 157–8
Cook, Moses 100
coppicing 46, 48, *48*, 50
    coppice stools *33, 34*, 38–9, *38, 39, 48*, 50, *62*, 76, 80, *80*, 156
coracles 87–8, *88, 89*
Cornwall 114, 136–7, 156
Cowley, Abraham 107
Cowpen Ash, Northumberland 101, *122*, 123
crafts *see* woodland crafts
Crécy, Battle of (1346) 90, *90*
Crossness, Essex 17
Crowborough, Sussex 114–15
Culloden, Battle of 132–3
Culpeper, Nicholas 102, 107
Cumbria, 68–9, 70, 106, 153–6, 175
Cury Great-Tree 136–7
Customs, Superstitions and Legends of the County of Somerset (Poole) 117
Cutsdean, Gloucestershire *28*

Dall, James 120
Dartmoor 107
de Havilland Mosquito 92
de la Mare, Walter 100
'Dead-Maid's Pool' (Dobell) 191
Deakin, Roger 202–3
Defoe, Daniel 130, 131
Department of the Environment, Food and Rural Affairs (DEFRA) 14
Derbyshire 43, 64, 67, 120–21, 123–4
    Derbyshire Dales 64–7
Derbyshire Courier 120
Devon 107, 111, 128, 139–41
Dictionary of English Plant-names, A (Britten and Holland) 114
Dictionary of Plant Lore (Vickery) 110, 113
Dictionary of Plant Lore (Watts) 107, 114
Dioscorides 106–7
diseases and parasites 162–77, 178–89
    ash dieback 9–10, 29, 39, 51, 64, 80, 139, 146, 163, 165, 178–89, *178, 180, 182, 183, 185, 186, 187, 188, 189*
    bacterial ash canker (*Pseudomonas savastanoi pv. fraxini*) 162
    bryophytes 172–3, *173, 174, 175*
    burrs 173, *176*
    galls 165, *165*
    mistletoe 103, 167, *167*–8
Dobell, Sydney 191
Doctrine of Signatures 102
Dodd, Ken 45
Domesday Book 40, 43, 44, 80
dool trees 134–5

Dorset 82–3, 107
Dorsetshire Folklore (Udal) 112
Dovedale, Derbyshire 64, *64, 65*
Drumnaminshog, Kirkcudbright 43
Dunbartonshire 131
Dundonnell River valley, Scotland 55–9, *56, 58, 59,* 171
Dutch elm disease 9, 67, 189
Dymock, Gloucestershire *107*

Earlsmill Ash, Morayshire 131–2, *132*
East Anglia 80–82
Eastern Arboretum, or Register of Remarkable Trees, Seats, Gardens, &c. in the County of Norfolk, The (Grigor) 14, 29, 122
Ebbor Gorge, Somerset 61, *61*
Edda Oblongata 106
Edlin, Herbert 50, 84, 86, 88
Eight Ash Green, Essex 43
elms 9, 67, 169, 189
Elvaston Castle, Derbyshire *122*, 123–4
Elwes, Henry John 49, 50–51, *50,* 123, 141, 175
Elworthy, F. T. 118
Ely Coucher Book 80
Epitaph for the Elm (Wilkinson) 9
Escrick, Yorkshire 40
Esher, Surrey 40
Essex 17
Evelyn, John *20,* 25, 27, 29, 32, 38, 84, 86, 100, 102, 106, 108, 130, 190
Evil Eye, The (Elworthy) 118

faggots 115–19, *118*
Faulkner, Peter *88*
felloes 90, 91
ferns 173
firewood 100, *100*
'Firewood Poem' (Congreve) 100
FitzRandolph, Helen E. 86–8
Five Ashes, East Sussex 43
Flora Scotica (Lightfoot) 112
Flowers and Flower Lore (Friend) 114
fodder 34, 101, *101*
Folk-lore Society Quarterly Journal 111
Folkard, Richard 107, 112, 119
Foll, Jack 44
Forby, Robert 112
Fordham, Pete *52*
Forest Hall Ash, Cumbria 153, *156*
Forest Trees of Britain, The (Johns) 101, 122, 136
Forester, The (Brown) 49
Four Ashes (Solihull, Suffolk and Staffordshire) 43
Fraxinus angustifolia 17
    'Raywood' 29, *29*
Fraxinus excelsior 14
    'Pendula' 29, 120–29
    'Pendula Wentworthii' 128
Fraxinus ornus 29
    ' Sarvar' *29*
Friend, Rev. Hilderic 114
froes 52
Fuller, John 194–5
Funcheon River, Cork 43

fungi 162–4, 168, 178–81
    Auricularia aricula-judae 164
    hairy bracket fungus (*Inonotis hispidus*) 139
    honey fungus (*Armillaria*) 165, *165*
    Hymenoscyphus fraxineus (syn. *Hymenoscyphus pseudoalbidus*) 178–89, *182*
    King Alfred's Cakes (*Daldinia concentrica*) *163*, 164
    mycorrhizal fungi 163
    Perreniporia fraxinea 164, *164*
    Polyporus squamosus 164, 165
    shaggy polypore (*Inonotus hispidus*) *164*
Funshin, Connaught 43
Funshinagh, Connaught 43

galls 165, *165*
Gardener's Magazine, The 124, 132, 139, 141
Geltsdale, Cumbria 175
Gentleman's Magazine, The 109, 112
George II, king of England 133
Gerard, John 107
Gilpin, Rev. William 30, 46, *25,* 27, 101, 131, 173, 175, 190
Gimson, Ernest 95
Glen Lyon Ash, Perthshire 146, *147*
Gloucestershire 173–4
good fortune 114
Goodhart, Honor 100
Gordon Castle, Moray 146–7
Gorget Tree, Applegirth Churchyard *134*, 135
Gosforth, Cumbria 106
Grafton, East *11*
Gregson, Phill 91, *91*, 199
'Grey and the Green, The' (Fuller) 194–5
Grieve, Mrs 103, 112
Griffith, David 167
Grigor, James 14, 29, 122
grikes 73, *73*
Guardian 186

Hageneder, Fred 104, 106
Hampshire 108
Hardy, Thomas 142
Hardy Ash, The 141–2, *142*
Hartburn, Northumberland *37*
Harvey, Dan 205
Hay, M. Doriel 86–8
Hayley Wood, Cambridgeshire *39*, 80–82, *80*
Heanton Satchville, Devon 139–41
hedgerow trees 32–3, *33*
Henry, Augustine 50, *50,* 123
Hepworth, Rev. Mr 120
Herefordshire 76–7, 83, 92, 95, 148, 159, 198
Heritage Trees of Scotland, The 146
Hertfordshire 17
Heston, Middlesex 115
High Wycombe, Buckinghamshire 94–5
Highgate Ponds, Hampstead Heath 128
Hilton, Dorset *33*
History of British Forest-Trees (Selby) 48–9
Hitchin, Hertfordshire 17
Hole, Christina 112
Holtye, Kent 80, *80*
hoop-making 87

hornbeams 61
Hull, Brian 124–5
Hundred Years War (1337–1453) 90
Hunter, Dr 102
Hutchison, Robert 18, 134, 135
Hyde, H. A. 50, 99

importation of plants 183–7
insects 165–6
    ash bark beetles (*Hylesinus varius*) 48, *48*, 162, 175
    ash bud moth (*Prays fraxinella*) 178
    cauliflower gall mite (*Eriophyes fraxinivorus*) 167
    Cryptophagus ruficornis 164
    emerald ash borer beetle (*Agrilus planipennis*) 183, 187
    gall gnat (*Diplosis botularia*) 167
Inshaig, Argyll 43
Inshaw Hill, Wigtownshire 43
Inshock, Forfar 43
Inshog, Nairn 43
Ireland 43, 97
Ivy Hatch, Kent *80*

Jacob's ladder 67
James II, king of England 130
James, Justine 128
Jameson, Robert 17
Jefferies, Richard 192
Johns, Rev. C. A. 50, 101, 122, 136
Johnson, Dr Owen 128
joug trees 135
Journal of a Naturalist, The (Knapp) 32–4

Kent 80, 204–5
keys *19*, 27–8, 102, 103, 112
Killyminshaw, Dumfriesshire 43
Kilmalie churchyard, Lochaber 132
Kincairney Ash, Dunkeld 123
King, Alice 118
Knapp, John Leonard 32–4
Knockninshock, Kirkcudbright 43
Knotty Ash, Liverpool 45
Koch, Karl 128

Lanhydrock, Cornwall *34*
Lathkill Dale, Derbyshire *66*, 67, *67*
Lauder, Sir T. Dick 131, 132
Ledbury Court, Herefordshire 95
Leeds Mercury 125
Leitz, Gudrun 95–6, *96*
'Levelled Churchyard, The' (Hardy) 142
lichens 58, *59*, 61, 69, *71*, 153, 168–72, *168*, *169*, *171*, *172*
    Lecanora argentata 168
    Lecanora conizaeoides 169
    Lecidella elaeochroma 168
    Lobaria amplissima 172
    Lobaria pulmonaria 172
    Lobaria virens 153
    Ochrolechia subviridis 59
    Parmelia sulcata 169
    Peltigera membranacea 172
    Ramalina fastigiata 168
    Ramalina farinacea 169
    Trentepohlia 169
    Xanthoria parietina 169
Lightfoot, Rev. John 112
lightning 114
Lillington, Warwickshire 44
'lime-ashes' 50
limestone pavements 30, *30*, 54, 55, 72–5, *72*, *75*
Lincolnshire 114
Lindridge Park, Devon 128
Ling Gill, North Yorkshire *23*
Linnaeus 103
Little Robin geranium 60
Little Stoke Woods 62, *62*
Liverpool 45
liverworts 61, 70, 172–3; *see also* bryophytes
Llanbedr-y-Cennin, Conwy 157–8, *157*
Lloyd, John 98–9, 199
Lloyd, Julie 98–9
Lodon Valley, Herefordshire *25*
Logierait, Perthshire, 134
'Logs to Burn' (Goodhart) 100
London Road Cemetery, Coventry *128*
Lord Vernon Arms, Pentonville Road 122
Lorton Ash, Cumbria 153, *153*
Loudon, John Claudius 86, 101, 102, 120, 123, 132, 139, 141, 147, 148
Lovelace, David 76
Loweswater Ash, Cumbria 153–4, *155*

Mabey, Richard 50, 75
MacLaren, James 95
Malham Cove, North Yorkshire 72–3, *72*
Man Who Made Things Out of Trees, The (Penn) 97
Manner of Raising, Ordering and Improving Forest-Trees, The (Cook) 100
'manorial affix' 40
Mareschall, Tom 199
Maxwell, Sir Herbert 43
Mears, Ray 164
medicine 102–3, 107, 108; *see also* superstitions
Meetings with Remarkable Trees (Pakenham) 146
Mendip Gorges, Somerset 60–62
Middlesex 115
Middleton-on-the-Hill, Herefordshire *48*
'Midland Oak' 44
Midsummer Hill *32*
mistletoe 103, 167, *167*–8
Mitchell, Alan 19
Moccas Park Ash, Herefordshire 148, *148*
Modern Herbal, A (Grieve) 103, 112
Monbiot, George 186
Monmouth, Duke of, *see* Scott, James, 1st Duke of Monmouth
Monmouth Ash 130–31, *131*
Monyash, Derbyshire 43
Morayshire 131–2, 146–7
Morgan, 'H.F.S.' 92
    Morgan cars 92–3, *92*, *93*
Morgan, Mike *98*
Morgan, Rev. H. G. 92
Morris 1000 Traveller 93
mosses 61, 70, *71*, 172–3; *see also* bryophytes

Moulin joug tree 134
Murray, Mungo 123
mythology 102, 104–19

Nash, David 199–204
National Forest Inventory for Great Britain 14
Natural History of Selborne, The 109
neuralgia 112
Nicholson, Sir Thomas 138
Norfolk 122, 181, 182
Norse
    legend 104–6
    place names 40, 43, 44, 70
North Runcton, Norfolk 122, *124*
Northumberland 101, 113, 128
Nottingham General Cemetery, 160, *160*
Nuttall, G. Clarke 167

O'Sullivan, Richard *98*
oaks 30, 44, 45, 84, 130, 165, 167, 190
    timber 84, 85
Oleaceae genus 14
omnibuses *92*
'One Tree' project 197–9
Onen, Monmouthshire 43
Opie, Iona and Peter 114
Ordnance Survey maps 43
Orford, Roger *93*
Owen, Sir Richard 111
Oxfordshire 113
oxlip 81

paddle-making 87–8, *88*
Pakenham, Thomas 146
Pankhurst, Maurice 70, 153, *155*
parasites *see* diseases and parasites
Parker Heath, Ian 43
Penn, Rob 97, 197–9, *197*, *198*
Penny Bridge Ash, Cumbria *86*, 153
Percival, Dr Glynn 182
Perthshire, 134, 146
Philpott, Hugh B. 94
'phoenix trees' *194*, 195
Pigott, Hugh 112
place names 40–5
Plant Lore, Legends and Lyrics (Folkard) 107–8, 112
Pliny the Elder 106–7
Poetic Edda 104
pollards/pollarding 32–8, *34*, 45, 50, 68–70, *68*, *69*, 76–7, *77*
Poole, Charles Henry 117
potash 101
Potter, Mark 198
Powerstock Common, Dorset 82–3, *82*
Powys 96
Presteigne, Powys 96
Purslow Ash, Shropshire *34*, 119
Putley, Herefordshire *188*

rabbits 48
Rackham, Oliver 39, 45, 80, 82, 156, 172, 191
railway carriages 92
rake-making 87

Rassal Ashwood, Scotland 54–5, *54, 55*
Remarks on Forest Scenery (Gilpin) 25, 131, 173, 175, 190
Rhyd-yr-Onnen, Gwynedd 43
Ribblesdale, North Yorkshire *30*
Richmond Park 111
Rock Ash, Llanbedr-y-Cennin, Conwy 157–8, *157*
Rock Ash, Wharfedale, Yorkshire 158, *158*
'Roderick' (Southey) 190
Rodney Stoke National Nature Reserve, Somerset 62
Rodolph, Charles, 19th Lord Clinton 141
romance 113
Ross-on-Wye, Herefordshire *89*
royalty 112
Rudd, John and Graeme 87
ruptures 108–11, *110*
Rural Industries of England and Wales, The (FitzRandolph & Hay) 86–8

salladding 102
samaras *see* keys
Schroder, F. R. 104
Scot's Gap, Northumberland *37*
Scotland 17–18, 43, 54–9, 131–5, 138, 146–7
Scott, James, 1st Duke of Monmouth 130–31, *130*
Scottish Land-Names; their Origin and Meaning (Maxwell) 43
Seathwaite, Cumbria 70
Seatoller Wood, Cumbria 68, *69*
Seaton Delaval Hall, Northumberland *127*, 128, *128*
Sedgemoor, Battle of 130–31
Selborne, Hampshire 108
Selby, Prideaux John 48–9
serpents *see* snakes
Seven Ash, Somerset 43
shrew ash 111–12
  Richmond Park *108, 109*, 111
  Selborne 112
Shropshire 133
Six Ashes, Shropshire 43
Small Talk at Wreyland 111
Smith, Dave *34*
snakes 106–7
  bites 107
Somerset 60–62, 107, 110, 118–19, 146
Somerset Archaeological Society's Proceedings 119
Southey, Robert 190
sporting equipment 97
  cricket stumps and bails 97
  hurleys 97
  pole-vaulting poles 97
  snooker cues 97
  tennis rackets 97, *97*
St Augustine 106
St Pancras Old Church 141–2, *141*
Stanley Hill, Herefordshire 95
Steven, J. 132
Stewart, Sir Michael Shaw 138
Stirlingshire 135
Stoke Ash, Suffolk 43
Stoke Lacy, Herefordshire 92, *93*
Stoke Woods, Somerset *51*
Strutt, Jacob George 137–8

Stuart, Charles Edward, 'Bonnie Prince Charlie' 132–3
Suffolk 43–4, 82
superstitions 106–19
Sussex 110, 114–15, 125, 138–9
Sylva (1664; Evelyn) 25, 29, 84, 100, 102, 108
Sylva Britannica (Strutt) 137–8
Systema Agriculturae, Being The Mystery of Husbandry Discovered and Laid Open (Worlidge) 85

Talley Abbey Ash, Carmarthenshire 148–51, *150, 151*
Tansley, A. G. 30
Tatton Park, Cheshire 197
thigmomorphogenesis 30
Thomas, Edward 192–4
Thorpe Cloud, Derbyshire 64, *65*
Three Ashes, Herefordshire 43
Tinnis Ash, Bowhill Estate, Selkirk 146
tool handles 98–9, *98*
Torr, Cecil 111
Toxophilus (Ascham) 90
traditions and customs 114–19
Traditions and Customs of Cheshire (Hole) 112
Transactions of the Highland and Agricultural Society of Scotland (Hutchison) 18, 114, 123, 134
Tree of Life *see* World Tree
Trees and How They Grow (Nuttall) 167
Trees of Great Britain and Ireland, The (Henry & Elwes) 49, *50*, 123, 138, 141, 175
Trees of the British Isles in History & Legend (Wilks) 135
'Trees' (de la Mare) 100
Tregoniggie, Cornwall 156, *157*
Trewin, Jan 191
Ty-uchaf Wall Ash, Usk Valley 159, *159*

Udal, John Symonds 112
utile 91
Uvedale, Dr 29

'Venus of the Woods' 30, 46
Vickery, Roy 110, 113, 114–15
Vikings 44, 104, 106; *see also* Norse
Vocabulary of East Anglia (Forby) 112
Voluspa 104, 106

Wales 43, 50, 88, 96, 98–9, 107, 148–51, 157–8
walking sticks 87, 112
Wartnaby, Jon 133
warts 112
Warwickshire 43, 44
Wasdale Head, Cumbria, *27*
Watendlath Wood Pastures, Cumbria 70, *71*
'water-ashes' 50
Watson, W. G. Willis 118
Watts, D. C. 107, 114
weather lore 114
weeping ash 29, 120–29, *120, 122, 124, 125, 127, 128*, 181
Welsh Timber Trees of 1931 (Hyde) 50, 99
Wentworth weeping ash 128
Wesley, John 139, 157
Wesley Ash, The 138–9, *138, 139*
Wharfedale, Yorkshire 158, *158*, 160, *160*
'Wheelwright, The' *195*

wheelwrighting 90–92, *90, 195*
White Peak, Derbyshire 64,
White, Rev. Gilbert 108–9, 111–12
whitebeams 61
Whitnash, Warwickshire 43
whooping cough 112
Whyle, Herefordshire 76, *77*
Wiggin's Tree 135–6
Wildlife in a Southern County (Jefferies) 192
Wildwood – A Journey Through Trees (Deakin) 202
Wildwood, The (Mabey) 75
Wilkinson, Gerald 9
Wilks, J. H. 135
Wilson, George Washington 133
Wilston *11*
Wiltshire *11*, 112
Wimpole, Cambridgeshire 120, 122
Winchelsea, Sussex 138–9
witchcraft 111, 112
Woburn Park, Great Ash *136*, 137
Wood, Robin 199
'Wooden Walls' (Evelyn) 190
woodland crafts 84–99, 195, 197–9
  arrow-making 90
  bow-making 90
  chair-making 94–6
  coach-building 92–3, *92*
  hoop-making 87
  paddle-making 87–8, *88*
  rake-making 87
  sporting equipment 97
  tool handles 98–9, *98*
  walking sticks 87, 112
  wheelwrighting 90–92, *90, 195*
  woodturning 195
Woodland Crafts in Britain (Edlin) 84, *97*
Woodlands – A Treatise, The (Cobbett) 30, 46, 119
woodpeckers 50
woodturning 195
Worcestershire *32*, 76–7
World Tree 104–7, *106, 107*
Worlidge, John 85–6
Wych elm 67

Yew: A History (Hageneder) 104
'Yggdrasil' 104–6, *104*
Yorkshire 44–5, 72–3, 113, 124–5, 158, 160
  Yorkshire Dales 72–5
Ystrad Meurig Ash, Ceredigion 151, *151, 152*
Yule log 115, 118

Acknowledgements

There are so many people who have helped to make this book possible so it is difficult to place anyone at the top of the list, but I will. Without the vision, support and energy of Stuart Dainton, Head of Innovation at Woodland Trust and Nick Johannsen, Director of Kent Downs AONB the whole project would never have got off the ground. Massive thanks to both of them, representing my two principal sponsors.

Also huge thanks to the three other financial supporters of this book, namely:
Ray Hawes, Head of Trees and Woodland Conservation, The National Trust
Jeremy & Roz Barrell of Barrell Tree Consultancy
Dave Jones, Group Marketing Director, Premier Paper Group

Dame Judi Dench for her kind support and foreword

My expert production team:
Sarah-Jane Forder – Editor | Chris Bell – Indexer | Chris Townsend – ABC Print Group | Jeremy Snell – L.E.G.O. UK

And to all the following wonderful folks who helped with research, guided me to or gave me permission to visit some stupendous trees, allowed me to photograph them at work and told me their stories, gave indispensable technical advice and information, and lent their beautiful images to make the book that extra bit special. If I have forgotten anyone then please forgive the oversight. You were all truly amazing:
Mike Abbott, Heather Ackroyd & Dan Harvey, Gary Battell, Sam Bosanquet, Simon Brett, Jonathan Briggs, Suzi Bullough, Lord and Lady Clinton, David Colwell, Prof Brian Coppins and Sandy Coppins, The Duke & Duchess of Devonshire, Ollie Douglas (The Museum of English Rural Life, Reading University), Dr Anne Edwards (John Innes Centre, Norwich), James Gilbert (Morgan Motor Co.), Lydia Gilroy (Chatsworth House Trust), Kim Gray (SCG Associates), Phillip Gregson, David Griffith, Paul Hipkin (Head Gardener, Heanton Satchville), Brian Hull, Justine James (The National Trust, Seaton Delaval Hall), Tim Kellett, John & Julie Lloyd (A. S. Lloyd & Son), David Lovelace, Dr Terry Mabbett, Robin Moseley, Tom Munro (Dorset C.C.), David Nash & Nia Roberts, Dr Caroline Oates (Librarian, The Folklore Society), Maurice Pankhurst (The National Trust, Keswick), Rob Penn, Dr Ana Perez-Sierra (Forest Research, Alice Holt), Donald Rice, Genevieve Rose, Dave Smith, Gwyneth Stevenson, Will Soos (Dundonnell Estate), Jon Stokes (The Tree Council), Jonathan Wartnaby (The National Trust for Scotland, Culloden Battlefield), Dr. Joan Webber (Forest Research, Alice Holt), Sue Wilson & Gordon Forster (Stanley Anderson Estate), Ray Woods, Guy Woolley.

LITERARY CREDITS
Extract from George Monbiot's article in The Guardian, June 2017 – p.186
Extract from 'The Ash Grove' by Edward Thomas - Alison Harvey (Archivist, Special Collections and Archives, Arts and Social Studies Library, Cardiff University) – p.194
Extract from 'The Grey and the Green' by John Fuller – p.195

EXTRA IMAGE CREDITS
Ackroyd & Harvey pp. 41, 204 & 205
Dave Pope Collection pp. 42 & 133 (top left)
Terry Rowell Collection p.94 bottom
Simon Brett – p.105
The Folklore Society (The Folklore Society Archives at University College London Special Collections) - pp. 108 & 109
Tim Winter Collection pp. 124 (bottom), 138 & 157 (bottom)
Gary Battell Collection p.124 top
Gary Battell p.182
Stanley Anderson Estate p.195
Tim Cochrane p.197
David Nash pp. 199 & 202
Madeleine Hodge p.205 (top)

Finally, as ever, I have to thank the love of my life, my wonderful partner Jan, for her constant support, patience and encouragement – she makes my day, every day.